NEW PRODUCT
SUCCESS STORIES

NEW DIRECTIONS IN BUSINESS

New Directions in Business books provide managers and business professionals with authoritative sources of ideas and information. They're designed to be a convenient and effective way to upgrade your skills in today's fast-changing world of business.

New Directions books cover current topics that leaders in every business need to know about. They focus on applied techniques that can be used today and they are written by leading-edge authors with academic and professional experience.

New Directions in Business Titles

Touchstones: Ten New Ideas Revolutionizing Business by William A. Band

The Smarter Organization: How to Build a Business That Learns and Adapts to Marketplace Needs by Michael E. McGill and John W. Slocum

Hands-On Strategy: The Guide to Crafting Your Company's Future by William C. Finnie

New Product Success Stories: Lessons from Leading Innovators by Robert J. Thomas

The New Competitor Intelligence: The Complete Resource for Finding, Analyzing, and Using Information about Your Competitors by Leonard M. Fuld

NEW PRODUCT SUCCESS STORIES

Lessons from Leading Innovators

Robert J. Thomas

John Wiley & Sons, Inc.

New York • Chichester • Brisbane • Toronto • Singapore

The student contributors to this book offer the following dedication:

This book is dedicated to the faculty who teach in the Georgetown MBA Program. Their wisdom, passion, and commitment have created an exceptional academic community that has greatly enriched our lives and careers.

This text is printed on acid-free paper.

Copyright © 1995 John Wiley & Sons, Inc.

All rights reserved. Published simultaneously in Canada.

Reproduction or translation of any part of this work beyond that permitted by Section 107 or 108 of the 1976 United States Copyright Act without the permission of the copyright owner is unlawful. Requests for permission or further information should be addressed to the Permissions Department, John Wiley & Sons, Inc., 605 Third Avenue, New York, NY 10158-0012.

This publication is designed to provide accurate and authoritative information in regard to the subject matter covered. It is sold with the understanding that the publisher is not engaged in rendering legal, accounting, or other professional services. If legal advice or other expert assistance is required, the services of a competent professional person should be sought.

Library of Congress Cataloging-in-Publication Data:

New product success stories : lessons from leading innovators /
    [edited by] Robert J. Thomas.
        p.   cm.
    Includes bibliographical references and index.
    ISBN 0-471-01320-X
    1. New products—Management. 2. New products—Marketing—
Forecasting. 3. Success. I. Thomas, Robert J., 1944–   .
HF5415.N3917   1994
658.5'75—dc20   94-26557

Printed in the United States of America

10 9 8 7 6 5 4 3 2 1

Preface

New product success has become increasingly important, especially to organizations in highly competitive business environments. Up to a third of an organization's annual revenues may derive from new products. Even for a new enterprise, survival depends on the success of the first new product. Unfortunately, the mediocre success record of new products and enterprises fosters conservatism among established organizations. They become unwilling to take chances to develop new products with truly new qualities that better satisfy consumer needs than products currently on the market—often when such innovation is needed most.

Overcoming this reluctance to undertake real innovation is the primary purpose of this book. By demonstrating that new product success is achievable in a variety of situations and with a variety of approaches, the stories told here perhaps can reduce the perceived barriers to innovation that plague many organizations and prevent venture capitalists from investing in new companies.

The book contains 24 new product success stories that show how innovative companies used a variety of approaches to achieve new product success. The stories illustrate wide-ranging ways of bringing new products to market—from orchestrating strategic business partners to define a new service (Calyx & Corolla) to spending hundreds of millions of dollars and 13 years to refine the technology for a new razorblade, then bringing in a product champion to resolve conflict and finally launch the product (Gillette Sensor). The book does not provide a "how-to" guide for new product success, but rather gives examples of how success can be achieved through numerous paths and by overcoming a variety of ever-present obstacles.

Structure of the Book

The book is organized into 10 chapters. Chapter 1 introduces the major themes of the book, with an emphasis on what can be learned from studying *success*—especially in a field where failure is more likely. Studying failure may not be helpful in situations where failure is more common than success! However, learning from mistakes that when corrected lead to success can be profitable. Chapters 2 through 9 consist of 24 new product success stories, three per chapter. Each chapter title represents a major theme that contributed to success in the stories.

The stories follow a general format of describing the success, briefly outlining the development process in as much detail as possible, and explaining the success in terms of various factors within or outside the organization's control. The last chapter of the book briefly summarizes some of the major lessons that can be learned from the success stories.

New product development is highly situational because of complex and rapidly changing business environments. The underlying thesis of the book is that, under such conditions, exposure to the factors explaining success across a variety of new product situations can sharpen new product thinking. Reading about how 24 new products emerged under a variety of market conditions can provide new insights for anyone involved in or studying new product development.

The 24 stories cover many types of new offerings, including repeat-purchase products, durable products, major technologies, retailers, and services. Also included are stories about well-known and less well-known organizations, old and new organizations, entrepreneurial and established firms, and global, national, and regional marketing situations.

The audience for the book is individuals concerned about new product development in their organizations and in society. Business proprietors, new product managers, senior-level executives, consultants, entrepreneurs, and venture capitalists should find value in reading the book. Also, professors teaching new product development courses may find that the book provides a type of "case study" in new product development and management that is different from traditional "problem-oriented" business school cases. Using success stories for retrospective analysis (identifying the success factors) and prospective analysis (projecting the future of the business on the basis of the success factors) provides a valuable stimulus for lively class discussions.

Finally, this book *is* a new product! It originated during 1992–1993 as a consequence of my teaching an MBA course on new product development at the Georgetown University School of Business. After discussing the general idea of the book, I formulated it into a concept that students used as a basis for selecting and developing success stories. Several of the stories include information from personal interviews conducted by students, which contributes to the originality of these stories beyond what is commonly known. Once the success stories were completed, they were reviewed and discussed by an advisory team of students prior to final editing. The students have agreed that all advances and royalties from the book are to be assigned to Georgetown University for use by students and faculty in the Georgetown MBA Program.

Acknowledgments

Much of the harmony in the Georgetown MBA environment that supports mutual learning between students and faculty emanates from the academic administrators. In particular, Martha K. DeSilva and Nancy D. Moncrief have continually guided students through their two-year experience with patience, caring, and good humor. Virginia N. Flavin, Director of Faculty Services, gracefully and without complaint always manages to get the entire business school faculty through each semester, often under trying circumstances.

The advisory board for this project deserves special acknowledgment. Its members are Susan Aiken, Leila Byczkowski, Katy Cancro, Mary Griffith, Luke Hodges, Wendy Hyer, Kathleen McCarthy, Soumitra Mukherjee, Freddie Smithline, and Elisabeth Watson. Unfortunately, an excellent project by Holly Darden and Bill Miller could not be included for proprietary reasons. I thank Robert White for his review of a previous version of the manuscript.

I am deeply indebted to Professor N. Craig Smith, who introduced the idea of using success stories in business school marketing classes at Georgetown. I am extremely grateful to Emily P. McNamara for her superb editing and constructive insights on the manuscript. The extra efforts of Luke Hodges and Kathleen McCarthy to coordinate this project with Georgetown MBA students and faculty on a continuing basis are greatly appreciated. Finally, this undertaking would not have been possible without the dedicated and unheralded legions of innovators who serve the organizations in the stories told in this book.

ROBERT J. THOMAS

Contents

1

Learning from New Product Success

It is possible to fail in many ways . . . while to succeed is possible in only one way (for which reason also one is easy and the other difficult—to miss the mark easy, to hit it difficult).

Aristotle, Nicomachean Ethics

The last thing any organization wants in a new product is failure. The Holy Grail of new product development is *success!* Although any kind of success is appreciated, it is most valued when it comes with a truly innovative new product. That kind of success gives an organization a platform on which to develop a family of profitable new products over the years. It is also the kind of success that gives a segment of consumers solutions to some of their problems and makes life easier for them in some meaningful way.

For example, consider Acuvue disposable contact lenses developed by Johnson & Johnson (J&J).[1] Many consumers who must correct their vision do not wear traditional hard or soft contact lenses on a regular basis because of the discomfort and the cleaning requirements. Through a patented manufacturing technology, J&J was able to produce high quality soft contact lenses at a relatively low cost. The lenses could be marketed at a sufficiently low price to allow consumer disposal after a week's use, yet still be competitive in cost with extended-wear contact lenses. Consumers found the lenses comfortable and easy to use, and cleaning was eliminated because the lenses could be replaced with a new pair each week.

1

When J&J launched its innovative lenses in 1987, it defined a new market because the new product satisfied the unmet needs of a segment of consumers. Although major competitors targeted this segment a year later, in 1992 J&J still held a 70 percent share of the $300 million market. Perhaps more important is the fact that J&J is using the new product and market position as a platform for continuously improved new vision care products—such as contact lenses that are disposable daily.

Pursuing innovations is not without costs, risks, and hard work to solve a succession of problems that arise during development and after launch. How a firm copes with and learns from these problems throughout development often determines the new product's success or failure. For example, J&J confronted a number of uncertainties and difficult issues during development of the disposable lenses:

- Did a market segment of consumers exist who would benefit enough from contact lens disposability to buy the new lenses on a regular basis?
- Could J&J manufacture the product at a sufficiently low cost to deliver the disposability benefit without sacrificing accuracy of vision?
- Could J&J persuade vision care doctors and other providers that the product was safe and that they would benefit financially from offering it to their patients?
- Could J&J persuade consumers of the logic of disposable contact lenses and get them to try a pair?

Fortunately for J&J, the answer to these questions was "yes," but getting to the answer almost always involved some form of learning. For example, in its first efforts to distribute the product, the company required the up-front purchase of inventory by eye doctors. After monitoring feedback, however, the company discovered that doctors did not like that requirement. Consequently, it developed a just-in-time network of distribution. That action reduced inventory costs for the vision care professionals and provided faster service for customers.

Not all of the learning that went on at J&J in developing Acuvue should be expected to work for every new product. Some lessons learned may be transferable to other situations, but others may not be. What J&J learned may not be relevant for a firm developing a new battery for an electric car or for a firm developing a new fat-free line of frozen dinners. In each situation, consumers are different, competitors are different, technologies are different, and so on. Studying one new product success may not be very informative. However, *exposure to a variety of different new product successes can provide insights on a range of success factors that, if considered for any particular new product, may positively affect its market performance*—which is the basic thesis of the book. Absorbing insights from 24 different new product successes might arm a person intellectually to undertake new product development.

WHAT IS A NEW PRODUCT SUCCESS?

Success is not always what it appears to be. Is a successful new product one that generates a 20 percent return on investment after its first year on the market? Is it one that breaks even in two years? Is it one that captures 10 percent market share from a competitor? Or are factors other than financial and sales objectives at stake in defining new product success?

Consider the case of Raytheon Company.[2] Perceiving a market opportunity for a fuel-efficient airplane, Raytheon set out to design and build one for the corporate aviation market through its Beech Aircraft division. Beech was not content simply to emulate corporate jets that dominated the market, but instead turned to new technologies to create a truly new airplane. The outcome was its highly innovative Beech Starship, made from carbon composites rather than traditional aluminum.

The new Beech aircraft has a unique design. The wings are far back on the fuselage and a propeller engine is mounted on each. The wing tips turn up in a stylish way at a 90-degree angle and there are two small wings on the nose of the plane. Pilots who have flown the plane love its handling, stability, cabin, and cockpit features. Consistent with the Starship name, the plane was marketed as a forward-looking, stylish, and fuel-efficient alternative to the traditional corporate jet, competitively priced at about $5 million.

However, by October 1993, some five years after FAA flight certification, only 23 planes reportedly had been sold—far fewer than the estimated breakeven of 500 planes. With an investment reported to be between $350 and $500 million clearly at risk, can the Starship be classified a failure?

Raytheon had acquired Beech in 1980 to reduce its dependency on government contract work. It installed its own managers at Beech and began the Starship project in 1983. Although the new aircraft apparently was within the general scope of the firm's business, the market in which Raytheon chose to compete—business organizations and corporate jets—certainly challenged its marketing experience. Many factors that determine strategic success in government markets can be very different in business markets. For example, government purchases typically are carried out in fairly well-defined bidding situations, whereas the purchase of corporate aircraft in business markets is a much more open and competitive process, often accompanied by intense personal selling and negotiations.

After years of dealing with government markets, Raytheon could not be expected to change its product development ways overnight. In this case, selling even one Starship might be considered a kind of success, albeit a costly one, signaling the company's ability to begin to satisfy the needs of a different type of market. With adjustments in its marketing, the Starship may even achieve limited long-run success on a financial basis. For example, Beech turned to an alternative market segment for its future marketing plans. Recognizing that the design of the advanced plane may be too showy for conservative business executives, Beech reportedly focused on the market defined by independent and successful entrepreneurs, who may be more likely to value a stylish and progressively engineered aircraft.

The experience was clearly not a loss for Beech because the company seemed to gain substantial insight into its own operations in competing in a nongovernment market environment. For example:

- During the five years of product development time (originally estimated to be two years), the business environment changed considerably. In particular, fuel prices that were lower than originally estimated eliminated the promise of fuel efficiency as a competitive advantage for the Starship. Beech learned that competitiveness in its rapidly changing markets requires accurate environmental forecasting of gas prices and/or fast product development.

- Unfamiliarity with the new carbon composites (versus aluminum) for the aircraft was cited as one reason for the delayed development. Ultimately, the organization engaged in a "crash" development program to focus resources and complete the project. The problems were solved, but the time and resources expended were substantial. Perhaps developing cross-functional teams very early in the development process to resolve technical, marketing, and manufacturing problems could have enabled Beech to avoid subsequent costly delays. In addition, special technical teams formed early in the process in anticipation of certain engineering problems may have been able to circumvent some of the technical difficulties.

- A new model launched shortly after the first model incorporated numerous improvements. Further, a price reduction of about 12 percent brought the plane's value more in line with the new market segment. These actions represent the flexibility needed to compete in a marketplace more difficult than government markets.

In any case, Beech did not terminate the Starship in the face of slow market acceptance. By considering price reductions, selecting a different market segment, and otherwise recognizing the strengths and weaknesses of the new product, the company was able to learn from experience. The delight of persons who have flown the airplane shows that it holds promise for satisfying its target segment, and Raytheon's investment in learning a new technology may pay off in future new products. Hence, though the Beech Starship may appear to be a failure in the business press, especially in terms of reported sales performance, it may be a long-term success for Raytheon. From Raytheon's point of view, the benefits of learning from experience how to renew the organization's competitiveness in the face of a declining government defense market may far outweigh the costs.

Clearly, new product success cannot be measured in absolute terms. It should be defined and interpreted according to realistic goals and objectives that reflect the specific new product situation. For example, in highly uncertain business environments, success may be defined in broader terms than it is in more stable situations. In any case, to truly understand what determines new product success, recognizing the general types of factors that may drive it is essential.

WHAT FACTORS LEAD TO NEW PRODUCT SUCCESS?

The study of new product success (and failure) has been a preoccupation of academic researchers for several years. A 1993 study of new product performance measures identified 61 research projects concerned with discovering the factors leading to new product success.[3] However, because these studies use different measures and cover a variety of industries and market situations, drawing valid comparisons and conclusions is difficult. Sound generalizations about the factors leading to new product success are therefore lacking, but two central points are clear: (1) *new product success is highly situational* and (2) *no one factor drives new product success.* Individuals and organizations developing new products must carefully analyze their situation and recognize that multiple factors may determine success. The following sections describe eight major categories of factors related to new product success.[4] These categories are also the basis for the next eight chapters of success stories.

Aligning Strategic Opportunities

Competitive strategy is the direction the organization pursues to gain a long-term advantage. New products are playing an increasingly important role in business strategy. In a 1990 study of new product development practices, respondents revealed that 32.6 percent of their sales in the previous five years came from internally developed new products and 8.9 percent came from products acquired from external sources.[5] They also indicated that over the next five years those proportions would increase to 38.8 percent and 13.3 percent of sales, respectively.

Perhaps the most important first step in new product development is conducting a *situation analysis* to help define the organization's competitive strategy. A situation analysis identifies and assesses an organization's strengths and weaknesses in relation to the opportunities and threats in its business environment. Aligning an organization's strengths and weaknesses with its opportunities and threats reveals valid strategic options. The extent to which new products fit into these options defines their strategic role. In particular, the synergy realized when a new product facilitates the alignment of an organization's competencies with its business opportunities may propel the product to success.

Black & Decker Corporation, for example, identified a market opportunity for a new line of high quality power tools among a segment of trade craftsmen.[6] However, the company ascertained that the Black & Decker name was not strong in that market segment. Consequently, to capitalize on the opportunity, it acquired a power tool business with a brand name strongly associated with quality in that market segment (DeWalt) and developed a new line of power tools for it. The products were very successful, despite heavy competition from an entrenched high quality Japanese competitor (Makita).

Black & Decker's acquisition of a high quality brand name helped to balance the organization's weaknesses in a particular market segment and accomplish long-term strategic objectives for the division. This example shows how success derives from the many factors that help an organization align its competencies with its opportunities through new products.

Capitalizing on the Business Environment

A business environment comprises numerous forces and mediators that interact to create market opportunities. Key environmental forces include trends in natural resources, population, cultural values, technology, economic systems, and laws and regulations. Politicians, regulatory agencies, financial institutions, mass media, industry associations, and various special interest groups (such as consumer activists and trade unions) mediate these global forces. Although environmental forces tend to be pervasive and to have long-term consequences, understanding the major trends in these forces and the actions of various mediators can reveal specific opportunities on which to build new product success.

For example, Rubbermaid, Inc. capitalized on trends in population, ecological concern for natural resources, and its own technological capabilities through the Sidekick "litterless" lunch box for children.[7] During the 1980s and into the 1990s, the post–World War II baby-boom generation began to settle down and have families, creating a sizable market of children. Through classroom discussions, these children became sensitized to ecological concerns, even to the point of lecturing their parents on the topic and becoming active participants at home in sorting garbage for more efficient recovery of resources.

Rubbermaid designed a new lunch box for these children that responded to the need to reduce waste. The lunch box included separate sealable and reusable containers for sandwiches, drinks, cookies, and other lunch items. Children could pack their lunch without using any paper, foil, plastic, or other throw-away materials. The new product was a major success with children (and in sales for Rubbermaid), even at a premium price in relation to traditional lunch boxes. Clearly, major environmental trends drove the opportunity, but a proactive product development capability was necessary to capitalize on it. Proper attention to the needs of potential buyers is central to this capability.

Pursuing Market Acceptance

The developer of a new product may believe that potential buyers are eagerly awaiting its arrival at local stores. Typically, however, market acceptance of new products is a slow process that is sometimes painful for the innovating organization. In fact, success often depends on interaction between the developing organization and potential buyers both before and after market launch. Such interaction is especially important for products that are really new to the market and require potential buyers to change their patterns of behavior.

For example, Apple Computer, Inc. launched its Newton MessagePad in August 1993 after a period of considerable marketing hype.[8] The MessagePad is a small hand-held computer operated with a pen instead of a keyboard. With a pen, or stylus, the user performs operations by tapping icons or writing on a small screen. The handwriting on the screen, whether text or numbers, is input to files and databases for processing. The MessagePad can be connected to a telephone for the electronic communication of messages and files (such as faxing). The Newton technology promised to bring together a variety of capabilities in a single hand-held device.

The acceptance of highly innovative products among potential buyers typically follows a diffusion process of growth. So-called *innovators,* a small proportion of the total potential market, are very eager to buy the new product, and do so. The hope is that *imitators* will soon follow innovators into the market and boost the volume of sales. However, if a product is relatively new, other buyers may be slow to follow, especially if the product's benefits and value are not entirely clear. The result is market growth that rises slowly at first, then accelerates rapidly as potential buyers learn more about the new product. Ultimately, sales growth slows as the market reaches its potential. This pattern of growth is the so-called S-shaped diffusion curve.

Critics began to pan the Newton MessagePad in their reviews even before launch. A popular comic strip in the daily newspapers (*Doonesbury*) ran a week-long series poking fun at the new product. One consequence of negative publicity can be uncertainty about the new product among potential buyers, which translates into delayed purchases. The major problem appeared to be that the handwriting recognition feature of the product did not perform according to expectations. The core benefit of a pen-based computer could not be realized. Although this deficiency was in part a product-refinement problem, Apple's extraordinary marketing hype had created expectations that greatly exceeded product performance, thus heightening uncertainty about the product.

The Newton MessagePad situation illustrates the pursuit of market acceptance in the face of widespread rejection. The business press expressed doubt about Newton's success. A stream of articles after the Newton launch appeared to document the rise and fall of the MessagePad. Consider the following article titles published in *The Wall Street Journal* from the date just prior to launch to about six months later:

7/30/93	"Imminent Debut of Newton MessagePad Has Apple Crowing and Critics Carping"
8/5/93	"In Newton, Apple Has the Germ of an Idea with Weighty Potential"
8/19/93	"Apple's Newton Moves Briskly in Early Sales"
10/1/93	"Apple Reports Brisk Sales of Its Handheld Computer"
12/13/93	"Sales of Apple's Hand-Held Computer Have Weakened Since Its Introduction"
1/25/94	"Apple's Sales Data Suggest to Analysts that New MessagePad Is Floundering"
2/3/94	"First Hand-Held Data Communicators Are Losers, but Makers Won't Give Up"

Part of the reason the makers did not give up was that they saw a market need for an easy-to-use hand-held computer. Although sales were less than expected, Apple sold some 80,000 Newton MessagePads during its first six months on the market. As a consequence, some competitors delayed launch plans for their new hand-held computers (to improve their performance), and analysts reduced estimates of market growth. Apple only had to recall its own experience with the innovative MacIntosh computer launched in 1984. Initially, the new computer with a graphical user interface and a "mouse" did not sell rapidly. However, with the advent of software that provided new applications and as buyers learned about the product's benefits, sales accelerated.

Market opportunity is open for the MessagePad and its competitors. As with many new technology-based products, however, acceptance by potential buyers may be slow as manufacturers improve product performance and buyers overcome their uncertainty and concern about product benefits. Successive generations of the MessagePad may better address buyer needs and concerns. Further, as in the case of the MacIntosh, new application software will enhance market acceptance of the new product. By working closely with potential buyers to understand their needs, innovating organizations can improve a new product's chances for success. Members of the organization must be motivated to discover buyer needs and revise the product or service design to meet them.

Motivating the Organization

Organizations bring stability to complex and dynamic business conditions. Not surprisingly, when faced with the problem of something new, they may resist change. Such resistance is especially common in the case of new products. For an organization's members, undertaking a new product project creates uncertainty and often involves taking on an additional workload.

Overcoming resistance to change is an important challenge in new product development. Recognizing difficulties in marshaling support for new products, organizations have begun to use new product development teams. The teams are cross-functional, usually composed of members from different parts of the organization who are important to new product development success. Members from research and development, marketing, design, engineering, and accounting are often led by a new product *champion*, who is given adequate resources and organizational support to carry out the important tasks of new product development.

The development of Microsoft's new Windows NT software operating system provides an example of the importance of motivating the organization to achieve success.[9] For Microsoft, Windows NT represented the ideal operating system. It would provide high speed processing of data, text, and graphics and be capable of performing multiple tasks simultaneously. It would be portable across a variety of computer and printer hardware platforms, compatible with current DOS and Windows software, and reliable in operation, whatever the system. To deliver these benefits, Microsoft had to build a very large and complex software program.

Recognizing the difficulty of the task, Microsoft recruited a programming expert with solid management experience to champion the development project. His management style, programming ability, and creativity impressed everyone with whom he would work, solidifying his leadership. After designing the general structure of the project, he organized several teams to tackle the various levels of the project. He then broke each of three primary groups (program writers, network designers, and user interface designers) into as many as 10 subgroups with three to four members in each. This action minimized hierarchy, delegated responsibility, and established controls to monitor the progress of the entire project on a daily basis.

Using a brusque style, which was compatible with the normally confrontational, but effective, Microsoft corporate culture, the Windows NT champion led the project with a motivational approach best described as creative conflict. Pitting very bright programmers against each other on complex issues hastened the resolution of difficult problems. The team apparently thrived on this conflict, working long hours and in some cases seven days a week. As deadlines grew near, meals were ordered in and team members slept in their offices. About 200 people were involved in the project and the financial commitment was estimated to be $150 million. The project met critical deadlines and resulted in a product favorably received by the market. Nevertheless, the process of ironing out problems continued beyond launch.

All ingredients necessary for development success are present in the Windows NT example: substantial corporate support from the CEO, a strong project champion, an integrated team approach built around the product's functionality, a motivational approach consistent with the organization's culture, and financial and human resources adequate to support the project. Clearly, a motivational approach based on creative conflict may not work in every organization. Each organization must recognize the situational nature of new product development and consider several paths to success.

Creating New Product Ideas

In the 1990 study cited previously, the survey of organizations revealed that of 100 new product ideas, 9.4 are commercially successful, or about one in 11.[10] The implication is that a large number of ideas may be necessary to yield a successful new product. For example, Amoco Chemical Company, a subsidiary of Amoco Corporation, found that out of 100 new product ideas, four eventually received sponsorship in the organization.[11] Further, evaluating whether these ideas were worthy of sponsorship took about one year.

A new product idea is an abstraction of a new product, preferably tied to the major need of a segment of potential buyers. A wallet-size telephone that can place and receive calls anywhere in the world is an example of a new product idea. Generally, families of related ideas may emerge around a particular segment need that defines a market opportunity. A wallet-size portable telephone with a visual screen for use as a small television or for two-way video calls is a new product idea related to the preceding example.

Numerous approaches can be used to generate new product ideas, including formal procedures tied to the new product situation (scenarios, consumption systems analysis, competitive analysis, technology), procedures designed to generate individual response (in-depth interviews, consumer complaints, inventors, creativity), procedures based on group response (focus groups, brainstorming, synectics), and procedures based on structural analysis of the new product and buyer needs (listing, attribute stretching, morphological analysis). Some of the most promising new ideas come directly from consumer problems.

For example, a Colorado river guide developed the highly successful Teva sport sandal to solve the problem of soggy tennis shoes for river rafters.[12] The ultimate product design involved a special Velcro nylon strap and buckle system that, with one pull, could tighten the sandal straps around the foot. Further, the straps and rubber footbed of the sandal provided drainage, traction, and stability.

Teva Sandals were adopted first by river guides and rafting enthusiasts, but soon became fashionable as a symbol of a rugged outdoor lifestyle. They became so popular for a variety of outdoor activities (such as hiking) and casual wear that they attracted major competitors in the shoe industry (such as Nike and Reebok). The premium prices for the sandals also attracted competition; in 1994 they sold at $60 to $100 a pair! Whatever the source of a new product idea, the ultimate goal is to realize its value through a process of testing and refinement.

Designing New Products from Concepts

A new product concept is a more specific description than an idea. It may be a written specification of product features that deliver consumer benefits, artistic renderings, models, or other characterizations of the new product design. Typically, concepts emerge from the most promising new product idea or set of ideas. Formalizing new product ideas into concepts forces a screening of many ideas into a feasible set and facilitates testing prior to major financial commitment for prototype development or manufacturing.

A variety of procedures can be used to evaluate alternative concept designs. The most promising ones evoke the response of potential buyers to the new product concept. Showing the concept to potential buyers in the context of focus groups, surveys, purchase laboratories, or other procedures provides a basis for measuring response. Typically, potential buyers are asked to express their intentions to buy. In simulated purchase situations, they may choose the new concept from a set of competing alternatives. Analyzing data obtained by these procedures produces estimates of market share and other measures of market response. These estimates provide the basis for sales forecasts for the new product.

Concept design and evaluation are especially important and valuable when the next step in new product development requires significant capital investment. For example, in a bid to become more market oriented in the early 1980s, Sunbeam Appliance Corporation decided to evaluate new product concepts before investing time and money in them.[13] The estimated cost for developing a working model of an appliance for testing purposes was between $5,000 and $20,000, and each model required about three to six months of time. Hence, testing 50 new concepts required about $625,000 (at an average working model cost of $12,500), a relatively expensive proposition.

To cope with the investment in time and cost, Sunbeam developed a two-step concept-testing procedure. The first step was the creation of "concept cards" that described the new product design in artistic renderings and lists of key product features. The second step was the use of concept cards to test a large number of concepts on a sample of consumers. The measures obtained gave managers important information about which concepts should be developed into working models for additional testing. Although concept testing has limitations (such as consumers' inability to experience the product's actual benefits), a properly developed concept-testing program can provide results that are useful in designing the new product.

Refining the New Product

Product superiority is always a dominant factor in new product success. A product that evokes a favorable level of consumer interest in concept or working model form must also be of sufficient quality to meet the needs of potential buyers. The total quality management (TQM) movement during the 1980s and continuing in the 1990s reflects organizations' efforts to match the high quality of products made by Japanese competitors. However, the pressure of launching a new product on time, or meeting other organizational objectives, may cause an organization to skimp on testing and thus sacrifice quality and performance.

For example, the launch of nicotine patch products in late 1991 promised to curb cigarette smoking.[14] Doctors prescribed the patches for patients to wear for extended periods of time. The patches cost up to $660 for a 20-week supply. Strong demand for these patches during 1992 far exceeded availability. However, by early 1993 some patch wearers had begun to show side effects and others were complaining that the patches were not effective in reducing smoking. Then the Food and Drug Administration (FDA) and attorneys general of 11 states began to pursue major suppliers of the nicotine patch for advertising the patch as a cure for smoking when apparently it was not. The consequences were a sharp decline in demand for the patches and a large marketing problem for their manufacturers.

The unfulfilled promise of the nicotine patch partly contributed to its difficulties. However, through more careful market testing, manufacturers of the patch might have been able to refine the product and avoid some of the difficulties that arose after launch. For example, most organizations usually undertake some form of *alpha testing,* the testing of a new product or service within the confines of the organization during development. Sometimes organizations use their own employees for testing, but often potential buyers are recruited to visit the organization on a regular basis to try the new product.

To carry the testing process further, *beta testing* of a product's effectiveness with actual users may be valuable. This type of testing over a long period might have revealed the side effects of the nicotine patch. Typically, beta testing involves placing the product with potential buyers in the context of their usage situations over a significant period to assess its performance. By monitoring consumer usage, the organization can obtain valuable information about the product's expected performance in a realistic setting.

Further, *gamma testing* of the patch and its marketing program (especially the advertising campaign) with the FDA and state agencies might have prevented some of the legal difficulties. Gamma testing involves exposing a product and its launch marketing program to market stakeholders involved in the new product's success (such as regulators, politicians, labor unions, and others). More substantial forms of *test marketing* can resolve questions that arise during alpha, beta, or gamma tests. Test markets typically involve selecting one or more test areas and exposing them systematically (often with controls) to one or more test programs. The results can be used to guide key decisions in the formulation of launch marketing programs. Finally, *delta testing,* or retrieving the product after extended use for further evaluation, may have helped further refine the nicotine patch and better understand its use among consumers.

Tracking the New Product

The new product development process does not end at launch; it merely continues. Careful tracking of a new product after launch involves establishing diagnostic measures that reveal the product's performance at all levels of the market, from manufacturing or operations to distribution channels to buyers. Collecting data on these diagnostic measures and comparing actual results with forecast results provides a basis for making changes. This control mechanism can save a promising new product that initially achieves only mediocre sales performance.

The General Motors Saturn automobile provides a good example of the importance of monitoring launch response.[15] For GM, the new Saturn represented an entirely new way of building cars. An investment of seven years and $3.5 billion promised the ability to compete strongly with Japanese manufacturers. However, production problems occurred immediately after launch in 1990, followed by a recessionary market, the Gulf War, and significant Saturn recalls (one of which involved recalling its entire output). Because the Saturn project was not well-loved among other GM divisions, these difficulties could have derailed the program and crippled its future success.

Despite the setbacks, Saturn stayed the course. Problems were identified and solved. Recalls were turned into opportunities instead of problems. For example, one recall was used as part of the Saturn ad campaign to show how concerned Saturn was about making its customers happy. Through continuous monitoring of customer and dealer response, a strategic commitment to a carefully crafted advertising program, and attention to the details of production and customer service, Saturn realized a significant sales increase during its second and third years on the market. As a result of this emphasis on getting Saturn right, even after its launch, GM received a third-place rating (behind the prestigious and more expensive Lexus and Infiniti cars) in the J. D. Powers and Associates 1992 survey of customer satisfaction.

Because the investment in Saturn was substantial, and because of the car's symbolic value to GM in competing with the Japanese, Saturn was very important to the organization (although other GM divisions felt it diverted resources from their brands). This importance justified careful monitoring and modification of the product after launch. However, continuous tracking of any new product after launch, whatever its importance to the organization, can lead to success.

WHY STUDY NEW PRODUCT SUCCESS?

In disciplines such as business, medicine, and law, learning comes with the study of problems presented in cases, projects, and other formats. A problem presented in the context of a realistic situation or experience provides an excellent opportunity to examine the underlying factors that give rise to it and suggest alternative ways to resolve it. In new product development situations, possible outcomes can be characterized in terms of success or failure. Learning can follow from studying problems that result in either success or failure. However, a strong argument can be made for studying new product development problems in the context of successful rather than failed products. Consider the following points:

- In new product development, the odds are against success. Recall that only about one new product idea in 11 becomes commercially successful! Hence, studying the problems and factors involved in a success means learning from products that have overcome the heavy odds of not surviving. Remember, missing the mark is easy; hitting it is difficult.

- In studying problems of failed products, determining what factors contributed to the failure is difficult. There are many paths to failure. However, studying problems of successful products shows at least what factors did *not* contribute to failure.

- Organizations do not like to share information about their failures. Managers are more likely to discuss the problems involved in and release data on their successes. They generally provide rich information that affords an understanding of the factors contributing to success.

Consequently, the 24 new product success stories in the following eight chapters are presented in the spirit of fostering the kind of learning and intellectual development needed to understand the factors leading to successful new products.

2

Aligning Strategic Opportunities

New product strategy can be understood best within the broader context of *competitive business strategy* and the role of new products in it. New products provide vehicles for building competitive advantage, leveraging resources and competencies, and capitalizing on strategic market opportunities. When the development of a new product helps to align an organization's strengths and competencies (as well as weaknesses) with market opportunities, the new product may have its greatest chance of success.

The three new product success stories in this chapter show how aligning competencies and weaknesses with opportunities can be an important factor in new product success. Though each story is different, they have a common thread: success could not be achieved by the innovating organization alone. Each needed partners or allies to capitalize on the market opportunity.

The first new product success described is Starbucks Coffee. To capitalize on a favorable market trend, Howard Schultz introduced consumers to coffee as a "consumption experience." Through the use of creatively designed retail outlets, he developed a way to communicate this experience to consumers and sell fresh roasted and brewed coffee in the process. At the core of this experience was the fresh roasted coffee. To deliver the best coffee possible, Schultz acquired a coffee roasting capability along with his growing chain of retail stores. As the number of stores grew, Starbucks gained buying power among the world's elite coffee roasters, thus obtaining the best quality beans. Then, to ensure the proper delivery of the consumption experience, Schultz offered his front-line employees

17

equity in the business as an incentive, even part-time employees. The development of alliances at the supplier, processing, retail, and employee levels was instrumental to Starbucks' performance.

The second new product success is Calyx & Corolla, an innovative fresh flower delivery service. Ruth Owades, the founder, was the first to offer flower delivery directly from growers to consumers. A colorful catalog that shows consumers what they are ordering, a toll-free 800 telephone number, and expedient delivery by Federal Express are major features of the service. Because the flowers are shipped within three days after cutting, they arrive fresher and with a longer life for consumers than those offered by traditional flower delivery services. To achieve this kind of service, Owades had to gain the cooperation of Federal Express and numerous key flower growers. Each had to change normal operating practices to make the flower delivery system work smoothly.

The third success is a new technology developed by Philips Electronics Corporation, the compact disc or CD. The story of the CD's success is somewhat dated (it begins in 1972), but it contains powerful lessons about the importance of establishing industry standards for a new technology. The strategic alliance between Philips and Sony was instrumental in bringing about the standard CD format. It also motivated CD player and recording manufacturers to bring products to the market to take advantage of market demand stimulated by Sony. Sony brought marketing, miniaturization technology, and access to the Japanese market to the alliance, and Philips brought its basic digital technology and prototypes. The resulting product was superior to traditional vinyl recordings in giving consumers high fidelity quality and value. Consumers responded favorably to the new technology and made it a resounding success.

Building partnerships to launch the three new products was not the only factor that contributed to their success. Numerous other factors were involved, many of which were both internal and external to the innovating organization. Each story therefore should be considered in great detail.

Starbucks Coffee Company

Leila M. Byczkowski and Kathleen S. McCarthy

> *We're not just selling a cup of coffee, we are providing an experience.*
> Howard Schultz
> Starbucks Coffee Company

A gourmet coffee craze swept the United States in the early 1990s, led by Starbucks Coffee Company.[1] Starbucks is a chain of coffee shops that originated in Seattle in 1971. Starbucks owned 11 stores in 1987 and had grown to some 280 stores by 1993.[2] Company sales revenue grew from $1.3 million in 1987 to $163.5 million in 1993! Profits in fiscal 1992 were $4.1 million, a 71 percent increase from the previous year. Perhaps most significantly, all of this growth was achieved without incurring any long-term debt.[3]

In May 1992, Starbucks announced an initial public offering of 2.1 million shares at $14 a share. Within two years the stock more than doubled and provided the capital needed to continue growth. Howard Schultz, president of Starbucks, is committed to making Starbucks the "nation's largest specialty coffee roaster and retailer."[4]

Several unique aspects of Starbucks' integrated marketing strategy led to its success:

- Providing a superior product through stringent quality control achieved through vertical integration.
- Adopting a successful niche strategy in a declining coffee market.
- Educating consumers to a new coffee taste to meet some underlying consumer needs.

- Providing incentives to build and maintain a workforce that is empowered to provide high quality service and impart enthusiasm about the coffee to customers.
- Leveraging the coffee shops as distribution channels for other Starbucks branded consumer products.

The essence of Starbucks' success is high quality coffee. To Starbucks, quality coffee begins with superior beans that are grown at high altitude, roasted in a slow European process, and protected from air at all stages of the production cycle. However, more than just high quality coffee was necessary for success. The coffee was part of the core of a new concept in the coffee business. To understand the success of Starbucks as a new concept, a review of the historically complacent coffee industry is useful.

THE COFFEE INDUSTRY

Coffee consumption in the United States peaked during 1962, when about 75 percent of the population drank coffee. Daily per capita consumption was 3.12 cups. Thirty years later, only 51.4 percent of the population consumed coffee and daily per capita consumption was down to 1.78 cups. Although a large market, retail coffee sales declined from a high of $7.4 billion in 1986 to $6.8 billion in 1992.[5] With declining per capita consumption, the dollar level of retail sales must be maintained primarily through price increases.

Yet, within the declining market, gourmet coffee sales grew from 10 percent of the total market in 1983 to about 20 percent 10 years later. The Specialty Coffee Association of America attributes this growth to "the educating of the American coffee palate."[6] Coffee experts predict that the gourmet coffee segment is here to stay. An appreciation for good coffee is returning as the quality of available coffee improves.

The slow emergence of this market began in the 1960s when U.S. coffee giants tried to reduce costs by purchasing inferior robusta beans and storing roasted beans so long that their quality became even poorer. This strategy left the coffee market wide open for gourmet competitors[7] that used superior arabica beans to ensure a marked difference in quality and taste between their coffee and standard canned brands.

Growth in the gourmet coffee market was also aided by broader distribution of gourmet coffees through supermarkets, introduction of new specialty coffee products by traditional coffee purveyors, and growth in the related gourmet food market.[8]

CAPITALIZING ON THE MARKET OPPORTUNITY

In response to the declining quality of mass-produced canned coffee, numerous independent coffeehouses sprang up in urban areas in the 1980s. Unlike the late-night folk-music coffeehouses of the 1950s and 1960s "beat generation," these shops were bright and operated throughout the day in high traffic areas. Thus, differentiation within the coffee market was already underway before Starbucks started as a small roasting shop in 1971. At the time, "two teachers and a writer began roasting beans in an old Pike Place Market junk shop."[9] The Starbucks name was adopted from Starbuck, the coffee-drinking chief mate in Herman Melville's classic novel, *Moby Dick.*

When Howard Schultz bought Starbucks in 1987 from the original owners, the specialty coffee retail market had numerous established competitors, but no dominant player. Schultz identified an opportunity to segment the gourmet/specialty market further. Building on Starbucks' core competency of purchasing quality beans and employing its unique roasting techniques, Schultz added the ambiance of an Italian espresso bar to the retail locations. His goal was to become the "premiere purveyor of specialty coffee and a national retail leader."[10]

Starbucks offers full-bodied, dark roasted beans purchased from exotic worldwide locations. It does not offer flavored coffees, which Schultz considers "a bastardization of the product, masking an inferior bean."[11] This policy excludes Starbucks from the fastest growing segment of the gourmet coffee market, but also differentiates it from Gloria Jean's Coffee and Barney's Coffees and Teas, the two largest national competitive chains of specialty coffee shops.

DEVELOPMENT OF THE STARBUCKS CONCEPT

Howard Schultz joined Starbucks in 1982 as director of retail operations and marketing. Located in Seattle, Washington, Starbucks was a local but highly respected roaster and retailer of whole bean and ground coffees. In 1983, Schultz traveled to Italy where he became enamored with the espresso/coffee bars and saw the potential in Seattle for the development of a similar coffee bar concept. He returned to Starbucks and convinced the founders to test the coffee bar concept at one of their new stores.

Because of the tremendous success of the test, Schultz decided to leave Starbucks and start several coffee bars of his own, which he named "Il Giornale." The stores offered brewed coffee and espresso beverages made from Starbucks' beans. However, in 1987, Schultz seized the opportunity to buy out the original owners of Starbucks. Because Il Giornale used Starbucks' coffee beans in acknowledgment of the excellent quality of its roasting operations, the acquisition made good business sense. More important, though, was the opportunity to integrate all operations vertically. Schultz combined the coffee bar, roasting, and retail coffee business into one outlet. He believed a coffee bar would be the best advertisement for his world-class coffees, thereby enhancing the sale of coffee beans by the pound.

His idea was to "transform Starbucks from a local roaster to the country's premier roaster and retailer of fresh whole bean coffee and coffee beverages, without compromising its tradition for quality."[12] Around this idea he would build the core product concept of a "consumption experience" through the selection of the retail location, the ambiance of the store, and the positioning of the Starbucks concept through imagery.

Through a Starbucks outlet, consumers could participate in the consumption experience by purchasing a variety of excellent exotic coffees, either by the cup or by the pound for home use. In 1987 and 1988, Starbucks began to expand into nearby Portland and Vancouver, British Columbia. Each store was designed for vertical integration of the coffee bar with the retail bean outlet. Old stores were strictly redesigned so that all Starbucks outlets would present a consistent image and character to the consumers.

DESIGN AND TESTING

Starbucks' special roasting process was retained after Schultz acquired the company. Some adjustment in roasting was necessary in changing from local roaster to national distributor, but the process itself remained the same. The exacting standards that had been firmly established in 1972 would be maintained. All roasting operations were centralized in the Seattle area to ensure maximum quality control of the Starbucks process.

The process of producing high quality coffees is "similar in complexity and detail to that involved in producing a world-class wine: there are many steps involved, and great care is required from start to finish."[13] Roasters have been highly trained to observe and control the roast. Roasting is done in small batches, controlled by the skill of the roasting staff rather than automated equipment. Each coffee is roasted to its individual peak flavor, a process perfected only after years of experience. "Roasters can smell the changing qualities in the wisps of smoke rising from the roasting coffee. They watch for subtle alterations of color and listen for the sound of popping beans."[14]

The senses, skills, and experience of Starbucks' roasters are essential to the success of the roasting process. Starbucks' freshness and quality standards are legendary. Roasts that do not meet the rigorous specifications and beans that remain in their bins longer than one week are donated to charities. Moreover, every piece of coffee-brewing equipment sold by the company is rigorously tested and evaluated. The company also tests and monitors new grinding devices as they come on the market.

The company continually searches for the highest quality beans. Its buyers scour more than 20 countries worldwide for beans that meet their exacting standards. Traditionally, European buyers have cornered the market for quality beans, but Starbucks has grown to be the largest U.S. purchaser of the high quality arabica coffee beans.

Starbucks works hard to keep all of its coffees in stock, but many of the varieties are rare and difficult to obtain. The company would rather run out of a particular coffee than substitute one of lower quality. It buys on the basis of taste alone, regardless of price, and can do so because the segment of customers attracted to Starbucks does not appear to be price sensitive. Starbucks' coffee buyers have consequently earned such an excellent reputation that coffee brokers send them hundreds of coffee bean samples every year for evaluation.

This reputation as an eager buyer enables Starbucks to develop unique coffee taste experiences through its "coffee blend" concept. Traditionally, blending is a cost-saving technique using "the smallest possible percentage of good coffee to mask the flavor of the largest possible percentage of mediocre-to-atrocious beans."[15] Starbucks combines only beans that retain their best characteristics, emphasizing nuance and balance to achieve a blend with unique character that is "greater than the sum of its parts."[16]

Coffee was not to be considered one standard product as it had been in the past. Schultz was the first to emphasize that coffee is a perishable good with a limited shelf life, in contrast to the traditional view that canned coffee has an unlimited shelf life. There were many varieties and roasting processes, and there was much to be learned. Schultz believed

Starbucks could set the standards and lead the gourmet coffee industry by listening to its consumers.

In-house product testing and market research are ongoing processes. Schultz recognizes that coffee tastes are slow to change, and he therefore relies heavily on his staff to stay close to customers, offering samples of new varieties and special blends for them to try. Starbucks thus gains valuable feedback while educating consumers to new coffee possibilities. This approach not only saves the company the expense of commercial market research, but also serves to pull customers in because they are eager to try the new coffees and expand their coffee expertise. They become part of the "coffee culture." By interacting with and staying close to its customers, Starbucks is able to meet their needs, spot changes, and stay on the cutting edge of innovation.

THE LAUNCH

With the acquisition of Starbucks and the formulation of a core product concept, Schultz set the stage for accomplishing his goal of making Starbucks the leading specialty coffee retailer. Three factors were instrumental in Starbucks' successful launch: (1) market attractiveness, (2) positioning, and (3) marketing strategy.

Market Attractiveness

Starbucks was not the first to enter the gourmet coffee niche, yet it still found the market attractive. By 1987, regular coffee sales were flat but the gourmet niche was growing at a rate of 20 percent a year. There were many local coffeehouses and a few national chains when Schultz envisioned becoming "the largest purveyor of gourmet coffee in the U.S." The market was ripe and competition was somewhat fragmented and limited. Even the three largest national purveyors of branded coffee (Procter & Gamble, Kraft General Foods, and Nestlé), with the resources to erect entry barriers, were relatively myopic about the gourmet coffee boom and benign to emerging competitors such as Starbucks.[17]

Positioning

With an attractive market opportunity and a superior product, Schultz still needed a strong image and positioning for Starbucks to realize his concept of a consumption experience. Because the new Starbucks was a combination of coffee bar and retail business, Schultz focused the launch on positioning Starbucks Coffee Company as an impeccable, world-class coffee company rejuvenating America's lost passion for coffee. Prices were kept at a premium to reflect the prestigious image of the coffee. Little advertising was necessary as Starbucks had tremendous brand equity in the Northwest. Publicity and word-of-mouth communication spread the Starbucks name and the company's community involvement helped bolster its image.

In combining two businesses, Schultz wanted an integrated marketing approach. The Il Giornale name was dropped in favor of the better known Starbucks name, and the logo and packaging were redesigned. The new packaging featured uniquely designed international stamps representing the coffees' origin and helped to promote a distinctive, worldly, and sophisticated image. The stamps of such exotic places as Arabia, Sumatra, Kenya, and Guatemala became so popular with customers that they are now sold through the company's catalogs in the form of kitchen magnets.

Schultz wanted to develop a coffee consciousness in his Starbucks customers. He hoped coffee drinkers would soon take fine coffee as seriously as wine connoisseurs take fine wine. Schultz wanted coffee drinkers to realize that fine coffee, like fine wine, varies in quality and quantity and can change from season to season. He wanted them to recognize that there are many different tastes, depending on the coffee's origin, and that some of the best coffees are meant to stand alone but others can be blended to derive unique flavor. Consequently, Starbucks' positioning was tied closely to the high quality of its product. Its positioning promise could be delivered with the right marketing strategy.

Marketing Strategy

To gain nationwide recognition, Starbucks needed to educate consumers about gourmet coffee and the coffee culture as well as Starbucks' superiority. To achieve this goal, Schultz emphasized the importance of the front-line sales staff. Starbucks' employees would be instrumental to the company's marketing strategy. They would not be simply order-takers, but a well-trained and persuasive salesforce. By initially providing 24 hours of product training followed by ongoing education, the company made sure that each employee became exceptionally knowledgeable about coffee and brewing products.

Customer service was also emphasized in training. As incentive, Starbucks gave all full- and part-time employees equity in the company. The decision to do so was based on thorough analysis. According to Schultz, "We did a regression analysis of the cost of hiring, training, and losing people."[18] The cost of benefits was less than the costs of hiring, training, and attrition. Employee ownership of the company created a system of values and infrastructure that has been well sustained.

From the start, employees (full and part time) felt tremendous loyalty to the company, which was readily apparent to customers. Schultz attacked employee attrition by making employment at Starbucks a career option instead of a temporary job. As a result, employee turnover was low, and "Schultz felt his people were their most important competitive advantage."[19] By empowering the front-line employees, Starbucks made them the best promoters of its various products.

Starbucks did not invest in traditional advertising during launch. The company relied instead on retail location and its knowledgeable, well-trained staff as the best communicators of the Starbucks image and products. This strategy proved successful for pulling customers in and educating them about the various coffees and Starbucks' superiority.

Consumer education was vital to Starbucks' success because its unique roasting process results in a coffee that tastes very different from the traditional thin, bland coffee made from stale beans. Starbucks coffees are distinct in flavor and aroma. In fact, *Consumer Reports* once criticized Starbucks coffee for having a "bitter charred taste." Indeed, for many people, Starbucks coffee, like wine, is an acquired taste. Starbucks believes that the more a person tries its coffee, the more that person will appreciate its subtle differences and superior quality.

Starbucks also became involved in each community in which it launched stores, as well as the broader world community. Besides donating coffee to charities, Starbucks offers a "CARE Sampler." Through a partnership with CARE, Starbucks donates part of the retail purchase price to various social programs in the developing countries that are the source of the coffee beans.

Starbucks' distribution of retail outlets follows a site selection plan based on high traffic, high visibility locations. Clustering large numbers of stores in each local area exposes the Starbucks brand name to the community and affords marketing and operational efficiencies. Each store is designed to add to the positioning ambiance and to ensure favorable merchandising of Starbucks products. Starbucks also uses direct mail distribution from its own catalog of coffee products and distribution through other specialty retailers (such as selected department stores) and institutional food services (such as colleges and airports).

Through an integrated and winning marketing strategy based on a premium product, customer service by an informed and cared-for workforce, and conveniently located and comfortable stores, Starbucks has created a favorable consumption experience for which consumers are willing to pay a premium price. Taken together, Starbucks' market entry timing, positioning, and marketing strategy have generated considerable "pull" for its product and have saved the company a great amount of advertising expense. As testament to the incredible pull of the Starbucks brand name, the Los Angeles Starbucks opened successfully in 1991 without major media advertising!

MANAGING THE PROCESS

Howard Schultz was definitely the product champion for Starbucks from conception to launch, but he soon incorporated teamwork into the decision-making process. Schultz stresses the importance of employee input as the vital link to consumer opinion and needs. Schultz also relies on a strong, interactive board of directors that has a high degree of operational involvement. The Starbucks management team assembled by Schultz has been together from the start and their decisions reflect an attempt to arrive at consensus.

Schultz cleverly planned ahead for Starbucks' exponential growth and store expansion by investing heavily in infrastructure between 1987 and 1989. He saw vertical integration as being key to achieving total quality control. The fact that each store is company owned ensures consistency of both product distribution and store image.

WHY DID STARBUCKS SUCCEED?

Any of a number of competitors will succeed to some degree in a growing market, but few achieve the rapid and relatively controlled growth of a Starbucks. Why? The reasons can be found in Starbucks' *competitive strategy* and the market's response to it. Competitive strategy defines how an organization decides to compete over the long run. Schultz was not out for a short-term profit, but took a longer-term view of the business and made decisions accordingly.

Competitive Advantage: Creating an Innovative Consumption Experience

If asked what business he is in, Schultz would emphatically say he is not in the business of selling coffee. Rather, he would say he is in the business of creating a consumption experience, of which coffee is a part. In Schultz's own words, a visit to Starbucks is "romance, theatrics, community—the totality of the coffee experience."[20] This carefully conceptualized vision of the business defines the innovation in the market that distinguishes Starbucks from its competitors and attracts customers. It is the basis for defining the product, building the necessary operations to deliver the product, designing the marketing program, securing financing, establishing human resource policies, and other related decisions.

Market Segmentation: Knowing the Consumer

Starbucks understood it could not market to the masses. It was content to start with a small but growing niche of the market. The Specialty Coffee Association describes gourmet coffee drinkers as young urban professionals ranging in age from 25 to 45 years who earn more than $35,000 a year. Their most significant attribute is education level. Consumers with some postgraduate education are an amazing 71 percent above average in gourmet coffee consumption! Starbucks further segmented this consumer market by targeting what the Association calls the "sophisticate." Sophisticates eat out more often than other segments and are prone to food experimentation. They are health conscious, like to travel, and identify with "gourmets." This segment comprises roughly 18 percent of all consumers.[21]

The Starbucks concept taps into the changing lifestyles and underlying needs of this sophisticated customer segment. In addition to the physical need of thirst that coffee fills, Starbucks addresses deeper social and psychological needs of increasingly health conscious consumers. For example, as alcoholic beverage bars lose favor as acceptable meeting places, Starbucks offers an elegant coffee bar as a social alternative. Alcohol sales are down in the United States, in what has been described as a "national thirst for sobriety."[22] This trend has resulted in a shift from the neighborhood pub to the neighborhood coffeehouse as the late-night hangout for young adults. In this lively social setting, Americans are expanding their coffee acumen, experimenting with new, exotic varieties of beans, and studying different roasting techniques.

On a more psychological level, Starbucks uses a knowledgeable but friendly staff to balance its image of exoticism, romanticism, and sophistication with consumer accessibility. Because an overly sophisticated or exclusive image could alienate or intimidate customers, Starbucks invites consumers into a warm and congenial environment to learn all about the exciting world of coffee. The *experience* is inviting, and customers return with their friends, who bring their friends, and so on! The rapid diffusion of personal information from satisfied users is much more credible in building a success than any form of mass communication.

Aligning Competencies

Schultz combined his strength in retail outlets (Il Giornale) with the Starbucks coffee buying and roasting strengths to create a vertically integrated business. With company-owned stores financed by a public stock offering, and opportunities for economies of scale in buying power, Starbucks was able to leverage cooperation with coffee growers and break into new markets more easily than its competitors.

Starbucks operated at a loss during its initial years. It invested its earnings in building a strong management team and the infrastructure (including information systems) necessary to control a far-flung collection of retail outlets. Also, the importance of buying power with suppliers cannot be overlooked as a competency. For years, Europeans dominated the specialty coffee markets, but now Starbucks can compete for the best beans and even outbid other American purveyors of gourmet coffee.[23]

Delivering High Quality to Keep Customers

The vertical integration enables the company to maintain exacting quality control of all operations. Franchising is avoided to maintain control; all stores are company owned. At the store level, front-line employees are trained, given equity incentives, and empowered to deliver the quality of service necessary to complete the consumption experience. Finally, by choosing high traffic urban locations and designing outlets with meticulous attention to detail, Starbucks ensures consistency in conveying its quality image.

STARBUCKS' FUTURE

Several lessons can be learned from the Starbucks story. First, a superior product can (and many people would argue *must*) be the core of a successful business strategy. Starbucks has developed a reputation for unrelenting commitment to quality and consistency, which has greatly enhanced its brand equity with consumers.

Second, a clear understanding of and, to the extent possible, interaction with consumers keeps an organization on the cutting edge of changes in the market. Starbucks stays close to the customer through consumer education and ongoing product testing. The company realized the need to educate consumers to a new coffee taste and culture. The continual interaction of staff and consumers gives Starbucks immediate feedback on products and service.

Third, employees should be thought of as assets, not expenses. Starbucks values its employees as marketers and educators for the Starbucks concept and treats all employees with respect, rewarding them with benefits and company stock. As a result, loyal employees are effective in promoting Starbucks, and expenditures on advertising media are low.

Although Starbucks has been a phenomenal success since 1987, its story is expected to continue. With the initial public offering in April 1992, Starbucks gained access to capital for increased expansion. The company plans to continue blanketing new markets in the United States and to launch an international presence.

The consequence of building a global presence can be the emergence of a global brand name that conveys all of the company's imagery and associations. Starbucks has an excellent opportunity to leverage the equity it is building into its name. For example, the company is extending its product line to include coffee mugs, coffee grinding and brewing equipment, chocolates, and syrups. With continued success, the Starbucks name may ultimately appear on premium branded consumer products in mass distribution channels, such as supermarkets, throughout the world.

Calyx & Corolla

Elisabeth A. Watson and Jennifer Zydney

What's in a name? That which we call a rose
By any other name would smell as sweet. (II, ii, 43)

This bud of love, by summer's ripening breath,
May prove a beauteous flower when next we meet. (II, ii, 121)

William Shakespeare, Romeo and Juliet

Today is Monday. Your loved one's birthday is on Wednesday, and you want a bouquet of flowers delivered to her on that special day. The problem is that you live in Phoenix and she lives in Philadelphia. What should you do?

One solution to your problem is to call the Calyx & Corolla toll-free 800 number and order the flowers from its colorful catalog. Calyx & Corolla has revolutionized the way flowers are sold and delivered. The company differs from the traditional floral delivery business on three dimensions: distribution, visual presentation, and service.

- Calyx & Corolla ships orders directly from growers to consumers overnight by Federal Express. Flowers arrive within 72 hours of being cut. Through careful planning and use of information technology, Calyx & Corolla eliminated the distributor/wholesaler channel common to all other floral industry businesses.

- Traditionally, flowers by wire are bought unseen by consumers. Calyx & Corolla provides a color catalog of the company's products (which include cut flowers, plants, and accessories) to enable potential buyers to visualize their purchase.

- To enhance the convenience of ordering directly from a catalog, Calyx & Corolla provides trained employees at its toll-free 800 number to answer questions about products or make suggestions about what to order for particular occasions or specific needs.

THE FLORAL OPPORTUNITY

Ruth M. Owades founded Calyx & Corolla in 1988. It was her second successful catalog venture. The first, Gardener's Eden, was a gardening supply catalog business. She sold it to San Francisco–based Williams-Sonoma in 1982 and remained with Gardener's Eden as president for five years. She then left to develop Calyx & Corolla, in part because she enjoyed flowers, but also because she sensed a market opportunity.

The Flower Industry

The flower industry is large and fragmented. About $1.5 billion is spent annually on sending flowers.[24] Typically, flowers are flown in (about 67 percent of flowers purchased in the United States are imported)[25] and sold to distributors. They are then shipped to wholesalers who sell them to retailers in large flower markets, usually located in major cities. This system has two important implications. First, distributors and wholesalers each require a margin, which increases prices to retailers and end users. Second, distributor and wholesaler relationships are generally not geographically cohesive.

In this distribution system, flowers travel long distances and are loaded and unloaded several times. The potential for spoilage is high. As a result of this system, the average retail customer buys flowers that have been cut as long as 14 days prior to purchase. End users can enjoy their flowers for only about a week in most cases. Therefore, market fragmentation and time to market provided potential opportunities for creative marketers.

Market Trends

Much of Owades' initial effort went into identifying and defining the market opportunity in the flower industry. She considered the following findings:

- Eighty percent of a florist's orders were by telephone.[26]
- The floral market was growing at a respectable 10 percent a year.[27]
- The mail order business had an annual growth rate of 15 percent during the 1980s, but the rate in the retail sector was only 5 percent.[28]

Library research also turned up relevant information. Women, with growing purchasing power, were increasingly purchasing flowers as decorative accents, gifts, or psychological boosts. Sixty percent of orders were placed by women.[29]

Another trend surfaced during the 1980s. Marketers were becoming convinced that a growing segment of consumers, many of them women, were dissatisfied with the hard sell of sex. Consequently, advertising became more emotional and romantic. Behind this trend was the fantasy of working women "to have it all without being consumed by work."[30] Supermarkets recognized this shift toward romanticism and began to offer cut flowers, which provided attractive profit margins. The mere presence of flowers in supermarkets helped to convince Americans that flowers are not just for special occasions.[31]

Owades predicted that flowers would be "the ideal gift of the 1990s; they are fat free, nonalcoholic, and politically correct!" Consequently, the corporate market appeared to offer additional opportunities for flowers as gifts. At the time of her research, the $1.7 billion corporate gift market was growing at 5 percent annually, in part because of employee recognition programs.[32]

Flower consumers were placing an increasing premium on convenience and delivery. One survey reported that 72 percent of respondents rated delivery most important.[33] These findings prompted Owades to pursue mail order and express delivery. Customers also wanted assurance that they were purchasing the "right gift." The ability to see the flowers in a catalog combined with an emphasis on service would meet that need.

Owades considered global factors. In 1988, Europeans were spending twice as much on flowers as Americans.[34] The fact that the Dutch were buying an average of 103 stems per capita per year[35] had encouraged Dutch growers to launch a successful marketing campaign in the United States. To Owades, the comparatively low level of flower consumption in the United States suggested an enormous opportunity if buying could be stimulated. A change in distribution and marketing communication might tap unperceived needs within consumers, encouraging them to view flowers as more than a luxury for special occasions.

Buyer Behavior

Owades correctly recognized that consumers place great emotional importance on flowers. Like no other gift, flowers connote emotion: romance, love, and redemption from guilt.[36] A news story demonstrates the powerful messages associated with flowers:

> [At a gathering of the National Women's Law Center honoring Anita Hill, a Washington attorney told Hill], "We sent you flowers; it was *therapy* for us because we were so angry." . . . "Let me tell you, it was *therapy* for me too," Hill replied. . . . "We took them to the nursing homes and the hospitals. This was one of the good moments, not only that we got the flowers, but that we could share them" [emphasis added].[37]

Clearly, the purchase of flowers is really the purchase of a good feeling, romance, or some other emotional need fulfillment. However, to satisfy their needs, consumers must overcome the uncertainty of the purchase process when ordering flowers. By offering a responsive flower delivery service, Owades created a concept to help consumers more effectively order flowers and satisfy their needs. As one of the Calyx & Corolla growers notes, even the act of taking the flowers out of the box and arranging them adds to the emotional aspect of receiving them.[38]

PRODUCT DEVELOPMENT PROCESS

The idea for a new concept in the flower business occurred to Ruth Owades while she was playing tennis! To reduce some of the uncertainty associated with ordering flowers and to lengthen the time consumers could enjoy their flowers, Owades developed the core concept of a new floral service around ease of ordering, speed of delivery, and responsiveness to customers. The key to implementing this concept was the design of an integrated and effective distribution system. The name "Calyx & Corolla" came as a last minute decision just before the first catalog was to be printed. It was taken from botany. The calyx is the part of the flower that protects the bud and the corolla is the petals.

Aligning a Creative Distribution System

Owades designed a distribution system that would eliminate distributors and wholesalers. It would increase the margins available to her and ensure delivery of flowers to retail customers within 72 hours of cutting. To implement it, she needed commitment from growers, a delivery service, and information technology for integration.

Flower Growers

Owades researched flower growers through trade journals and approached them with her concept. She identified ones who produced the varieties she needed and had a reputation for quality products. In many cases, the growers were enthusiastic and referred her to others. Her proposal to the growers required them to meet quality specifications set by Calyx & Corolla. Flower quality is determined by stem length and the size of the bulb, or bud.[39] Only by specifying premium characteristics and using quality growers could Owades ensure that her products would meet consumer expectations.

Her proposal also required the growers to make fundamental changes in their way of doing business. If they signed on with her, they would have to cut flowers to order and package them for individual customers. These tasks were traditional responsibilities of retail florists. However, growers were receptive because they were looking for a means to expand their business and distribute more efficiently.[40] Further, Calyx & Corolla agreed to pay growers for some of the traditional "florist" functions.

Delivery by Federal Express

Owades targeted the Federal Express delivery service because she believed its status as a premier reliable service would give credibility to Calyx & Corolla. The next step was to persuade Federal Express to establish multiple terminals at the growers' sites for daily pickup. She required other exceptions to its standard operations: Saturday deliveries, leaving packages at the door if customers are not at home, and guaranteed delivery dates.

Federal Express executives were skeptical of the new service at first. It was not clear that Calyx & Corolla would generate sufficient demand to justify his company's efforts. Owades countered by noting that the potential volume and the opportunity for Federal Express to learn about the growing business of shipping perishables would make the venture worthwhile.[41] Because of the quality of her presentation and an agreement that Calyx & Corolla would accept liability for packages left, as well as some persuasion in the form of flowers she sent on two occasions, the executives were convinced.[42]

Information Technology

To control the distribution process, Calyx & Corolla uses an electronic ordering system. Customer orders are sent by computer to the major growers who provide more than 80 percent of the flowers. Orders can also be sent by fax or Federal Express to the other growers.[43] Product quality determines which grower gets a particular order. Once orders are shipped, Federal Express can track them through its sophisticated tracking system to let customers know the exact location of their flowers should they request that information.

Packaging

The growers cut the flowers and package them in boxes designed by Calyx & Corolla and Federal Express. The packaging is designed to protect the flowers in transit. Roses are put in individual water vials and lie on "ice pillows." Gerbera daisies are packed with straw casings to protect their fragile stems. Federal Express picks up the orders each afternoon and ships them overnight to the customers. The high quality of the product is maintained by the packaging and the speed of delivery.

Communication Program

With a distribution system in place to ensure speedy delivery of freshly cut flowers from growers, Calyx & Corolla had to create a communication program that would enable potential buyers to visualize their purchases and execute their orders easily. The Calyx & Corolla catalog became the realization of its product concept. It removes much of the uncertainty of flower ordering by giving potential buyers a visual presentation of the products. The text in the catalog is a source of information about all aspects of the purchase, including the flowers and plants, ordering, delivery, and the company.

The award-winning catalog is also the firm's primary promotional vehicle. Its colorful, visually appealing photographs of beautiful flower arrangements encourage readers to place an order. The catalog's success as a form of direct mail advertising depends on carefully pruned mailing lists that correctly target potential customers. For example, to launch Calyx & Corolla, Owades rented and tracked 50 lists.[44] She also states that the beauty of selling flowers through a catalog is that she can use a wide variety of mailing lists representing such diverse consumer groups as gift, apparel, and book and record buyers.[45]

Other forms of direct and personal communication complement the catalog to generate sales and build awareness. For example, Calyx & Corolla participated in a copromotion with Bloomingdales for Mothers' Day. Bloomingdales advertised fine crystal such as Lalique and Waterford and offered purchasers complimentary orchid bouquets from Calyx & Corolla. Calyx & Corolla gave Bloomingdales a good price on the orchids and offered its guarantees of quality and timeliness. Owades claims that such copromotions are successful, especially when they communicate a quality image with such prestigious firms as Bloomingdales and Lalique.

Corporate accounts represent a growing opportunity for sales. Flowers are excellent incentives. They are visible, convey sincere appreciation, and are universally welcome. Companies also use flowers as office decoration, which improves the working environment and conveys class and sophistication to visitors. Corporate accounts are a source of large sales and continuing contracts. They enable Calyx & Corolla to use its competitive advantage in building relationships to attract loyal customers. Moreover, corporate accounts increase awareness, as employees are certain to notice the flowers and will think of Calyx & Corolla when they want to make individual purchases.

Relationship Building

Essential to each step in the product development process was Owades' ability to develop strong relationships with the growers and Federal Express. Maintaining quality control and reliability in the widespread supply network is driven by the relationship between Calyx & Corolla and the growers. The growers must believe that their business is enhanced by supplying Calyx & Corolla customers. The growers' ability to reach new markets with quality products is key to the relationship. To maintain the relationship, continuous improvements to the distribution system must be made and ideas for reaching new markets must be generated.

The creation of special packaging and the scheduling of pickups depended on a strong relationship with Federal Express. Federal Express wanted to increase its share of the perishables market and Calyx & Corolla provided an opportunity to do so. The Federal Express logo is featured in the Calyx & Corolla catalog as an integral part of the quality message. Federal Express is continually working with Calyx & Corolla to identify and meet the company's needs.[46] Most important, Federal Express believes in Calyx & Corolla. Linda Luttrop, marketing manager for direct marketing, states that "Federal Express is an integral part of Calyx & Corolla."[47] Together, they have developed an innovative means of managing damage claims, which Federal Express has imitated with other customers.

HOW SUCCESSFUL HAS CALYX & COROLLA BEEN?

As a privately held company, Calyx & Corolla provides limited financial data. However, there are signs that the company's success has been sizable since its launch in 1988. After a January 1994 interview with Ruth Owades on *Working Woman*, a television talk show, the narrator revealed that Calyx & Corolla had grown from a $5 million to a $15 million business in its first five years. Such growth is remarkable during relatively slow economic times. Retail flower sales growth has flattened since 1990, but Owades believes flowers, beer, candy, and ice cream are the four most recession-proof commodities that Americans buy.[48]

Another indicator of Calyx & Corolla's success is its increasing number of competitors. For example, though not a direct competitor, 800-Flowers has used aggressive television advertising targeted largely to male buyers in the 25 to 45 age group to sell flowers through local florists (much like FTD).[49] More recently it has instituted shipping by UPS for next-day air delivery, "FloraMinder" to remind customers when to send birthday and anniversary flowers, and interactive multimedia ordering through online computer services.[50]

PCFlowers is a computer online service with computer-generated photographs that lets potential buyers visualize flowers and place an order. In 1991, Flowers Direct emerged as a competitor by connecting callers directly to local florist shops (presumably to eliminate the charges of middlemen). Even FTD launched a new service, Direct Access, which features an 800-SEND-FTD telephone number and a "Florist Finder" service that helps link a caller directly to an FTD florist. Reportedly, this service lost money in its first year ending January 1993.[51]

Another indicator of success is the low level of customer complaints. Owades reports that her complaint level is only 2 percent,[52] a rate that is difficult to achieve when selling perishables. All purchases are unconditionally guaranteed and backed by an extensive and well-trained telephone marketing and customer service staff. The firm prides itself in helping consumers solve their problems, whether before or after the sale. Coupled with the sales growth and competitive response, the low customer complaint rate indicates that Calyx & Corolla has achieved its original mission of providing quality goods and service to a premium market segment.

KEY FACTORS IN THE CALYX & COROLLA SUCCESS

The most obvious factor that led to success for Calyx & Corolla is simply its execution. Owades had to secure a cooperative commitment from selected growers and Federal Express to implement a system with perishable products. Aligning key players in the distribution system was critical to the new company's performance. Maintaining those relationships is crucial to continued success. If the relationships dissolve, so will the business.

Market research also played a critical role in launching Calyx & Corolla. Owades discovered fragmentation in the flower industry and lack of coordination between suppliers and retailers. She discerned major market trends that were favorable to flowers. She learned about the nuances of buyer behavior in the purchase of fresh flowers. She tested 50 lists to ensure that she was communicating with her most likely buyers, and continues to refine her list to find ways to encourage repeat purchases.

Communication is another key factor in the company's success. Many people have promising ideas for new products, but they often fail to execute their vision through a refined communication strategy. Clearly visualizing the delivered product for consumers by means of a high quality catalog helped to communicate the potential benefits of ordering the flowers. Complementing the catalog with an effective array of holiday promotions and direct marketing to large accounts helped to increase awareness and purchases. Further, Calyx & Corolla made extensive use of public relations, with Ruth Owades frequently featured in the popular and business press.

Finally, the success of Calyx & Corolla depends on *quality*. For example, its packaging is an essential part of quality assurance. During the development stage, working closely with the Federal Express packaging engineers was crucial. Then it was critical to work with the growers to change their traditional packaging system. The product is delivered in specially designed boxes that are as environmentally sound as possible (the flowers are shipped in excelsior for protection against bumps and bruises) and appealing to the recipient. Packages have a painted ribbon and bear the

Calyx & Corolla logo. The distribution system, product guarantees, and trained customer service personnel also ensure that the quality promise is kept.

Perhaps the most important lesson for anyone looking for ways to create successful new products or services is the attention Calyx & Corolla gives to the entire marketing program. Unlike companies that achieve success with breakthrough products, Calyx & Corolla's success is centered on its innovative *delivery* concept based on distribution and promotion. Customers had an unmet need to see what they were purchasing when ordering flowers and to be assured that they were sending the appropriate message to the receiver. Growers wanted to reach their markets more directly, and the market for perishable fresh flowers was ripe for innovation in speed of delivery. By focusing on customer needs and then delivering the best product available at a competitive price, Calyx & Corolla has upgraded the flower industry's standards and provides significant added value to the end user. Innovation that brings lasting improvement is sure to be the hallmark of a successful venture.

CONCLUSIONS AND FUTURE ISSUES

Maintaining Calyx & Corolla's success may be difficult because of the company's continued growth, increasing competition, changing market conditions, and environmental factors. Like any growing company, Calyx & Corolla must work continually to improve the quality of its operations. Because Federal Express does not pick up or deliver on Sunday and does not find holiday delivery to be cost effective, Calyx & Corolla cannot schedule deliveries on Mondays or holidays. These limitations affect Calyx & Corolla's gift business, especially because major gift-giving occasions are on Sundays or holidays.

All catalog firms are plagued by problems with the U.S. Postal Service in the form of increased postage expenses and delays. In 1991, delays cost Calyx & Corolla "hundreds of thousands of dollars" in lost business because fall and holiday catalogs, scheduled for delivery two to three weeks apart, arrived within days of each other.[53]

Other issues facing Calyx & Corolla are external. Weather conditions affect the business. In October 1992, Hurricane Andrew knocked out South Florida flower growers' operations and caused delayed and limited shipments. Because many flowers are imported from South American countries, their cost is subject to rapid inflation and/or currency devaluation.

Calyx & Corolla is dependent on Federal Express and its growers. For example, should Federal Express have labor or operational problems, Calyx & Corolla would be unable to do business. If key growers decide to give preferential treatment to the company's competitors, Calyx & Corolla could be at a disadvantage. Finally, the sustainability of Owades' own abilities to maintain the company's essential relationships can determine future success. Relationship building is time-consuming and requires considerable effort.

Calyx & Corolla also faces strategic challenges. Can a segment of flower consumers who value premium flowers and service be found around the world as it was in the United States, thus giving Calyx & Corolla an opportunity to expand globally? Further, though they are not currently planned, product extensions may become important to sustain growth. For example, calendars and datebooks, which could take advantage of the company's visual imagery strengths, might be possible line extensions.

Partly as a result of Ruth Owades' actions, the flower industry is changing, and information technology and innovation are accelerating the changes. An increasing number of competitors will be able to emulate Calyx & Corolla's source of competitive advantage, thereby reducing its potential for continued growth. Clearly, to continue its success, Calyx & Corolla must stay on the leading edge of innovation in the industry, using the same approaches that led the company to success in the first place.

Philips Electronics: The Compact Disc

Corain E. M. McGinn and Kristina Nordsten

How many quadraphonic sound records do you own? When quadraphonic sound was introduced, it was supposed to replace stereophonic sound in the same way stereo displaced monaural sound. Unfortunately, quadraphonic sound failed miserably in the market, which is why you probably own few, if any, such records.

Not surprisingly, because of quadraphonic sound and other major market failures, the home electronics industry tends to have a conservative attitude toward new recording technology. Launching a new technology that will successfully replace a current technology is very difficult. The reason is not only the way such technology is brought to market, but also consumers' entrenched buying habits and their inventories of records in a particular medium. A consumer with a fine collection of Beatles records in stereo would not be likely to replace them with a new quadraphonic collection. Hence, Philips Electronics was understandably apprehensive about introducing a new compact disc technology to the audio market.[54]

The new technology appeared in the form of a smooth-surfaced, digitally coded disc less than five inches in diameter. When the disc is inserted into a player, its surface is read by a laser beam for accurate reproduction of the digital encoding of recorded sound. The disc is protected with a coating of plastic to give it a very long life.

The new product was originally called the digital audio disc (DAD), but has become better known as the compact disc (CD). The technology incorporated in the compact disc process had been available in experimental form since the 1950s. However, a combination of a market ready for innovation, an alliance of key industry leaders, and a superior product had to be aligned strategically to provide any kind of reasonable business opportunity for this new product.

Fortunately for Philips and its collaborators, the technology and its product were so effective, and the collective industry launch strategy so successful, that the audio compact disc not only superseded the traditional vinyl disc but contributed to its gradual disappearance. Consumers replaced their collections of vinyl discs and tapes with CDs! More than one billion CDs were sold in 1991 in contrast to 1.3 million traditional vinyl discs. The CD also increased the total size of the music market in terms of both dollar and unit volume.

The compact disc generated excitement in the previously stagnant audio hardware market. Turntable sales had been decreasing since 1975 because of minimal improvements in sound technology. The CD player gave the hardware market a needed boost. How did this success with a major new sound platform come about given the high risk of failure for such new technologies?

THE SITUATION PRIOR TO THE SUCCESS

The CD was developed during the 1970s and brought to market in the 1980s. It was launched in Japan in 1982. During the 1970s and early 1980s, the audio equipment manufacturing industry had become highly competitive and was reaching maturity. It was dominated by a few Japanese companies with a reputation for superior quality, design, and value. A worldwide economic recession in the late 1970s contributed to declining sales in the audio equipment industry.

Demographic trends in the 1980s led to the emergence of a new kind of consumer as the result of the post–World War II baby boom. Referred to as "yuppies" (young urban professionals), these consumers enjoyed collecting a variety of electronic devices (among other things). Their energetic and demanding lifestyles required portable high quality stereo tape players, hand-held TVs, cameras, computers, and portable telephones. An emphasis on high quality among these consumers fueled demand for components to complement the basic home stereo unit. Consumers were ready for new concepts that would enhance the sound quality of their music.

The electronics industry was eager to develop new products. For three years prior to April 1981, 49 Japanese, American, and European companies tried to standardize the digital recording format through the Digital Audio Disc Council. This attempt failed to produce a common format. Instead, three digital formats emerged as leaders: the compact disc of Philips and Sony, the minidisc of Telefunken of West Germany, and the audio high-density technology (AHD) of Matsushita's JVC division.

Weary of new technological formats, the large electronics firms proceeded very cautiously. For Philips, an expensive lesson had been learned from the video compact disc (also known as the laser disc) introduced in 1978. The laser disc provided an audio and video capability on a video disc player. Consumers could not record on the machine, only play movies or other videos. Further, players were not widely available through distribution channels, and promotion and publicity about the new technology were limited. Meanwhile, consumers were responding favorably to the heavily marketed and lower priced video cassette recorder (VCR), which had playback and recording capabilities. The Philips video laser disc failed in the market.

Sony had a similar story. The company developed its own VCR product and introduced it as the Betamax system as early as 1975. Even though the product provided quality superior to that of the competing Matsushita VHS video cassette system, the latter dominated the market. Sony held Betamax as a proprietary technology for its own distribution, whereas Matsushita licensed VHS to a variety of companies, thereby opening the market and setting the industry standard. This experience led Sony to recognize the potential benefits of working with common industry standards.

Failures of the magnitude of those experienced by Philips and Sony would prompt any firm to rethink how it develops and introduces breakthrough products and technologies. For example, building strategic alliances absorbs some of the market risk and facilitates the establishment of industry standards. Major market failures also suggest the need for a more integrated organizational response to innovation; marketing support and production capability are as important as research and development for success. Finally, a major market failure signals that an organization may be out of step with its market. In developing any major new technology, an organization needs to focus on markets in which consumers are eager to adopt new products. Because of their experiences, both Sony and Philips had strong motivation to collaborate on the development of the compact disc technology. Their collaboration would become a major factor in the success of the CD.

THE NEW PRODUCT DEVELOPMENT PROCESS

Figure 2.1 is an approximate timeline of Philips' new product development process for the CD. Although it is a simplified abstraction of the actual process, it provides a useful overview of some key events.

The Idea

The compact disc originated in 1972 as a spinoff from Philips' work with the video laser disc. The video laser disc technology could be used to create a long-playing analog audio disc. However, the initial idea was rough. Then

1972	Philips invents initial idea for CD system
1973	
1974	
1975	
1976	
1977	
1978	Prototype is accepted by the Philips board of directors
1979	CD is presented to press; strategic alliance with Sony announced
1980	Japanese DAD Council accepts CD as industry standard
1981	October: first public prototype presented at Japanese Audio Fair
1982	November: CD introduced into Japanese market
1983	February: CD introduced to European and U.S. markets
1984	
1985	3 million CD players sold worldwide
1986	9 million CD players sold worldwide
1987	
1988	
1989	
1990	
1991	Over 1 billion CD players sold worldwide
1992	

Figure 2.1   Timeline of CD new product development.

Dr. Kees Schouhamer Immink of Philips Research Laboratories, who was important in the standardization of the CD, realized that using a digital (instead of analog) approach provided significant benefits. Digital coding of sounds is the equivalent of the zero-one binary coding used in computers. It affords great accuracy and flexibility in reproducing sound. Thus began a technological innovation that would lead to the development of a family of new products.

Prototype and Board Approval

In 1978, after six years of technological development work, a prototype with one hour of playing time was presented to and accepted by the Philips board of directors. Its benefits were obvious: very high quality reproduction of sound (without the hissing and noise heard on vinyl records and tape) and a compactness that made possible a range of player sizes (from portable, to car, to home sound systems).

Assembling the Primary Team

Cor van der Klugt, at the time a director and later president of Philips, played an important role in the concept development for the CD. As the designated product champion, he assembled a high level cross-functional team with people from marketing, research and development, engineering, the recording company, and other areas. The members of this team then led other teams working on critical aspects of project development.

The cross-functional team was crucial in the development of the CD. Because of previous difficulties in product development, Philips wanted to improve communication between the R&D department and the rest of the company. Much of the technical research was done in its corporate headquarters in Eindhoven, Holland, although marketing and other divisions were located elsewhere. By putting major players on the primary team, van der Klugt linked the key organizational functions despite their physical locations. With the technology and organizational players in place, the final version of the CD was presented to the world press in the spring of 1979.

The Philips/Sony Alliance

Despite progress on the CD, van der Klugt realized that Philips alone would have difficulty turning its concept into a world standard. After considering alternative partners, Philips chose Sony to become its counterpart for three reasons. First, Sony was recognized as one of the leading and most progressive audio equipment manufacturers in the world. Second, the company was Japanese and provided access to the important Japanese market. Third, and perhaps most important, van der Klugt and Sony's CEO, Akio Morita, had a personal relationship.

The Philips and Sony strategic alliance began in the summer of 1979 and led to several technical and marketing achievements. Together the companies developed the microchips necessary for the modulation, control, and correction of the digital signal. Sony also developed three integrated circuits that eliminated 500 microchips, thereby making the CD player more compact and affordable.

Establishing CD Standards

Learning from their previous experiences with difficulties in establishing a common format, Philips and Sony managed to get their key electronic chips adopted as the standard by the influential Electronic Industries Association (EIA) of Japan. After an effective presentation to the Japanese Digital Audio Disc Council, the Philips/Sony standard was adopted and the other two major competing systems (Telefunken and JVC) withdrew to become licensees. Philips and Sony then moved quickly to make the technology available to other manufacturers. However, the record industry was still reluctant to buy into the new technology, in part because of a three-cent royalty that Philips and Sony wanted for each CD sold.

To overcome this resistance, Philips and Sony used their resources to present the CD concept directly to the world press to build consumer awareness and interest. The idea was to stimulate demand for the technology in the market and *pull* it through the channels. The CD was revealed to key audiophile groups and their influential trade magazines. This pressure stimulated consumer and trade interest and ultimately persuaded the industry to commit to the Philips/Sony CD standard.

The Launch Dates

In 1981, the CD was introduced at audio equipment exhibitions around the world. The introduction of the CD into the Japanese market was set for November 1982, to be followed by the introduction in Europe and the United States in February 1983. By the end of 1982, some 32 companies had licensed and launched models of compact disc players.

Readying the Market

Setting the standard and launching the CD was the first hurdle that Philips and Sony had to overcome. The second was ensuring that a steady supply of recordings and players would be available to meet market needs. Consumers would buy CD players only if they had a large selection of readily available recordings (featuring their favorite songs and performers). Many of the consumer electronics giants had developed relations with music companies. Philips owned PolyGram in Hanover, Germany, and Sony had a relationship with CBS. Through these relationships, both partners were able to produce compact discs and influence the development of catalogs of CD recordings.

Philips and Sony sensed that consumers would respond favorably to the CD because it filled a perennial audio need: high quality sound reproduction that would not deteriorate over time with usage. The CD provides a low noise, accurate, and portable reproduction medium. Further, the disc has a very long life—so long that markets for used CDs have emerged. Its advantages to the consumer over the larger, heavier, and more fragile vinyl disc were clear—no more snap, crackle, and pop while listening to one's favorite tunes!

In addition to consumers, retailers had to be convinced of the value of the CD. Philips and Sony believed that the opportunity to market the new CD players in place of the maturing vinyl-record turntables would make the new technology acceptable to retailers. They expected that with adequate profit margins as incentives, retailers would welcome CDs and CD players. Also, because a clear standard was common to all manufacturers, retailers did not have to worry about which ones consumers wanted. Retailer support and willingness to make the product available would be critical to the success of the CD.

The New Product Launch Program

Whereas Philips brought forth the new technology, Sony took on the marketing of the CD. Consumers would recognize that Sony, with its highly successful Walkman, was certainly capable of producing another major electronic innovation. This reputation helped pave the way to consumer market acceptance. The Sony name eventually became synonymous with the CD in the marketplace.

The strategy for introducing CDs to the market varied by segment. Initially the industry targeted lead users such as audiophiles, retailers, and key radio stations. At launch, the cost of the CD players was kept high to give the product a high quality positioning. This strategy also allowed time to accelerate production and distribution of recordings. Within two years, when the quality reputation was established and music titles were available, CD player prices were cut, making the product attractive to more market segments.

Most competitors planned to launch their CD players at the same time. Marketing was therefore a crucial factor for success. To differentiate its brand and quickly capture market share to gain a market leader position, Sony embarked on an education strategy to inform the market about the benefits of CD players in comparison to the conventional analog audio equipment.

In the past, the Japanese market had adopted new technology readily, so the CD was introduced in Japan four months before its launch in Europe and the United States. The introduction in the United States and Europe involved creating awareness and interest among audiophiles, who were regarded as early adopters of sound innovations. Interest was aroused through promotional activities and efforts to convince and educate potential buyers, as well as retailers, about the benefits of CD. An atmosphere of anticipation was generated by promoting the CD as "the future of recorded sound." Initially, the emphasis was on the quality of the sound, and later on price.

Launch promotional activities included the use of album-oriented classical and rock FM radio stations in about 20 major U.S. markets. Sony supplied a CD player to each station and discs as they became available. In return, the stations promoted the CD format and the Sony name on air every time a CD was played. The stations were required to do a two-hour special on digital sound reproduction in which Sony was prominently featured. Sony also established the Sony Consumer Digital Audio Club. Consumers were invited to join the club for a $15 fee and in return received a variety of promotional materials (newsletters, books, sample CDs).

Sony spent heavily on media advertising for the launch program. For example, during the 1984 holiday season, Sony spent $3 million on 30-second prime-time network TV spots on such shows as CBS's *60 Minutes*, NBC's *Hill Street Blues*, and National Football League games. For the introduction of the D-5 portable CD unit in November 1984, Sony ran a month-long advertising campaign on MTV that included 56 commercials. Sony also teamed up with three CD recording manufacturers on a promotion that offered a grand prize of a Sony digital CD system. After 1984, the marketing program was rolled out gradually to other markets, with adjustment as necessary during launch.

SUCCESS OF THE LAUNCH

By any standard, the introduction of the CD sound system was successful. Once industry support was gained, sales exceeded all expectations. In 1982, Philips and Sony forecast a worldwide industry sales volume of 10 million CD recordings during 1985, but that figure was revised to 15 million in 1983. Actual CD sales totaled 59 million units by 1985 and grew to 136 million in 1986!

The conservatism of the original forecasts was related partly to the worldwide recession that seemed to be ending in 1982–1983. Actually, the new product could have been launched during 1981 (the depth of the recession), but introduction was delayed until it became apparent that the world economy was improving. The CD player had similar results. In 1985, three million units were sold. Nine million were sold in 1986, a number that earlier Philips' forecasts indicated would not be reached until 1990.

WHY THE CD SUCCEEDED

As in the case of any successful new product or technology, multiple factors accounted for the CD's success. For Philips, the most important ones were market readiness, a strategic alliance, and a superior product.

The Market Was Ready for an Innovation

The maturing recording industry needed a new product that could raise declining profits. A new kind of consumer was entering the market who appreciated high quality sound and was willing to pay for it. The population and income of this consumer segment were increasing substantially throughout the 1980s as the new CD players and recordings were becoming available. Manufacturers and retailers could see the profitability in a new recording format, provided that clear industry standards were adopted that would not confuse consumers and inhibit purchase.

A Strategic Alliance of Major Players
Guaranteed an Industry Standard Format

The cooperation between Philips and Sony provided a union of strong technology with marketing. Each company had experienced difficulties in trying to set the industry standard for a major new technology. Bringing together their strengths created a dominant competitive force in the market (against the major format competitors Telefunken and JVC) and convinced all major stakeholders that if the product delivered its promised quality, everyone could benefit from its adoption. The successful promotional program ultimately convinced the industry to support the CD as the world standard.

In addition to manufacturers of CD players, record companies had to be persuaded to risk the necessary financial investment to provide broad availability of needed CD recordings. However, record manufacturers were reluctant to transfer production facilities from vinyl records to the CD on economic grounds. The cost of a CD pressing plant was double the cost of a conventional one. Moreover, a switch of production to CDs from conventional records would make the companies' manufacturing experience obsolete.

A major benefit of the Philips/Sony alliance was that both firms controlled production capabilities to press the new discs: the CBS/Sony plant in Tokyo and the PolyGram plant in Hanover, Germany. Although their output would not be adequate to meet world market demand, they could use the operating results of their plants to prove the economics of production to other would-be CD manufacturers. By holding prices high and managing demand in the first year after launch, they could meet that demand and also attract other firms to convert their record catalogs into CDs. This approach spurred rapid growth of record supply to meet the demand stimulated by Sony's consumer marketing program.

A Superior Product

Although market readiness and the strategic alliance were important for success, the product had to deliver to consumers a real improvement over currently available sound technologies. The CD player had to perform well and be easy to use, but also had to be compatible with existing stereo equipment. It is not surprising that it took about six years of product refinement to develop a prototype of the new CD player, and another four years to launch the actual product.

CONCLUSION

Several factors combined to make the compact disc a success. Perhaps the most important was Philips' strategic alliance with Sony. It would have been difficult for Philips, Sony, or any other firm to succeed alone. The Philips and Sony alliance was necessary to bring about the industry standard format. This standard helped to secure retail cooperation and reduce consumer uncertainty about adopting the new product.

However, risks accompany an alliance. Although Philips realized an overall business success, it did not have the same kind of marketing success as Sony. Philips developed the original technology, but the CD became synonymous with Sony. Sony shared in the technological development, but gained tremendous market value for its brand because of its aggressive marketing effort. It was much more difficult for Philips to market CD players under its own name. For example, to enter the U.S. market in 1985, Philips had to use the Magnavox name to compete with the stronger Japanese brands. Therefore, a company must balance the benefits and risks of sharing knowledge in an alliance to further an innovation.

To balance benefits and risks, a company needs to understand the alignment of strategic resources in the new product development process. Perhaps Philips should be content to work with partners strong in marketing and other skills so it can focus resources on developing next-generation technologies. For example, photo CDs, CD-ROM (read only memory), recordable CDs, and mini-CDs are examples of new directions in CD technology. For an alliance to succeed, each party must bring complementary and balancing strengths to the innovation process.

3

Capitalizing on the Business Environment

The business environment for a new product defines its market opportunity. It includes the less controllable factors that tend to be global and pervasive in their effects and must be managed or otherwise mediated to realize the opportunity. For example, *natural resources, population, cultural values, technology, economic systems*, and various *laws and regulations* are less controllable factors that can create or threaten market opportunities.

One philosophy of management is to accept the global environmental forces as given and develop products accordingly. Another, more proactive, philosophy is to influence the mediators whose decisions and actions have an effect on the trend and magnitude of those forces, thereby gaining some control over the environment. For example, *politicians, regulatory agencies, financial institutions, mass media, industry associations*, and other *special interest groups* may be in a position to alter many of the basic forces in the business environment.

In this chapter, three different new product success stories reveal the importance of environmental factors in creating market opportunities for new products, as well as creating barriers to success. Each story shows how some less controllable force in the market environment provided a new product business opportunity. To be successful, the innovating firm had to respond to the opportunity before, and more effectively than, competitors.

The first story documents the emergence of a major new telecommunications technology—mobile telephones. Cellular One began when a small paging company was selected by Motorola as a partner in testing a new version of the technology in the greater Washington/Baltimore metropolitan area.

Although technology is important to the success of mobile telephones, the Federal Communications Commission (FCC) was instrumental in bringing about its orderly and timely market development.

The rules established by the FCC for granting an operating license created the possibility of a drawn-out legal battle among five applicants. Cellular One created a partnership to avoid a legal battle and bring the technology to market sooner than expected. Its development process and launch marketing program caught its single major competitor, Bell Atlantic Mobile Systems, off guard. Cellular One managed its regulatory environment for competitive advantage.

The second story involves Ault Foods Limited, a Canadian company that launched Sealtest Parlour 1%, a new frozen dessert. Many aspects of the business environment were important to the success of Parlour 1%. Consumers were being pressured by the medical community through mass media to reduce fat and cholesterol in their diet. They enjoyed the taste of high fat foods, but felt guilty about eating them. This concern touched off a technology race to supply fat substitutes that could be used in foods to provide good taste, but without fat.

Because of Ault's commitment to technology, it was able to develop a dairy-based fat substitute (Dairylight™) that delivered the rich, creamy taste of ice cream without the fat. However, a surprise occurred during market testing. Consumers had difficulty believing that ice cream that tasted good could also be fat free. Consequently, Ault developed a 1-percent fat content product instead, a product with reduced fat, but one consumers would find credible and purchase!

The third story describes the creation of a new sport, paragliding. It clearly shows the importance of understanding the business environment in terms of cultural values. Paragliding was launched at almost the same time in Europe, where it succeeded, and in the United States, where it did not. Europeans and Americans had different values that influenced their interest in free flight. Europeans, pressured by economic integration (Europe 1992) as a possible threat to their freedom and cultural traditions and hence their basic identity, perhaps saw the free flight of paragliding as a way to regain their freedom and identity. This difference is only one of many identified in the story, but it shows the risks of new product development, not to mention marketing and business strategy, in a global context.

Cellular One

Taylor T. Simmons and Duk-Ki Yu

When at last this little instrument appeared, consisting, as it does, of parts every one of which is familiar to us, and capable of being put together by an amateur, the disappointment arising from its humble appearance was only partially relieved on finding that it was really able to talk.

James C. Maxwell, The Telephone, *1878*

On December 16, 1983, Cellular One became the first non–Bell-owned company in the United States to offer commercial cellular telephone service, that is, mobile telephones. The story of Cellular One's success began in 1977, when Motorola approached American Radio Telephone Service (ARTS), a small Baltimore paging company, and formed a partnership to offer experimental mobile telephone service in the Washington, DC, and Baltimore metropolitan areas.

Test marketing for the experimental service began in 1980. By 1983, ARTS (which had then become American TeleServices or ATS) needed only to obtain a license from the Federal Communications Commission (FCC) to begin offering full commercial service. The license was granted to the ATS-led Cellular One partnership in September 1983, and on December 16 Cellular One went "on the air." Cellular One's subsequent growth and its impact in building the entire cellular telephone industry clearly demonstrate that the launch of Cellular One was a new product development success.

THE BUSINESS ENVIRONMENT PRIOR TO SUCCESS

The genesis of truly mobile telephones began with an emerging market need, new technology, and the intervention of a regulatory group, the FCC.

The Need for Mobile Communication

Business managers are estimated to spend 90 percent of their time communicating, and 65 percent of that time using voice communication channels.[1] The recessionary period in the late 1970s and early 1980s put pressure on businesses to become more efficient and effective. That pressure made it increasingly important for managers and others to make the best use of their time.

Not surprisingly, anything that could make "dead time" (such as being stuck in traffic or in transit between locations) productive was attractive to people who valued time. Results of marketing research and test marketing revealed that a mobile communication service would be welcomed by the segment of business people who spent a great amount of time both on the phone and on the road.

Because people in such fields as construction, real estate, and sales spend much of their time traveling to appointments, there was a major unmet need for mobile phone service among occupation-based segments. In addition, the desire to avoid mistakes in communication and missed opportunities due to not having access to a phone created an environment in which an affordable and reliable mobile phone service could succeed. Prior to the advent of mobile communication, many managers and salespeople spent considerable time on pay phones, hotel phones, and even their clients' phones, just trying to catch up on missed calls.

Technological Developments

The need for some sort of mobile communication was being met by several technologies. One was the tone pager or "beeper." In the early 1980s, most paging units did not have numeric digit display or vibrating options. When users got beeped, they had to first call their office or designated message center for the number or message, and then call the person who left the message. Carrying a pager meant hunting for a telephone, fumbling for pocket change, and the potential embarrassment of having the beeper interrupt an important sales presentation or other meeting.

Another technology, citizen's band (CB) radio, enabled two or more people to communicate from mobile locations. However, a CB radio was necessary not only for the traveler, but also for everyone with whom he or she wanted to communicate. This system afforded little privacy, as anyone with a CB or a CB scanner could hear somebody else's conversation. If privacy was necessary, communication could not take place on the

CB. Finally, two voices could not talk simultaneously because CBs lacked the duplexing function found in regular (and cellular) telephones.

A third option available was mobile telephone service (MTS), which later became improved mobile telephone service (IMTS). It required operator assistance. IMTS had only 44 channels available at one time, and many users had to share the same channel. Delays in obtaining a channel coupled with the high price and limited availability made IMTS an unattractive mobile communication option.

The lack of private, accessible, and affordable mobile communication paved the way for new technologies and pioneers such as Cellular One.[2] The technology of cellular communication as the basis for a mobile telephone system was first introduced by Bell Labs in 1971. What differentiated cellular telephone service was its ability to increase the capacity for mobile phones in a given geographic area within the limited frequency range assigned by the FCC. The same frequencies could be used simultaneously throughout a metropolitan area, thus ensuring private conversations rather than the free-for-all common on CB channels.

The cellular process works by dividing a city or county into small areas, or cells, which can range in diameter from one mile to 20 miles, depending on terrain and capacity needs. Each cell has a low power radio transmitter/receiver, which is connected to the local telephone network through the cellular company's switching center. By adjustment of the power of the transmitter, the same frequencies can be used in nearby cells with little chance of interference. As a driver crosses a cell border, another transmitter takes over and quality mobile telephone communication is maintained.[3]

The new cellular technology had the familiarity of a telephone without the connecting wires. It also afforded communication privacy, unlike the CB, and was more accessible and affordable than any of the other technologies. To telephone service carriers, cellular mobile telephone service increased the available capacity for car phone usage and thereby opened new markets and uses for mobile communication. In sum, cellular mobile telephone service was based on a *breakthrough* technology that provided potential benefits to consumers and business opportunities for the companies developing it.

Regulatory Participation

The Federal Communications Commission (FCC) was established by the Communications Act of 1934. Its primary responsibilities include the regulation of interstate and foreign communication by radio, television, wire, cable, and satellite in the public interest. For example, the FCC was involved in setting the standards for high definition television (HDTV) in 1994. In addition to standard setting, the agency is involved in pricing. For example, during 1994 the FCC ordered a 7 percent reduction in the fees cable television operators charge subscribers.

The emergence of cellular communication technology clearly involved the FCC. A primary concern was the orderly development and operation of the new technology in the public interest. Accordingly, on June 7, 1982, the FCC accepted applications for licenses to operate cellular mobile telephone systems in the top 30 U.S. markets.[4] To encourage competition and efficiency in the provision of the new service, the FCC ruled that one firm (designated a "non-wireline" carrier) would be selected in a comparative hearing process. This firm would become the sole competitor in a specified geographic area against a "wireline" carrier (essentially one of the Bell operating companies).

In anticipation of multiple applicants in each market area, the FCC required each party to submit a comprehensive application that would be judged against a set of "comparative criteria." The Commission wanted to examine the financial, technical, and marketing capability of each applicant, as well as estimates of market demand and the setting of prices, with special attention to how well the public would be served. The FCC then would decide which firm would be the major competitor in each market area. That decision would influence the direction of many investors and business organizations.

DEVELOPMENT OF CELLULAR ONE

In 1980, prior to the FCC's intervention in the mobile telephone licensing process, the Motorola/ARTS partnership began experimental service in the Washington/Baltimore market. It obtained participants by mailing 75,000 folded flyers with cut-out business reply cards to "likely users." Participants could rent a car phone and obtain cellular service for $185 a month plus a $200 installation fee. One hundred minutes of use was included, with additional time billed at 45 cents a minute.

More than 1300 people responded to the test and eventually more than 200 people signed up, including many influential Washington, DC, dignitaries. Many of the trial participants were salespeople, construction personnel, and real estate professionals who spent a lot of time in their cars.

Interestingly, lawyers and doctors, originally envisioned as the most likely early adopters, were among the last to embrace the service. This experimental approach helped the users to learn about mobile telephones and the providers to remedy problems in the system. It thus minimized the possibility that technical difficulties would occur after the licenses were granted.

Competition

In the infancy of the cellular communication industry, the competition facing ARTS, which preceded Cellular One, came from two levels. On one level was Bell Atlantic, the regional telephone company, which was planning to launch the Bell Atlantic Mobile Systems cellular service in 1984. With the support of AT&T, Bell Atlantic would become the major competitor for any "non-wireline" carrier selected through the FCC process.

On the second level of competition were other non-Bell firms that also applied for the non-wireline carrier license for the Washington/Baltimore market. These firms included The Washington Post, Metrocall, Metromedia, Graphic Scanning Corporation, and Metropolitan Radio and Telephone Service. A very small part of the Washington area cellular market would also be served by Bell-owned Contel Cellular, rather than Bell Atlantic, but that firm did not pose a major threat to ARTS.

New Product Management within the Organization

In 1980, ARTS was a relatively small company with about 40 employees, most of whom worked on the paging and telephone answering service side of the business. The team developing cellular service in Washington consisted of four employees from Motorola and six from ARTS, including three product champions: Wayne Schelle, Al Grimes, and Emily Nelms. Nelms stresses that the organizational atmosphere was entrepreneurial and the team was fully cross-functional, with each member sharing all of the responsibilities of development.[5]

In 1981, the FCC issued its final rules for cellular licensing, dictating that each market would be served by two carriers: the present Bell-owned local telephone company (Bell Atlantic) and one non-wireline carrier. Despite its technological lead and its experimental system with Motorola in the Washington/Baltimore area, ARTS, which had become American TeleServices (ATS), had no better chance of obtaining the license than the other five applicants. The other applicants did not have the technology, but did have the foresight to apply for an FCC license in an attempt to cash in on the budding and potentially lucrative cellular industry.

Faced with competition from the wireline carrier and a potentially drawn-out FCC licensing process, ATS President Wayne Schelle weighed the value of trying to win the competition against the possibility of forming a partnership with the other five applicants.[6] After considering the results of a comprehensive market entry timing analysis and other factors, he decided to form the partnership to avoid the risk of missing out completely and to launch full cellular service before Bell Atlantic.

In September 1983, after 15 months of negotiations, the Cellular One partnership was formed, with ATS owning 40 percent and the other non-wireline applicants (Metrocall, Metromedia, Graphic Scanning, MRTS, and The Washington Post) owning the rest. The partnership became the Washington Baltimore Cellular Telephone Company, trading under the new name "Cellular One."

With the Cellular One partnership in place, the final obstacles to launch were overcome. The FCC's lengthy application review and the litigation that was likely to have resulted from an award to any single applicant were averted. Having resolved the issue of competition from its non-wireline peers, Cellular One could now concentrate on positioning itself to compete against Bell Atlantic Mobile Systems.

Launch Marketing Program

On December 16, 1983, Cellular One officially launched commercial mobile telephone service in the Washington/Baltimore market with eight cell sites in the region and a switching station in Columbia, Maryland. The early entry was an effective marketing strategy and "caught Bell Atlantic with its phone off the hook."[7] Mike Bollinger of the DDB Needham advertising agency recalls the initial campaign for Cellular One:[8]

> Beginning on the day of the launch, we ran full spread ads in *The Washington Post*, both to make a lot of noise and to tell the story of how cellular phone service worked. It was like a brochure, in that it explained the concept in detail and told readers exactly how they could subscribe. The ad was entitled "Cellular One Introduces the Perfect Phone for People Who Live Their Lives in Overdrive," and thanks to the ad, Cellular One's offices were swamped with orders for car phones priced at $2600 plus installation and monthly fees.

Because Bell Atlantic had yet to launch its own mobile telephone service (it was constrained by an old AT&T construction schedule), Cellular One's launch campaign focused on convincing consumers of the benefits of its service. The initial ad was followed by a three-part series illustrating rush hour on the beltway around Washington, DC. For example, a print ad entitled "The Day the Earth Stood Still" contained a powerful image of commuters caught in the usual beltway traffic jam, fuming about the wasted time. The mobile telephone provided a productive solution to this problem.

When Bell Atlantic finally arrived on the market in April 1984, it faced an established, technologically superior competitor with ample financial resources. Cellular One exploited its technological lead. It ran radio and print ads touting the difference in quality between the two carriers. For example, one full-page newspaper ad stated: "Test Drive Bell's Car Phone System and Here's What Will Happen to Your Conversation," with the print on the last five words breaking up and fading out. Radio ads demonstrated to listeners the actual difference in sound quality, with Cellular One's phone reception remaining clear for miles and Bell Atlantic's first growing weak and then fading out completely. Bell Atlantic had rushed to launch its service with only two transmitters, incurring a technological disadvantage that lasted five months. Cellular One's strategy to achieve early entry had paid off.

Building Awareness and Credibility

Recognizing that the local telephone company still had much greater overall consumer awareness than Cellular One, Wayne Schelle decided in March 1984 to license the name to other non-wireline carriers of cellular service around the United States. According to Cellular One's general manager at the time, Al Grimes, "they won't be part of the same company, but we are hoping that eventually the name will become synonymous with 'not the phone company.'"[9]

To encourage other non-wireline carriers to use the Cellular One name, the licensing cost was set at just one dollar plus legal fees. By facilitating the development of a nationwide Cellular One network, the Washington company increased the awareness and credibility of the Cellular One brand name. It also gave customers and potential buyers the advantage of being part of a larger nationwide system.

DIAGNOSING THE SUCCESS

By the time Bell Atlantic Mobile Systems finally launched its own cellular service in April 1984, Cellular One had 4,000 subscribers. By May 1985, Cellular One had 10,000 subscribers. A year of aggressive marketing doubled the number of subscribers to 20,000. By 1992, Cellular One still maintained a slight lead over Bell Atlantic with close to 200,000 subscribers in the Washington/Baltimore market. In addition, Cellular One maintained wider area coverage than Bell Atlantic.[10]

Although there are many reasons for Cellular One's success, four are central: managing the regulatory process for early market entry, use-testing the technology, licensing the Cellular One brand name to create a recognizable identity, and organizational vision and leadership.

Managing the Regulatory Process

The basic charter of the FCC guaranteed its involvement in the development of cellular mobile telephone service. The effect of regulatory involvement in markets can be delay. Agencies often engage in cumbersome processes to serve the public. For a technology that is ready to be launched, time delay results in financial loss. The analyses and actions by the leaders of Cellular One to create a partnership that circumvented a potentially long regulatory process demonstrate that such processes can be managed.

In this case, forging a partnership among the non-wireline competitors afforded a degree of control over time to market entry. It eliminated the need for lengthy FCC deliberation about who should receive the license. The resulting early market entry attracted the most important innovators, who influenced other consumers to adopt the Cellular One service. It led to market share advantages against a formidable competitor that were still evident almost 10 years later.

Testing the New Technology with Users

As discovered in the Cellular One case, careful testing and monitoring of a new product can lead to surprises. For example, learning who early users are from the test of the new product helps to focus early marketing efforts on key marketing segments. Recall that the assumed importance of doctors and lawyers as early adopters was contradicted by the results of the test offer. Also, monitoring consumers' usage experiences helps to identify and solve the numerous problems that can arise in a new technology. Determining the power of a system and the proper location of antenna towers helped to guide subsequent decisions in building the network.

Building Early Brand Awareness and Credibility

Establishing an easy-to-recognize brand name was another key to Cellular One's success. The initial partnership and its subsequent licensees all shared the identity of the Cellular One name. The name conveyed the actual technology rather than the effect of the technology, thus attracting innovators to become customers of Cellular One. Mobile telephones are often called "cell phones" by users. More important, by licensing its name, Cellular One established an image as a solid organization with nationwide offices and service centers. "Cellular One" is still the most recognizable name in the mobile telephone communication business.

Maintaining Organizational Vision and Leadership

The emergence of an exciting new technology can bring out all sorts of investors and schemers, and consequently a rigorous regulatory process. Amid the turbulence, developing a competitive business requires a continually clear vision of the outcome, and leadership to assemble the teams and resources needed to implement the vision. For Cellular One, the vision and leadership of its founders and early team of leaders provided the focus and concentration of resources necessary to succeed in such a business environment.

ISSUES FOR THE FUTURE OF CELLULAR ONE

The initial cost and size of cellular telephones have declined dramatically in the last nine years (from large $2,600 devices in 1984 to small hand-held phones offered practically free today), although service fees declined just 27 percent between 1985 and 1991. One reason service fees remain relatively high is to discourage subscribers from being on the phone too long. Because cellular companies place about 25 subscribers on each channel, accessibility and capacity are still somewhat limited. However, rates will continue to decline as the cellular system technology improves.[11] For example, the industry may convert from analog to digital switching in the future. Also, improved capability for networking among its systems has enabled Cellular One to become part of the North American Cellular Network, through which a subscriber can be reached anywhere in North America with one number. This nationwide system will be developed and linked by McCaw Communications, Inc.[12]

Although fierce competition will continue, Cellular One's future looks very favorable because of the company's strong subscription base and growing recognition. Moreover, car phones have become so popular that automobile manufacturers are beginning to include them as options in their new cars. The U.S. cellular communication industry continues to grow rapidly, having achieved 10 million subscribers in November 1992 and acquiring 6,400 new subscribers every day. Some experts estimate that the number of subscribers will not approach saturation until the year 2000. With so many satisfied customers, and many more potential customers, Cellular One's cellular telephone service appears poised to continue growing into the 21st century.

Ault Foods Limited: Sealtest Parlour 1%

Soumitra Mukherjee and David Sanchez-Garcia

Let it be the finale of seem.
The only emperor is the emperor of ice cream.

Wallace Stevens, The Emperor of Ice Cream

Sealtest Parlour is the leading Canadian ice cream, marketed by Ault Foods Limited. On August 31, 1991, Ault Foods announced the launch of Sealtest Parlour 1%, a new product extension of the Parlour line. It was the first frozen dessert product in the market to use the new Dairylight™ technology. This technology enabled the product to have the rich, creamy taste of premium ice cream while having only 1 percent total fat content.

The market opportunity for Parlour 1% was based on consumers' concerns about fat intake in their diet and their general distaste for the current low fat dessert products. Ault sought to give consumers a product that was healthy yet tasty, thereby creating value for those concerned about fat and cholesterol intake. Although numerous factors drove the success of Parlour 1%, its primary advantage was based on technology. Blending the many ingredients of ice cream to deliver the benefits of taste and low fat clearly challenged Ault's product development capabilities.

COMPANY BACKGROUND

Ault is Canada's leading dairy products company. It began as a small family dairy in 1891. The Toronto-based company employs more than 3,000 people, operates 17 plants, and owns 20 distribution centers across Ontario and Quebec. Ault produces, markets, and distributes a complete range of dairy and related products through its fluid, refrigerated, frozen, and industrial divisions.[13]

In 1968, Ault became part of John Labatt Limited, a high profile Canadian company with interests in brewing, food, and entertainment. The Labatt connection provided the financial strength and management resources for Ault to acquire new businesses and invest in leading-edge technology. Ault's domestic and international sales total more than $1 billion (Canadian) annually. According to Graham Freeman, Ault's CEO, "The achievements that have made us market leaders can be boiled down to three crucial factors: Quality products. Innovative technology. And highly skilled, resourceful people."[14] To understand how this philosophy works and how Ault achieved its success with Parlour 1%, examining the business environment for ice cream is helpful.

THE BUSINESS ENVIRONMENT FOR ICE CREAM

The market, the industry competition, and the technology for low fat foods are critical aspects of the business environment for ice cream.

The Ice Cream Market

The Canadian ice cream market had almost no growth in the last half of the 1980s. From May 1990 to May 1991, the market actually decreased by 1 percent. The only segments that were growing were frozen yogurt and light ice cream, an indication of increasing health concerns among consumers.

Consumers' attitudes toward food changed during the 1970s and 1980s. To the mid-1980s, consumers were becoming increasingly concerned about certain aspects of nutrition, such as their intake of calories, cholesterol, sodium, and artificial sweeteners and other ingredients that are not "natural." Since the late 1980s, consumers have become even more conscientious about nutrition and health and more concerned about what they eat.

As a consequence of consumer concerns about health and the environment, the demand for natural and healthy food has increased. Such foods have gained considerable shelf space. Low fat foods in particular are available in great variety. For consumers, the problem with low fat foods is taste. They still enjoy the taste of foods with high fat content.

The conflict between the pleasures of good taste and the prescriptions of the medical community to eat low fat, high nutrition foods creates a feeling of guilt in consumers who crave high fat foods. However, consumers in the United States and Canada still consume and enjoy whole-milk products such as ice cream and cheese. With some exceptions, the available low fat products have not been able to deliver the same taste as whole-milk products with high fat content.

The Industry

The emergence of consumer concern about fat and nutritional matters in general during the 1980s touched off a race in the food industry to develop products to address dietary problems. Many firms rushed into the market with weight-loss diet products (especially liquid foods and frozen meals) that implied sacrifice: "Have a can of liquid for lunch and you can eat real food for dinner."

The weight-loss dietary approach does not solve the problem of consumers who do not necessarily want to lose weight, but want to reduce fat intake. Such consumers would like to maintain their current eating habits without ingesting fat, cholesterol, sodium, or other nutritionally undesirable substances. Of course, these consumers would like to do so without losing most of the taste of the food!

Estimates about the size of the fat substitute market range to about $1 billion (U.S.).[15] During the 1980s, many companies rushed to capitalize on the "less fat, same taste" market opportunity and began conducting research to develop fat substitutes. For example, Procter & Gamble spent many years developing a fat substitute called Olestra. Nutrasweet did the same with an Ault-developed substance called Simplesse™. ConAgra bought the patent rights to an oatmeal-based fat substitute called Oatrim (used first in low fat ground beef products).[16] By 1992, fat substitutes were also being offered by Unilever's National Starch Company (N-Lite), Hercules (Slendid), A. E. Staley (Stellar), and Pfizer (Veri-Lo), and the Kraft division of General Foods was developing one (Trailblazer).[17]

The food processing industry was certainly feeling pressure from consumers to provide low fat products, and would consider any of the new fat substitutes offered. However, the actual use of those substances in consumer products was problematic for a variety of reasons. Some had to be approved by the U.S. Food and Drug Administration (FDA), which delayed their market entry. Others were natural substances that did not require FDA approval, but posed certain processing problems. For example, processing that involves heat may render some fat substitutes unstable.

Ault Technology

Ault has an established reputation in the development of natural low fat products. In 1979 the company discovered by accident a substance, Simplesse, that had the apparent taste and feel of fat but only a third of the calories. Ault sold the worldwide (but not the Canadian) rights to Nutrasweet Company, now part of the Monsanto group, but Ault's R&D team continued research on fat substitutes. The technologies it has created differ from others in the kind of ingredients and the process used in the substitution of fat.

Such ingredients as gums, cellulose, oats, and air are used to reduce the fat content of food. Depending on the application, the results have been mixed. For example, the Simplesse technology used nondairy ingredients such as heated and blended egg whites. Although the product appeared promising for the creation of a broad range of tasty and healthy food, its benefits were best realized in selected processed foods. For example, frozen ice cream products created with Simplesse apparently produced a different feeling in the mouth than regular ice cream, making it more challenging to use in those types of applications.[18]

On August 28, 1991, Ault announced a technology breakthrough—a 100-percent milk-based fat substitute containing no chemicals or additives. Called Dairylight, this substance enables dairies and food processing units to produce a range of low fat and fat-free dairy products. The technology is unique because it uses fresh milk as a starting material. Unlike fat replacements made by chemical modifications of food materials, Dairylight is 100 percent dairy based and is produced by traditional dairy methods. Using the traditional dairy processing steps, Ault scientists discovered a unique and gentle way to process milk proteins that enabled them to reduce butterfat in dairy products.

A significant reduction of the fat content of dairy foods would reduce the calories and cholesterol in those foods. If Dairylight could be incorporated into good-tasting food products, it would enable consumers to consume more of their favorite dairy products more often if they so desire.

Ault used rheology, the measurement of eating qualities of food products, to answer key new product development questions about how well the new substance would meet consumer expectations. For example:[19]

- How does a low fat dairy product taste in one's mouth?
- Is it rich and creamy?
- Does it have the right flavor?
- If it is a frozen dessert, how fast does it melt in one's mouth?
- How cold does it feel?
- Does it give the same eating sensation as a full-fat dairy product?

These were the kinds of questions that had to be addressed in the Parlour 1% new product development process.

PARLOUR 1% DEVELOPMENT PROCESS

The development of Parlour 1% began in 1979 with the accidental discovery of Simplesse. After the sale of that technology to Nutrasweet Company in 1982, Ault assigned a special team to conduct research in fat substitutes. The trend of consumer interest in low fat products was increasing and could no longer be ignored.

The project received strong support from top managers because the link of R&D with market needs was clear and it could be the basis for a market-driven business strategy. For example, the first product from Ault's R&D team was called Lactania Pure & Simple. In 1989, it was the world's first pure light butter. It had 52 percent less fat and 46 percent less cholesterol than conventional butter, and no artificial preservatives or emulsifiers.

The Dairylight Development Surprise

Although product development is normally a tedious and incremental learning process, there are occasional surprises, both good and bad. The research team started the development of Dairylight in 1990 and to the surprise of everyone, including the R&D team, the technology was ready in less than one year. This achievement is significant in light of the fact that the development cycle time for such technologies can reach 10 years. Extensive cooperation between Ault's R&D and marketing departments made it possible. Also, the R&D team benefited from accumulated experience with the technology, thus achieving high levels of productivity from small efforts. The technological success can also be attributed to a focus on a major market need. Consumers wanted a low fat ice cream with the taste and texture of regular ice cream, and Ault's R&D team focused on creating a technology to satisfy that need.

The Consumer Taste-Testing Surprise

The use of Dairylight in ice cream resulted in a product with no fat that tasted as good as regular premium ice cream. When the new product was taken to the market for testing, consumers' reactions to it were excellent. However, when consumers learned that the product had no fat, they did not believe it was all natural and began to worry about its actual ingredients. In other words, consumers did not believe that a product tasting so good could have no fat! Consequently, the marketing team decided to develop instead a more consumer-credible 1-percent fat content ice cream. The R&D team then set to work on what would ultimately become Sealtest Parlour 1%.

The Core Product Concept

The core concept was defined at this stage: *Same Parlour ice cream taste with 1 percent fat.* Every stage of the development process and all major decisions were based on this core concept. Ault chose the name "Parlour" because it had an excellent image and brand equity among Canadian consumers as a premium ice cream product. Of course, failure of the new product could jeopardize this strong market position. In consumers' minds, the Parlour name is associated with such qualities of ice cream as creamy, tasty, and rich. Because Parlour 1% was to be developed to have those qualities, managers decided to allow it to share the Parlour name despite the risks.

The marketing team targeted a broad set of consumers for the new product. Included were women and men concerned about fat intake, people who consume ice cream infrequently or have stopped consuming it for health or other reasons, and ice cream lovers who want rich, creamy ice cream taste *more often*, rather than as an occasional taste treat. Once the market segments were identified, more comprehensive testing began.

Testing, Testing, Testing

The marketing department determined the flavors consumers wanted through market analysis and focus groups. R&D produced and tested laboratory samples and conducted blind taste tests among employees. Subsequent product testing included microbiological tests, shelf-life tests, shipping tests, and ice crystal tests. R&D also worked on matching taste to that of the original Parlour ice cream.

Independent taste tests among target consumers indicated a favorable reaction:

- Measuring purchase intent for the Parlour 1% concept revealed that 86 percent of the consumers who tried the product would *probably or definitely buy* (62 percent was the norm of purchase intent for such concepts).
- The purchase intent rate for Parlour 1% at regular price was 54 percent among consumers who had tasted the product, as high as that for regular Parlour ice cream.
- The purchase intent rate after an in-home test was a favorable 79 percent.
- In-home taste tests showed that 63 percent of consumers who tasted Parlour 1% liked it as much as or more than their regular premium ice cream.

Other taste tests compared Parlour 1% with a Baskin Robbins ice cream made with Simplesse. Consumers preferred Parlour 1% in a ratio of 3-to-1 over the Baskin Robbins product. Dairylight significantly outperformed Simplesse in all categories tested. Its product was considered better tasting, smoother, creamier, and richer by consumers. The final Parlour 1% formulation contains 38 percent fewer calories, 86 percent less cholesterol, and 90 percent less fat than regular Parlour ice cream.

Launch Marketing Program

Given the spectacular results of the market research, Ault decided not to test market the product but to go directly to national launch. The company was very confident about the new product. On balance, the expense of a test market, the benefits of an early launch, and the risk that test marketing would tip off competitors led to the launch decision. Ault's Parlour 1% marketing program consisted of the following elements:

Core product concept:	Same Parlour ice cream taste with 1 percent fat.
Segments:	Women and men concerned about fat intake, former and infrequent ice cream users, ice cream lovers who want rich, creamy taste more often.
Product:	Parlour 1% in four flavors: vanilla, butterscotch, marble, and chocolate cherry mint.
Packaging:	Graphic design to differentiate between regular and 1% Parlour ice cream, yet keep the concept within the Parlour family. Highlight "1%" logo.
Price:	Same as that of regular Parlour.
Promotion:	Public relations, television advertisement, in-store and in-mall sampling, cents-off allowances.
Distribution:	Payment of fees to ensure shelf space among small retail stores and large supermarket chains.

Ault defined two major objectives for the promotional program: to make sure that consumers did not perceive Parlour 1% as a diet product but as a mainstream product, and to induce consumers to try the new product. TV advertising had an important part in the achievement of these objectives. Two different commercials were aired, one to convey the message of increased frequency of consumption and the other to convey the message of increased quantity.

To induce trial, Ault used an extensive sampling program. Research had indicated a very positive consumer attitude toward the product after trial. Consequently, for successful market development, Ault wanted to make sure that consumers would try Parlour 1%. To develop a favorable image of Dairylight, Ault used public relations to generate extensive newspaper and TV coverage. Creating a good image helped Dairylight to gain acceptance among consumers, the health care community, and food companies.

To ensure product availability in retail outlets in major market areas, Ault gained retailers' cooperation by offering slotting allowances or listing fees to obtain good freezer space position. It created brochures and display cards that the salesforce could deliver to retail buyers to explain and illustrate the performance of Parlour 1%.

THE SUCCESS AND REASONS FOR IT

The product was launched on August 31, 1991. It outperformed initial expectations and gained 2 percent of the Canadian ice cream market in less than five months. It is second only to regular Parlour as the best-selling ice cream in Canada and represents 13 percent of total Parlour sales. Almost no cannibalization from regular Parlour or Parlour Light occurred.

The market for ice cream had matured, but Parlour 1% generated incremental volume by bringing back people who had stopped consuming ice cream and winning customers from competitors. The product contributed to a 32 percent volume increase for Parlour from the previous year's level. On balance, several factors contributed to its success, but only the major ones are considered here.

Capitalizing on a Favorable Health Trend

Even though Ault, working with John Labatt Limited (the parent company), stumbled onto Simplesse in 1979, it did not attempt to rush a fat substitute product into the market. In retrospect, selling Simplesse to Monsanto was a shrewd strategy because it provided time and resources to pursue newer technologies. When the health trend favoring reduction of dietary fat became more substantial during the 1980s, Ault wisely stepped up its efforts in fat substitute technology. Medical reports about the dangers of fat and cholesterol in the diet generated a frenzy of publicity on TV talk shows and in newspapers, magazines, and other media.

Consumers' ability to live a long and healthy life seemed threatened by the very food they were eating. They would consider trying new products with less fat, but did not want to sacrifice taste. The stage was set for new technologies that could meet this challenge.

Capitalizing on Technological Strengths

Technology was part of Ault's corporate mission and the vision of its leader. Along with quality and people, technology was one of the three factors that provided direction for everyone at Ault. Hence, when the market need for fat substitutes appeared to increase, Ault could quickly marshal the resources needed to achieve its R&D goals. The fact that Ault could develop Dairylight in such a short time highlights the value of making technology and innovation part of an organization's basic mission. The discipline imposed shortens new product development time, thus affording a competitive advantage in a turbulent business environment.

Capitalizing on Brand Equity

In Canada, the Sealtest Parlour name carried brand equity. Especially when associated with ice cream, it had a strong image among consumers. A strong brand image can leverage the introduction of new products, but failure of a new product can damage a brand's reputation. For this reason, Ault engaged in substantial testing to be very sure the new product could meet the standards set by the Parlour name. This effort reduced Ault's risk and, as it turned out, may have strengthened the brand's image in the market.

Executing a Strong Launch Marketing Program

Understanding market needs is a prerequisite to success in marketing a new product. The effective use of marketing research enabled Ault to discover consumers' credibility problem with a totally fat-free product and encouraged the development of a 1-percent fat content product instead. The core concept of a low fat product with all the taste of real ice cream was central to all development efforts and the launch marketing program.

Given the brand equity of the Parlour name, Ault had only to build awareness and knowledge of the benefits of the new product and generate trial. Taste testing had shown that trial would lead to repeat purchases. Ault relied heavily on advertising, couponing, and publicity to accomplish these goals. This major effort also stimulated support from the distribution channels, which saw the potential of a product in a growing category (low fat frozen desserts). Ault was able to achieve 93 percent distribution penetration in its major markets by the launch date. In addition, Ault paid retailers high listing fees or slotting allowances as part of trade promotion to get good freezer space.

CONCLUSION

The success of Parlour 1% began with Ault's ability to capitalize on a growing market opportunity through an emphasis on technology. Then, the new product development process emphasized extensive testing to ensure that the product met consumer needs and did not jeopardize the Parlour brand's market position. Finally, a well-executed launch program gave consumers the chance to try the new product and discover its benefits, thus fostering repeat purchasing—an absolute must for a food product.

Because of the overall size of the potential market for fat substitutes, Ault cannot expect to go unchallenged. Retailers and consumers will be swayed by the promotions of competitive products as they enter the market. To maintain its competitive edge, Ault and its parent, John Labatt Limited, will have to continue its ongoing process of innovation in fat substitute technology, constantly improving its products and marketing.[20]

Paragliders

Jonathan W. Kohn and Gregory Schooley

In 1982, Larry Walters, a 33-year-old truck driver from San Pedro, California, sat down in his Sears aluminum lawn chair in his back yard. Moments later he flew into history. He had strapped 42 weather balloons to his chair and, pellet gun in hand, cut the cords that attached him to earth. He spent two hours at 16,000 feet before popping enough balloons with his gun to begin his descent. Walters spent all his money orchestrating the adventure. He had never before in his life done anything risky.

A great variety of aircraft have been created to fulfill the human desire to fly. Paragliders are among the simplest types of aircraft. They have no motor, no heavy and cumbersome frame, no sensitive steering devices. Although they look like rectangular parachutes, paragliders are large, floating wings that create lift just as the wings on airplanes do. They are made from nylon cloth and Kevlar strings that clip onto a harness. When folded, they weigh less than 20 pounds and can be carried in a medium-size back pack.

The rectangular nylon canopy of a paraglider is composed of sewn chambers that, when inflated with air, form a large wing. Unlike parachutes that retard a fall by trapping air and creating resistance, paragliders soar as the wing moves horizontally through air. With a paraglider, one can fly alone in silence for as long as desired. That activity may be the closest thing to flying like a bird that humans can experience.

Since the launch of paragliders in 1985, they have realized more than $300 million in cumulative sales in Europe. Today paragliders are much more popular than hang gliders, with more than 100,000 active pilots.

From this success, paragliding has been dubbed "the air sport of the nineties." However, the success has been largely in Europe. Even though the paraglider was launched at about the same time in the United States and Europe, the U.S. market has been slow to develop. Finding out why is the basis for this story.

THE EUROPEAN ENVIRONMENT

In the early 1980s, the proposed economic integration of Europe created a positive, yet contentious spirit among its different cultures. The opportunity for paragliding emerged from a European environment with three primary characteristics: cultural integration and change that created basic needs related to identity, a population that traditionally sought challenging outdoor activities, and available opportunities to satisfy those needs, including hang gliding, the forerunner of paragliding.

European Identity: The Need to Fly—Or Be Free?

The human desire to fly is difficult to explain. Solo flying takes people out of their everyday life into a new environment; only in water and air can people move in three dimensions. But what makes people want to fly is a mystery to the paraglider industry. Clearly, deep human needs are involved, but they are difficult to uncover. One study reporting on high risk leisure consumption through skydiving casts the experience as a classical *drama* with a protagonist, an antagonist, and a catharsis.[21]

A variety of dynamic motives, behaviors, and experiences can be identified to explain high risk leisure consumption. For example, the reason a high risk endeavor is undertaken for the first time may simply be *social pressure* from other people, along with the *thrill* of the experience and the satisfaction of *survival*. As the experience is repeated, social pressure gives way to a feeling of belonging to the *group* who engage in the activity, accompanied by feelings of *pleasure* and *achievement*. Ultimately, the risk taker acculturates into the group and gains a sense of *community*. Pleasure and achievement lead to *flow*, or a higher level of Zen-like involvement, and new personal *identity* consistent with the risk-taking culture one has joined. Hence, among the reasons for engaging in high risk leisure consumption is the development of one's identity.

Whatever the motives for paragliding, one of its advantages over hang gliding, skydiving, and other forms of flight is its relative safety. A person can experience the drama of flight with less risk than is present with other aircraft. In the 1980s, this drama may have been attractive to Europeans, who were facing the prospect of a pan-European world. Personal flight may enable a person to cope with a threatened loss of cultural identity and to develop a stronger personal identity. Moreover, paragliding may have been consistent with Europeans' fondness for outdoor activities.

The European Outdoor Culture

Europeans have always been involved in a variety of outdoor activities such as mountain climbing, kayaking, hiking, skiing, and camping. Such activities are part of any European's culture and are viewed as an important part of a person's lifestyle. With the European standard of four to six weeks of annual vacation, people participate in these activities often and throughout the year.

The level of participation in outdoor sports became so great that Europeans began to find it difficult to experience untamed nature. Over time, virtually all virgin wilderness areas had become civilized. Most mountaintops could be reached in 10 minutes by anyone who had enough time and money to ride the gondola to the summit. It is not unusual for mountain climbers, in the middle of a difficult climb, to come upon a roped and well-maintained footpath crowded with strolling tourists! Such experiences severely compromise a climber's communion with nature and the perceived challenge of the climb.

Also during the 1980s, the ecological movement was becoming very strong in Europe. A focus on nature and a shift away from some urban activities were evident. New political parties emerged solely on a platform of conserving the environment. More than ever before, outdoor activities were fashionable, especially sports involving an experience with nature. People were looking for new ways to enjoy the outdoors. Finally, Europeans have always been fascinated by the ubiquitous mountains that surround them. The mountains are accessible and well suited for flight of all kinds—the perfect environment for quiet little flying devices.

The European Hang Gliding Scene

The outdoor recreation industry in Europe was mature, yet offered large growth opportunities to innovative sports. The paraglider's predecessor, the hang glider, had been successful in the late 1970s, but by the early 1980s sales had begun to decline. This decrease in popularity was due to the difficulty of flying the hang glider, which requires a high degree of control and awareness. The craft is steered by the shifting of the pilot's weight from side to side for turning, and forward and backward for diving and climbing. The need for exacting control during flight to avoid catastrophe discourages many people from pursuing hang gliding.

Furthermore, launching the hang glider is difficult for beginners. A hang glider is made of aluminum tubing, wire cables, an elaborate harness, and heavy nylon material. It weighs about 60 pounds, making transport difficult. To take off, a pilot must support the entire weight of the apparatus while running at full speed down a hill and into the wind. Consequently, a pilot must be coordinated and physically fit to use a hang glider.

Hang gliding became an exclusive sport among its participants. Frequent flyers wanted more performance and the industry responded. Listening to advanced users and not beginners, manufacturers made hang gliders more user-responsive to handle extreme flying. The beginner was forgotten and hang gliding became a sport for a shrinking number of experts. However, even with the decline in popularity of hang gliding, Europe still had more hang glider pilots than any other part of the world. Evidently, Europeans had a desire to fly that had not been satisfied by fixed-wing aircraft or hang gliders.

THE DEVELOPMENT OF PARAGLIDERS

The first paragliders were designed in the 1950s by Francis Regalla, a NASA engineer stationed in North Carolina. He took part in NASA's effort to design space vehicle re-entry devices. Paragliders were considered as alternatives to parachutes because, instead of dropping their load vertically, they could move horizontally during descent. Regalla hoped to use the horizontal velocity of paragliders to skip a spacecraft along the surface of the ocean and keep it from sinking. Regalla was not successful and NASA used parachutes to land the Apollo spacecraft after the moon missions.

Late in the 1970s, paragliders were still an idea filed away in NASA's warehouse. Then, in Europe and the United States, new technology and advances in parachute maneuverability led to the first foot-launched parachute descents. Mountain climbers were among the first to attempt them. They used parachutes to jump off the cliffs they had climbed and got home in time for dinner, a bath, and the 10 o'clock news. In Switzerland, Laurent de Kalbermatten was among the first innovators in foot-launch parachute design. He built his own hang gliders and was curious about the possibilities of improving parachute designs exclusively for foot-launching use.

Who actually designed the first foot-launch paraglider is uncertain. However, Kalbermatten was among the first to create a modern paraglider. His first paraglider was made of different materials than parachutes.[22] Initially, performance was only slightly better than that of parachutes. Kalbermatten was encouraged by a group of friends, hang glider pilots, climbers, and skydivers to improve on his design. As his paragliders became better, more of his friends bought them and taught themselves to fly. They were a close-knit group of fun-loving individuals who played on the hills surrounding Lake Geneva and the ski slopes of Switzerland.

For Kalbermatten, new product development was a continuous process of generating ideas, prototyping, testing, and experimenting. He was attempting to combine performance with the safety of an open parachute. The design tradeoff was safety for maneuverability and increased glide ratio[23] to accommodate foot launching. Paragliders left the parachute class once the profile of the canopy could create enough lift to suspend the pilot. This breakthrough achievement made paragliders comparable to hang gliders. In fact, today the French classify paragliders as class III hang gliders.

Among the pioneer paraglider pilots was world renowned skydiving stuntman Philip Bernard. Bernard had already jumped from planes and performed stunts in the name of countless heroes, including James Bond. He and a partner opened the first paragliding school. They sold Kalbermatten's gliders, but only to students who successfully completed their course.

Paragliding was a new way of flying. Kalbermatten's gliders, through Bernard's schools, were the first ones available to the public. The aviation industry was captivated by the new product. Ailes-De-K, Kalbermatten's new paragliding company, fascinated the aviation magazines and media. Ailes-De-K got free press all over the world. The beauty, freedom, and convenience of paraglider flight took off from the hills above Lake Geneva. Paragliding had begun!

The Core Concept

The core concept of paragliding is solo flying that is safe, easy, and available to anybody. Paragliding is the easiest way to enjoy personal flight. The French called it *vol libre*, free flight. Paragliders are relatively safe because they are much more passive than hang gliders. Paraglider pilots sit in a harness and control flight by using their hands to pull strings that adjust the tail end of the canopy. Pulling down on the left side causes the glider to turn to the left. If the pilot does nothing, the glider floats down to earth in a straight line.

Paragliders are easy to use in two ways. First, with their light weight and backpack size, they can be easily transported to and from the flight site. Second, taking off on a paraglider requires only a few unhurried steps. Kalbermatten knew that hang gliders did not reach their full potential in Europe because of their difficulty to use. He realized that the paraglider could offer what had been lacking: easy learning and use. However, for the concept to be implemented, a marketing program would be needed to make paragliding available and affordable.

The European Marketing Program

Launching a new product as comprehensive as the paraglider required a bundle of equipment and services. The market potential that could be realized depended on reaching novices and teaching them to fly the paraglider safely and effectively. Only in this way could a company achieve the volume and profit margins necessary to support ongoing development. Ailes-De-K needed a carefully designed marketing program based on a clear understanding of *distribution* to make paragliding available, an array of *products* suitable for users from beginners to experts, *promotion* to build awareness and trial, and a *price* to generate profitability and value to the buyer.

Distribution

Initially, Kalbermatten chose to use flight schools as the distribution channel to reach potential buyers. He decided that consumers should purchase a paraglider only after having completed a beginner's training program. Use of a paraglider by an untrained pilot posed as great a danger to the paraglider industry as to the pilot. A string of paraglider accidents in the early years could have given the sport a reputation of being dangerous. Besides being ethical in terms of saving lives, this decision created a natural alliance between flight schools and paraglider manufacturers.

The individuals who were part of the original clique of the sport provided a pool of available instructors. Therefore, Kalbermatten and his friends took the flight school idea one step further, actively pursuing possible locations for additional schools. Because Europe has teleferiques and gondolas to the tops of many mountains, dozens of sites were available. The criteria for site selection were flying conditions, transportation to the mountain summits, spectacular scenery, and proximity to cities or tourist centers.

Some companies tried to distribute gliders directly to end users, but that strategy consistently failed. Typically, companies sell their gliders through distributors to schools, where the instructors sell the gliders to the end users. The novice paraglider pilot knows little about the sport and is unlikely to buy the expensive new product without some expert guidance.

Product Design and Production

During the early years of paragliding, manufacturers were able to make huge technological advances through continuous new product design. Competitions were held that fostered new design and promoted awareness of the sport. World champion brands leap-frogged over the competitors and captured market share, only to be dethroned by a new winner. This design competitiveness enhanced the quality and effectiveness of the paraglider without loss of the basic benefits of ease of use and safety.

Manufacturing operations grew from one in Switzerland in 1985 to more than 10 worldwide by 1987. Paragliders were manufactured in Asia, Europe, and Israel. As the number of manufacturers and schools increased, a need for distribution networks developed. Schools began to carry many different brands of gliders. Distributors were owned by the manufacturing companies and distributed only their own gliders. In the early years, demand was so great that companies had two- and three-month order backlogs.

Promotion

The spectacular sight of a paraglider in flight attracted considerable attention. Paragliders quickly became the new fad of European aviation. Countless articles were written about these new flying devices that could be easily used and mastered after only a few lessons.

An unexpected synergy developed. Teleferique companies, mountaintop restaurants, landing-site restaurants, tourism bureaus, and other organizations encouraged paragliding because it attracted tourists and built business. The paragliding pilots were a small group in comparison to all the people who would travel to see them fly. Paragliding became a money-making attraction at many resorts, especially those where tourists could share a ride on the gondola to the top of the mountain with the paraglider pilots, thus sharing the camaraderie and excitement of the sport.

Kalbermatten was the first to sponsor performance pilots to showcase his paraglider designs. These individuals exhibited their skills at popular resorts to build awareness and interest in the sport. Later, he organized cooperative events with resorts, such as competitions, charity shows, and exhibitions. For example, in 1987 Kalbermatten organized the first World Championships of Paragliding in Switzerland. He invited the top sponsored fliers representing each of the 10 paraglider manufacturers to compete against each other in a variety of events.

With the rapid increase of public interest, Kalbermatten helped create paraglider associations throughout Europe. These associations promoted events, disseminated information about the sport and new products, and enabled manufacturers to target users with advertisements for the first time. Later, paraglider magazines emerged for members of the associations, providing the perfect avenue for introducing product extensions and advertising current product lines.

Price

Paragliders were introduced at a price range of $3,400 to $4,000 (U.S.), roughly half the cost of a hang glider and a fraction of the cost of a private plane. The total cost of becoming a pilot was about $5,000, including lessons, the harness, and the emergency reserve chute.

As paragliding became more popular, manufacturers became more competitive and prices dropped. By 1993, the total package cost less than $3,000. As the industry matured, manufacturers were forced to differentiate. Some pursued the beginner market and others pursued the advanced pilot market. All companies tried to become price competitive. The result was a migration of paraglider manufacturing to countries with cheaper labor.

Ailes-De-K attempted to cut costs by selling directly to instructors and end users. This strategy was short lived, as Ailes-De-K quickly lost its market leadership position. The company that eventually emerged as the leader was a French firm that subcontracted its manufacturing to a Korean firm. Today that Korean firm has learned how to make its own gliders, has dropped its French client, and makes one of the top beginner gliders in the world. Ailes-De-K has not been able to regain market leadership. It still manufactures in Switzerland and makes top quality paragliders. It charges a premium price and caters to a high end niche market.

DIAGNOSING SUCCESS IN EUROPE

Could paragliders have succeeded anywhere but in Europe? Why not in the United States? Most of the key reasons for the European success are related to the opportunity created by the environment.

The European Culture

In Europe, free flight of all kinds seems to have struck a highly resonant chord in the culture. Because of the dense concentration of population, Europe has few open, expansive spaces in which people can escape and feel free from their current reality. The rise of environmentalism in Europe in large part reflects concern about the declining quality of the remaining natural resources. Further, Europeans are facing a future of economic integration in which traditional nation-states may be subsumed within a pan-European culture.

It is understandable, then, that Europeans would flock to the ultimate escape—leaving the earth and flying free over the countryside. Paragliding became a way to meet the need for escape safely with a thrilling new activity. Suddenly, in their own backyard, Europeans could find a new challenge that stirred feelings of individual identity, freedom of spirit, and closeness to nature.

The European Geography

European cities are close to excellent paragliding sites. The Alps run from France into Italy, Switzerland, and Austria. There are other mountain chains in Spain, Germany, Scandinavia, and Central Europe. Because so many people go to the mountains, most mountaintops are accessible by teleferique or tram.

The European Legal Environment

European countries impose few legal constraints on paragliding. European legal systems discourage suing. Landowners are not liable for accidents that may happen to paraglider pilots landing or taking off from their property. Under European law, it is difficult to prove negligence. Lawyers are not paid on a contingency basis, but instead must be paid in advance for their services regardless of the outcome. This requirement discourages people from hiring lawyers.

Eventually the national aviation authorities in each country began to regulate paragliding. They established pilot licensing, site selection, and canopy rating criteria. However, the regulators did not interfere with the growth of the sport. By setting standards and approving the activity, they validated and encouraged paragliding.

A Committed Champion

Although he may not have been the founder or inventor of paragliding, Laurent de Kalbermatten was its champion. His designs implemented the basic technology and stimulated early interest in the sport among a group of flying enthusiasts. He envisioned the need for a flying capability that was safer, easier to use, and easier to learn than current free-flight approaches. Then he established the organization and distribution network through flight schools, providing the market infrastructure to support the business. Kalbermatten was clearly the visionary who championed the success of paragliding.

WHY PARAGLIDERS DID NOT SUCCEED IN THE UNITED STATES

Paragliders were introduced in the United States at about the same time they were launched in Europe. Although an identical marketing approach was implemented, the outcome was completely different. Only about 1,000 paragliders have been sold in five years of sales in the United States, in contrast to more than 50,000 units in Japan and more than 100,000 units in Europe. There are several reasons for this poor performance.

The U.S. Culture

The need to fly, to be free, to regain one's identity may simply be less compelling in the United States than in Europe. The American identity may not have been in as much flux as the Europeans' during the late 1980s. Americans have a strong sense of freedom, mainly because of the large size of their country, their historical and political roots, and their relative geographic isolation from other countries.

Even concern about the environment is less intense in the United States than in Europe. Attitudes toward sports are also very different. Mountain climbing, hiking, kayaking, and windsurfing are special interest sports in the United States, but in Europe they are common, everyday sporting activities. Americans enjoy watching football, baseball, tennis, and other sports on TV more than playing them. The segment of consumers who spend time outdoors may be much smaller in the United States than in Europe.

However, attitudes may be changing. In a 1993 *Newsweek* article on lifestyle, the writers observe:[24] "Your father's station wagon won't cut it anymore. On bikes, rafts or in free fall, Americans are looking for adventure." Participation in bungee jumping, paragliding, skydiving, rock climbing, and white water rafting has increased, especially among people in their forties. Ironically, many of the activities are undertaken to improve performance at work—to be tougher, more competitive, more energetic. However, if the changing attitude simply represents sampling from a menu of adventures rather than commitment to specific outdoor sports on a regular basis, paragliding may remain just a tourist phenomenon.

The U.S. Geography

The logistics of paragliding are much more difficult in the United States than in Europe or Japan. First, the U.S. population centers are not close to mountain resorts. Not surprisingly, paragliding is most popular in Colorado and California. Second, mountain resorts in the United States do not have gondola services like those in Europe. Paragliding therefore involves much more time, effort, and planning in the United States than in Europe. Although ski resorts may use their facilities and ski lifts for an off-season paragliding business, such opportunities are limited.

The U.S. Legal Environment

The legal environment in the United States is a challenge for the sport of paragliding. Property owners in the United States are much more concerned about potential lawsuits than those anywhere else in the world. If a person were injured after launching or landing on someone's property, the property owner could be held liable and could lose everything. Property owners therefore refuse to allow paraglider launches or landings.

The lack of launching areas exacerbates the logistical problem faced by paraglider pilots in the United States.

In Europe, paragliding is regulated by national aviation authorities. The rights of paraglider pilots are thus formally recognized by the government. The lack of formal recognition by the U.S. Federal Aviation Administration (FAA) leaves American paraglider pilots without the backing of the government. Finally, several well-publicized deaths of paraglider pilots in the United States soon after the product's introduction discouraged sales and reduced the excitement surrounding paragliding. These deaths heightened property owners' concern about the legal implications of this new sport.

THE FUTURE OF PARAGLIDERS

The market for paragliders in Europe may be maturing. Paraglider performance is becoming increasingly difficult to improve through design. Certainly the breakthrough performance enhancements that enabled one company to leap-frog all others will be less common, if not impossible. As the limits of technical paraglider performance are reached, manufacturers will have to rely on other factors to compete, including outstanding safety records and price/performance ratios.

The future of paragliders in the United States and other countries may depend on the removal of legal and regulatory barriers. The emergence of designated paragliding areas (as at Aspen, Colorado) that combine paragliding flight school, lifts to the mountaintops, and resort accommodations may alleviate some of the logistical and legal problems. However, even if the barriers to paragliding are removed, it will not be successful in the United States unless people experience a need to fly and are willing to take the risks associated with doing so. Hence, both cultural factors and basic human needs will determine the future of the sport. As reported in *The Wall Street Journal*, Gunnar Breivik, Norway's leading philosopher of sport, states it this way:[25]

> Man must exist in a state of balance between risk and safety. Pure risk leads to self-destruction. Pure safety leads to stagnation. In between lies survival and progress.

4

Pursuing Market Acceptance

A common pitfall for a new product or business is the assumption that a large and interested market of potential buyers and other stakeholders is eagerly awaiting its arrival. Potential buyers are likely to have well-established behavior patterns for satisfying many of their needs. When confronted with an innovation, no matter how beneficial, they may need time to learn about the new product before committing to a purchase. Immediate market acceptance of a new product is unusual. Typically, acceptance must be pursued—over time and under a variety of market circumstances.

Guidelines for good business practice emphasize the importance of identifying what consumers want, then giving it to them. That approach generally works well when consumers know very clearly what they want. However, when they feel a need but do not know exactly what they want or how to describe it, the new product developer may come up short, especially with traditional marketing research techniques. In such cases, the new product may be outside the realm of the potential buyer's experience.

To succeed in such situations, new product development must become an *interactive* process, that is, one in which the new product developer works very closely and continuously with potential buyers and other key stakeholders in an almost partnerlike relationship. Consumers' reactions to new product ideas and concepts can be gauged through a variety of creative methods. Their suggestions can be incorporated into revisions of the concept. This interactive process can and should continue throughout new product development to obtain consumer input on prototypes, early product formulations, advertising, pricing, and other marketing program factors.

In this chapter, three new product success stories show the importance of pursuing consumers to gain their acceptance of new products. The first new product success presented is Slim-Fast dietary products, developed by Thompson Medical Company. A large and growing market for dietary foods emerged in the 1970s. Consumers showed very little loyalty to any particular dietary approach. Instead, they adopted each new diet fad, even to the point of risking their health in some cases.

Thompson had considerable experience with dietary products. However, because of regulatory concerns about liquid diets, the original Slim-Fast powder lost its market as sales dwindled despite its safety and favorable initial response by consumers. How Thompson responded to this experience with a more carefully developed and researched concept six years later reveals the importance of persistence in understanding the consumer and other market factors to achieve new product success.

The second new product success is The Body Shop International. The Body Shop concept was based largely on assumptions about the existence of an environmentally concerned segment of consumers that could support a global chain of retail cosmetic specialty shops. Rather than researching the idea for the business, Anita Roddick, the founder, quickly launched a first shop. In so doing, she learned about the business by using the store as a vehicle for interacting directly with the market. This experience enabled her to shape and develop the new concept to carry out her business philosophy and at the same time satisfy consumer needs for personal care products. The success of The Body Shop represents a classic case of positioning a new concept directly opposite the industry standard to create a clear difference in the potential buyers' minds.

France Telecom's Minitel videotex system is the third new product success considered in this chapter. The remarkable aspect of Minitel is that it is the first and only major videotex system of its kind to be developed and widely used by a relatively large population. Attempts to develop videotex systems in the United States have failed. The product took several years to develop, partly because of efforts to work closely with users to improve system design and delivery.

The final Minitel system included hardware and software that were very user friendly and delivered a large selection of information services in addition to telephone directory assistance. How France Telecom motivated consumers to adopt the new Minitel system and simultaneously stimulated information providers to develop new services for inclusion on the system reveals an interesting path to new product success, albeit one that benefited from state subsidized resources.

Slim-Fast Foods Company

Jennifer Sagawa and Fredrica Smithline

"But wait a bit," the Oysters cried,
"Before we have our chat;
For some of us are out of breath,
And all of us are fat."

Lewis Carroll, Through the Looking Glass

Despite a difficult start in 1977, the Slim-Fast product line has become phenomenally successful. In 1991, Thompson Medical Company's Slim-Fast products had revenues of approximately $650 million.[1] Its New York-based Slim-Fast Foods Company is estimated to control between 76 and 80 percent of the diet aid market.[2] Slim-Fast had achieved an incredible 96 percent brand awareness and 90 percent brand recall among weight-conscious consumers by 1991.[3]

Thompson Medical took advantage of the diet craze of the late 1970s by introducing in 1977 the original Slim-Fast formulation, a product that met dieters' needs at that time. It was convenient, safe, and tasted better than its competitors. Most important, it worked. Although regulatory concerns for liquid dietary products dampened demand nine months after its initial launch, the success of a reformulated Slim-Fast product came quickly after its relaunch in 1983.

By 1990, the "Slim-Fast Way of Life" had become synonymous with weight reduction and maintenance for as many as 30 million of the 72 million Americans who follow a weight loss plan.[4] Among the reasons for this phenomenal success was Thompson Medical's persistence in trying to meet an important need among consumers. This effort helped propel Slim-Fast to market leadership and fostered the development of a new "meal replacement" food category. Appetite suppressants had dominated the dietary market until the 1980s, but by 1984 they comprised only about half of the market and by the 1990s their role was minimal. Meal replacements have become the major category in the market.[5]

IN SEARCH OF THE MARKET: DIETING AND THE CONSUMER

Consumers, particularly women, became increasingly aware over the past several decades of a "need" to be thin. Thinness came to be associated with acceptance, attractiveness to the opposite sex, and love. This basic need drove the diet market to new heights during the 1960s, when two pop culture icons took America by storm: Twiggy and the miniskirt.

As hemlines rose and more body-defining clothing became popular, women's desire to be thin intensified. The image of Twiggy, the superstar model of the era, was hailed as the new ideal of the modern woman. The delicately slender beauty quickly became the envy of American women, and her popularity launched an obsession of a new generation: to be thin.

At the time, and continuing throughout the 1970s, nutrition was not considered an important aspect of dieting. The dieting concept was simple: take the weight off quickly through calorie-cutting—in essence, fasting. This "quick-fix" mentality on the part of consumers lasted nearly 15 years and was the basis for a proliferation of dieting products. Appetite suppressant pills quickly became the dominant diet product on the market, with Thompson Medical's Dexatrim leading.

Other diet fads grew in popularity during the middle and late 1970s. The macrobiotic diet, the Pritikin Diet, the Stillman Diet, the grapefruit diet, the Scarsdale Diet, and the Chinese tea diet flooded the market, each offering fast weight loss. Perhaps the most popular, and the most controversial, was the Last Chance Diet, based on a book published in 1976 by Dr. Robert Linn. Its concept, a "protein-sparing fast," was simple: by ingesting just enough protein to keep the body going without breaking down lean tissue, the dieter could live off of his or her own fat. Weight loss of up to 10 pounds a week could be achieved by limiting intake to six to eight ounces of liquid protein a day (plus as much water as desired).[6]

Dr. Linn's liquid protein diet became an instant success, enticing as many as four million Americans to purchase and consume the "foul-tasting" formula.[7] The diet was effective in causing weight loss, and the consumer did not need to count calories (intake was restricted to 300 calories a day of the formula). It seemed to be the answer to dieting. However, during 1978, Dr. Linn's diet was put under investigation by the U.S. Food and Drug Administration (FDA) as the cause of death of 59 people. Sustained use of liquid protein products, such as Prolinn, Gro-lean, and Cherrmino, caused heart arrhythmia—abnormal heartbeat.[8] The FDA's investigation spurred distributors to cancel orders and retailers to remove the products from their shelves. As a result of the deaths, consumers grew suspicious of liquid diets.

The Slim-Fast plan was first introduced in 1977 and faced problems for several years because of the controversy over liquid protein. Retailers feared placing it on their shelves. Even though the Slim-Fast plan offered more nutrients and calories, in the minds of consumers it was too similar to liquid protein products to be safe. This delay of a strong introduction did not hurt Thompson Medical, however, as its success in appetite control products was booming. Its Dexatrim was number one in the appetite suppressant market and provided ample resources to sustain the business.[9]

In the early 1980s, another diet fad reached new heights in the meal replacement market. The Cambridge Diet, similar to Slim-Fast in product concept, entered the market as a powder that was mixed with water and used as a substitute for meals. However, its number of calories was significantly lower—330 a day—and one could not eat any food or a regular dinner with it. Because of pressure from the FDA, Cambridge Plan International later increased the daily caloric intake in the diet to 800. The product was well received by consumers; by 1984, the diet had garnered more than five million customers.

The success of the Cambridge Diet was due largely to its innovative distribution channels. "Counselors," local neighborhood people, sold the diet powder door to door, thereby effectively reaching more potential customers than was possible through traditional distribution channels.[10] Witnessing the success of Cambridge, Thompson Medical took advantage of the market opportunity evidenced by renewed interest among consumers for easy-to-use diets. Thompson relaunched Slim-Fast in 1983.[11]

Although liquid protein diets had lost their popularity by 1983, consumers still wanted convenience and ease of use from their weight loss plans. In the 1980s, consumer income and spending increased. More women entered the workforce. Because of their hectic lifestyles, consumers needed a diet that was quick and easy. Weight Watchers, in the diet business for more than 21 years, required consumers to weigh their food and eat meals prepared separately from those of their families. Alternatively, Slim-Fast offered simplicity, nutrition, and convenience. The powder, which was mixed with skim milk, could be used at home or brought to work. It was a perfect dieting product for the woman of the 1980s. These features became Slim-Fast's competitive advantage in the young and rapidly growing meal replacement market.

THE PRODUCT DEVELOPMENT PROCESS

Slim-Fast's founder, C. Daniel Abraham, began working at his uncle's small drug company in 1945. However, he soon realized that his talents were not in pharmaceuticals, but rather in business. His first entrepreneurial venture, the purchase of an itch-relieving ointment manufacturer for $5,000 in 1947, proved to be an important one. That company became Thompson Medical, which later produced the original Slim-Fast drink mix.[12]

In 1956, Abraham produced his first diet product, Slim-Mint gum. It served to dull the appetite through an ingredient called benzocaine. Realizing the potential of the diet market, then $50 million and steadily growing, Abraham quickly followed Slim-Mint with his first diet capsules four years later. Thompson Medical introduced several appetite suppressants and other health care products over the next four decades, including such products as Control, Aspercreme, and Cortizone-5. Not until 1976, however, did Abraham have his first major success. In that year, he bought out Dexatrim, a one-dose-a-day appetite suppressant pill. The heavily advertised product quickly became the number one diet pill and its sales reached $50 million in 1979.[13]

The Reluctant Idea

Just as Dexatrim was gaining momentum, *The Last Chance Diet* came onto the shelves of bookstores, promoting the benefits of liquid protein dieting. Many of Thompson Medical's retail accounts saw the potential in this new segment of the market and tried to push the company into it. Having more than 30 years of experience in the diet and nutrition field, Thompson certainly had the background and loyal retail customer base to be successful in the new market. However, Abraham was very hesitant to develop a liquid protein diet. He felt it was very unsafe for people to ingest only liquid protein and dangerously few calories.[14]

The American Medical Association (AMA) conceded that although the all-protein liquid diets could achieve beneficial weight loss results, they also could have very dangerous side effects such as "nausea, vomiting, dehydration, muscle cramps, hair loss, and dry skin." Similarly, the AMA was concerned about the risks of these liquid diets because they were sold over the counter, without the supervision of a physician.[15] Generally, the liquid products tasted terrible, further motivating people to fast and lose even greater amounts of weight.

The pressure from distribution channels, coupled with the controversy surrounding liquid diets, prompted Abraham to research the best product for the market. He worked with a nutritionist to help Thompson Medical formulate a new and different product. Rather than concentrating on low calorie, high protein liquid, Abraham wanted to produce a nutritious powder. He solicited the help of Dr. George Blackburn of Deaconess Hospital at Harvard. Together they researched and developed a powder that, when mixed with milk, provided adequate calories and protein (and other nutrients such as fiber and calcium), as well as a superior taste, which eventually became Slim-Fast's competitive advantage.[16]

Product Testing

Surprisingly, Thompson Medical did little formal taste testing of the product. Because of time constraints and pressure from retail outlets for immediate launch, testing centered on company employees. Abraham himself tested packaging and package copy by soliciting the opinions of pedestrians on the street in front of the company's New York City offices! Changes were made on the basis of input from persons interviewed. Although Abraham's methods were not traditional, they were effective in enabling Thompson Medical to bring Slim-Fast to market within one year of its formulation.[17]

The First Launch

Nine months after the Slim-Fast launch in 1977, the FDA released a study warning against the use of three "well-known" brands of liquid diet. The FDA believed these liquid diets contained protein of "extremely poor quality."[18] Concern deepened when a few dieters, under their doctors' supervision, died while on the liquid diets. Despite lobbying efforts in Washington to show that Slim-Fast was not like the other liquid diet products, Thompson Medical could not prevent many of its accounts from dropping the product. Although the company continued to market Slim-Fast, sales steadily decreased because of the bad publicity.

The Relaunch

The success of the Cambridge Diet six years later encouraged Abraham to resurrect the Slim-Fast brand. Building on its product claims, Thompson Medical positioned Slim-Fast as being superior to Cambridge: better tasting, conveniently available in retail stores, and more nutritious to drink. The company believed that re-entering the market after the market leader and positioning the product as superior to the leader would actually benefit the company in the long run. By learning from the leader's mistakes and correcting them, Thompson could develop a strong competitive advantage.

The relaunch marketing program was much better planned than the original launch of Slim-Fast. Thompson Medical conducted an extensive pilot test in its California retail accounts (such as Walgreen and Thrifty drugstores). There they ran a comparison campaign showing the differences between the Cambridge Diet and the Slim-Fast Plan, emphasizing the superior benefits of Slim-Fast. The test results proved positive, with the sales of Slim-Fast surpassing those of the Cambridge Diet. Consequently, Thompson Medical launched the product across the country, using the same comparison campaign.[19]

Product Line

The early success of Slim-Fast led to a variety of product line extensions. Hot chocolate and pudding were introduced in 1984 and Ultra Slim-Fast in 1988. Ultra Slim-Fast quickly became the line favorite, accounting for most of the Slim-Fast product line's sales. Other line extensions were ready-to-drink shakes, popcorn, cheese curls, shelf-stable entrees and frozen dinners, candy bars, and dry soup mix. Each promotes Slim-Fast's program and enables people to control their calorie intake with a nutritious product.[20]

Positioning Slim-Fast in the Diet Aid Market

Slim-Fast was positioned to be very different from its competitors, especially Cambridge. Rather than establishing it as simply a weight loss product, the positioning messages centered on taste, convenience, and nutrition. Slim-Fast was promoted as better tasting than Cambridge, widely available in retail outlets, costing considerably less than Cambridge, and being more nutritious (higher in fiber, vitamins, and nutrients).

The positioning concept was palatable to dieting consumers and focused on a balanced lifestyle: "A shake for breakfast, a shake for lunch and a balanced dinner." The concept of a "shake" has favorable connotations and fits a busy lifestyle because a shake can be consumed in a relatively short period of time. Mixing the product with milk requires just enough consumer involvement in the product to convey a feeling of having "prepared" a meal. Also, milk has an image of being a complete and healthy food that is lacking when a powder is mixed with *water*. Finally, sacrificing traditional foods for breakfast and lunch is compensated by the idea of a "balanced dinner."

Advertising

Being second in the market, Slim-Fast needed to communicate its positioning against the Cambridge Diet effectively to consumers. On the basis of market research, the ad agency created an advertising campaign that established Slim-Fast as "a better tasting alternative with more nutrients than the popular brand sold door-to-door." It also stressed that Slim-Fast was less expensive than Cambridge, which appealed to the consumer.[21]

Unlike the diet pills and liquid crash diets that had flooded the market in the 1970s and early 1980s, Slim-Fast did not become associated with a slimness obsession. Thompson Medical wanted every woman and man to relate to the Slim-Fast concept of a balanced lifestyle. The thousands of letters received from happy customers with "before and after" photos stimulated an ad campaign featuring people grappling with common weight problems. These testimonials, a new concept in the diet industry, were well accepted by consumers. They were even extended to include personalities with everyday weight problems. For example, in 1988, the company convinced Dodgers manager Tommy Lasorda to lose 30 pounds with Slim-Fast and used his testimonial for an advertisement.

Distribution

In addition to unique positioning and advertising, Slim-Fast developed an intensive distribution strategy to make the product available wherever weight-conscious consumers shopped. Slim-Fast was placed not only in drugstores, but also in supermarkets and specialty stores. The success of the comparison campaign highlighting the deficiencies of the Cambridge Diet persuaded former retail accounts of the late 1970s to restock their shelves with Slim-Fast. The company eventually negotiated enough shelf space to place "Slim-Fast Food Centers" in retail outlets. The centers were simply an entire block of shelf space or a special section devoted strictly to Slim-Fast products. This intensive distribution strategy created a strong competitive advantage. Dominating limited shelf space makes it difficult for competitors to gain access to consumers.

DIAGNOSING THE SUCCESS

Despite its delayed market entry after Cambridge, Slim-Fast and its sister product Ultra Slim-Fast have been remarkably successful. Since its re-launch in 1983, the number of people using Slim-Fast, its market share, sales volume, and brand awareness have skyrocketed. Approximately five million people were using Slim-Fast in 1985. That number grew to more than 23 million in 1990, just five years later.[22] Some analysts believe Slim-Fast products had between 76 and 80 percent of the $1 billion diet aid market in 1991.[23] Reported brand awareness and brand recall levels at 96 and 90 percent, respectively, are high for any business. Four major reasons for this considerable success are briefly reviewed here.

Understanding Consumer Needs in a Large Market

Part of Slim-Fast's success can be attributed to the sheer size of the dietary market (both overweight and average-weight people) and the strong, almost obsessive, needs of its target consumer. Of the more than 100 million overweight Americans,[24] 72 million follow some type of weight loss program. The very strength of their desire to be slim (established in the 1960s), which is based on their need for beauty and attractiveness, has supported the Slim-Fast business. Understanding consumers' basic needs and how to meet them in simple, effective ways was essential to Slim-Fast's success.

Persisting for Market Acceptance

In many markets, success depends on patience and persistence, especially in appealing to a large market with a strong consumer need. Resources must be adequate to sustain market development over time. Thompson had ample resources because of its other businesses.

The lesson of patience is clear from Thompson's approach to Slim-Fast. It was not easy for Thompson to lose the market for its new product in

1977, especially because the product worked well and could truly help consumers lose weight. The company faced regulatory barriers, competitive barriers, and other market difficulties. Its eventual willingness to re-enter the market six years later and invest in a new product development and marketing program shows that persistence can pay off. Nevertheless, C. Daniel Abraham was appropriately reluctant to take the risk, requiring substantial information before committing Thompson.

Following the Leader

Some of the risk of Thompson's relaunch was mitigated by a delayed entry timing strategy. Because Abraham was uncertain about the market's receptivity toward a liquid diet product (after the liquid protein controversy), it was advantageous for him to allow Cambridge Plan International to launch its products first. Through Cambridge's experience in the marketplace, Thompson Medical was able to learn about market response to liquid diet products in the 1980s and to find out what was missing in Cambridge's products.

Cambridge helped to build consumer and regulatory confidence in liquid diet products, thereby lessening the burden for Slim-Fast. Cambridge bore the cost of educating the market, whereas Slim-Fast gained valuable information about both the market and its main competitor. Market research gathered during the delay period helped Slim-Fast develop its effective advertising strategy.

Using Advertising Effectively

Many of the successful dietary programs up to the launch of Slim-Fast used personal methods of communication. Weight Watchers initially relied on group meetings, and Cambridge used dietary "counselors" to sell its product door to door in neighborhoods. Alternatively, Slim-Fast followed in the earlier tradition of Metrecal (a canned dietary liquid) by using national television advertising.

National television advertising made sense for Thompson given the large size and geographic dispersion of the market for dietary products. Such advertising becomes very efficient when a large number of consumers are tuned into selected programs. It also made sense given the simple message that Thompson wanted to communicate about Slim-Fast. Television facilitates the communication of before-and-after visual testimonials that show the efficacy of a product. The effectiveness of the aggressive advertising programs became evident in the high awareness and recall rates among consumers in the diet market.

FUTURE CHALLENGES

Once Slim-Fast was launched, a host of imitators flooded the market in the hope of capturing part of its large market share. Products such as Carnation's Do-It-Yourself and Slender, JB Williams Company's Protein, Vitamins, Minerals (PVM), and Lederle's Dynatrim entered the market soon after Slim-Fast. Although they initially stole market share from Slim-Fast, none were able to sustain it. Competitors could not build their own distinct competitive advantage in the market.

The more successful competitors were in the "diet support segment," including firms like Jenny Craig and Nutri-System that provide therapy, support, and food. The success of these competitors revealed the increasing segmentation of the diet market. Consumers entering the market may have needs and problems that are not completely solved by Slim-Fast. For example, needs may be shifting from losing weight to a broader concern for health. How many times will customers repurchase Slim-Fast to fight off the weight they have regained multiple times? For some consumers, losing weight may not be just a three-month project, but a commitment to a particular way of life that includes proper diet, exercise, and eating in moderation. An emphasis on nutrition, exercise, low fat, low cholesterol, low salt, and other factors may be perceived as an alternative way to look slender and attractive. These shifts, coupled with new food technologies, have expanded the meaning of competition for Slim-Fast. Everyday foods like bread, salad dressings, yogurt, milk, pretzels, crackers, soups, and ice cream have begun appearing in "light" and nonfat versions and, in effect, compete with the Slim-Fast concept.

In the near future, a wealth of information about diet and nutrition may become readily available to consumers through information technology. Consumers may become empowered to make better nutritional decisions, and hence may rely less on structured programs and specific diet plans like Slim-Fast. Further, the medical community may extend its research to the point of discovering genetic predisposition to overweight and other nutritional problems. Should such conditions prove to be correctable with gene therapy, the entire diet aid market would change significantly.

The challenge to Slim-Fast Foods Company will be to respond effectively to increasing competition, changing consumer behavior, segmenting markets, and new technologies, medical and otherwise. Should the company continue to build equity in the Slim-Fast brand name and product line extensions or add new products to satisfy emerging needs and other pressures? In either case, the new product success of Slim-Fast has provided the company a solid base from which to build in the future.[25]

The Body Shop International

S. Luke Hodges and Diane E. Knaut

In the factory we make cosmetics; in the store we sell hope.

> *Charles Revson*
> *Revlon Inc.*

We make and sell our naturally-based products which cleanse, polish,
and protect the skin and hair . . . [The cosmetic industry] . . . is
run by men who create needs that don't exist. There is not one product
on the market that will make you look younger. It's impossible. If you
want to look younger, live in space.

> *Anita Roddick*
> *The Body Shop*

From its inception, The Body Shop International has been an extension of
Anita Roddick's beliefs and values. Even with its expansion into international markets, the company has never compromised its founding principles:

- Naturally-based products;
- No animal testing;
- Minimal packaging; and
- Reuse, refill, recycle.

On these principles The Body Shop has built its reputation and entered
into the intensely competitive cosmetics market with an innovative product line and a new philosophy of business.

The Body Shop is Anita Roddick's vision of how a business should be
run. Her drive and determination broke the traditional business formula

created by the cosmetics industry. Prior to starting The Body Shop, Roddick had traveled extensively around the world. She and her husband Gordon owned a restaurant and hotel in Littlehampton, England. In 1976, while her husband was fulfilling a lifelong dream of riding horseback from Buenos Aires to New York, she conceived the idea of opening a shop to sell simple, naturally-based skin and hair care products inspired by practices she encountered in foreign cultures during her travels.

Using the hotel as collateral, she took out a $7,000 loan to begin her new business and hired a local chemist to develop naturally-based lotions. With no market research, limited testing on family and friends, and only a handful of products, Roddick opened the first store, called The Body Shop, in Brighton, approximately 30 minutes from Littlehampton. Within six months the shop was a success.

THE BODY SHOP SUCCESS

By 1994, the company had opened more than 1,000 shops worldwide. Shops are located in 45 countries, trade in 23 different languages, and perform well in most markets.[26] In fact, for the first time since the company had entered the U.S. market in 1988, operations in its 78 U.S. stores finally produced an operating profit of £1.5 million in 1992.

Net sales in 1994 for the total company were approximately £195 million, a 16 percent increase from the previous year's level, with a profit margin of 15.4 percent.[27] Even more phenomenal is that as of 1990, "for over a decade sales and profits continued to grow on average some 50% a year."[28] These figures had a positive impact on the trading of the company's stock. The Body Shop went public in 1984 with five million shares and the shares have since split five times.

Despite this financial success, the focus of The Body Shop is not simply on the numbers. According to its corporate philosophy, "we are not motivated solely by profit. We are as concerned with people's safety and welfare and the protection of the natural environment as we are with making good products."[29]

THE ENVIRONMENTALLY CONCERNED CONSUMER

At issue for Anita Roddick in developing The Body Shop was her assumption that a large and supportive segment of environmentally concerned consumers would share her enthusiasm for the new store concept. When she opened her first store in the mid-1970s, an environmentalism movement already existed but no one knew how it would evolve. The path of environmentalism since that time has been a winding one.

Broad concern about the natural environment arose in the United States during the mid-1960s after publication of Rachel Carson's *Silent Spring* in 1962. It grew through the 1970s, but slowed somewhat during the 1980s. However, in Europe, concern about the environment intensified during the mid-1980s. Consumers in West Germany were much more concerned about ecological matters than those in other European countries, even to the point of achieving a political party based on the environment, the Green Party.

Subsequently, the "green revolution" regained momentum in the United States in the 1990s. One survey in 1991 found that some 86 percent of 1,514 respondents voluntarily recycled newspapers, glass, aluminum, and motor oil.[30] About 82 percent said they bought products made from or packaged in recycled material. The study also showed that the cosmetics business was among the lowest rated for concern about the environment. An interesting aspect of U.S. environmentalism in the 1990s was its popularity among young people, who were especially interested in recycling and avoiding waste.

Environmentalism is clearly a global phenomenon. It is manifested on a variety of issues (waste, nuclear energy, air quality, rain forests, and the "greenhouse effect"), at different times, in different geographic areas of the world, and in varying degrees of intensity among consumers. Reaching a segment of consumers who could be living anywhere in the world and who would respond to an environmental appeal for personal care products would be a challenge.

DEVELOPMENT OF THE BODY SHOP

The Body Shop is much more than just a place to purchase bath and skin care products. One of the most important features of The Body Shop is its commitment to environmental and societal concerns. In fact, the company has become almost as well known for its commitment to environmentalism as it has for its products.[31] It has achieved this recognition by integrating environmental issues in the core product concept for the business to create "The Body Shop Approach" by which its products are developed and produced.

The Body Shop Concept

As Anita Roddick's idea for The Body Shop began to take form, various concepts for it emerged. First, she believed strongly that she could find consumers who had environmental concerns similar to her own—an environmentally concerned market segment. Second, she believed she could find and develop products that were naturally-based and to which the environmentally concerned consumer would respond. Her ideas included producing and selling skin creams, shampoos, and lotions made from fruit and vegetable oils, not the animal fats typically used in traditional cosmetics.[32] Her concept also included use of minimal packaging to reduce unnecessary waste and offering a range of sizes to meet customer needs.

Designing Naturally-Based Products

Many of The Body Shop's new skin care ideas and formulas are developed and documented through Roddick's continued travels and the efforts of the company's anthropology and research and development departments. Unlike most cosmetic products on the market, many of the products in The Body Shop are naturally-based. Research is an ongoing process to find plants, herbs, fruits, flowers, seeds, and nuts to create new products. This research includes identification of ingredients that come from renewable sources. Careful studies are done to ensure that using the raw ingredients will not negatively affect the natural environment. Resulting products include, for example, mango body butter and banana hair putty!

Although many of the products are naturally-based, they do contain preservatives and other man-made substances. Preservatives are added to ensure the safety of the products by keeping the natural ingredients fresh and effective and preventing contamination. Synthetic ingredients are used occasionally as substitutes for natural ingredients to produce the desired results without cruelly or carelessly extracting oils from animals or from plants that might be jeopardized environmentally.[33]

Testing New Products (No Animal Testing)

From the beginning, The Body Shop has been opposed to animal testing in the development of its products, whether in its own research facility or by suppliers of raw materials and products. The Body Shop does not buy any ingredient that has been tested on animals within the last five years. This position is unconventional in an industry with a history of using tests such as the Lethal Dose 50 and the Fixed Dose Test. These tests consist of force-feeding rats with product formulas or raw materials until 50 percent of them die, or exposing them to a greater amount of formula than that to which a human would likely be exposed.

The Body Shop uses modern product-testing methods that are reliable, effective, and do not endanger animals or people. These methods include:

- Incorporating into formulas only ingredients with a long history of safe human use.
- Analyzing ingredients according to structure, properties, and compatibility with other ingredients through The Body Shop's own database examinations.
- Microbiological testing of all raw materials by the latest analytical techniques.
- Developing and using alternative in vitro testing methods such as a tissue culture protein test to predict human reaction.
- Final formulation screening on volunteer members of staff at The Body Shop Product Evaluation Clinic in England.

If these tests are passed, the formulations are sent to the University of Wales for final tests by independent dermatologists.

The Body Shop is totally committed to the development of safe products, but firmly believes that "it is neither right, necessary, nor scientifically accurate to test skin and hair care products on animals."[34] This strong stance was challenged by a television documentary in England. However, Roddick won a libel suit filed against the company that produced the documentary, vindicating her company's image and its testing practices.

Packaging (Reuse, Refill, Recycle)

The Body Shop takes full responsibility for its wastes. Consequently, its packaging is minimal and practical. Plastic bottles are used because they are safe, durable, and light. They can also be refilled or recycled. The approach was taken initially because of lack of funds to keep adequate stock. The Body Shop has always offered to refill or recycle its plastic bottles. As the impact of waste on the environment has become more evident, waste reduction has become an integral part of all aspects of the company's operation. In addition, the company continues to encourage customers to reuse, refill, and recycle, offering cash discounts to those who refill old bottles.[35]

Supplier Relations

Beginning in the late 1980s, fair trade with suppliers became an important focus of the company. Committed to helping people help themselves, The Body Shop works with communities in need to implement trade links (producing products or ingredients that can be sold in The Body Shop) that are economically feasible and beneficial to the communities.

Building strong trade relations with the company enables these communities to "acquire the tools and resources they need to support themselves."[36] Following the sentiment of "doing well by doing good," The Body Shop not only helps less developed countries, but also generates steady suppliers and opportunities for discovering new ingredients and products. Supplier relations are an often neglected aspect of new product development, especially as sources for new ideas.

Marketing Program

The cosmetics industry tradition of being global and highly competitive necessitates continual new product development and marketing. Success often comes at the expense of a competitor's market share. The push for new products has resulted in higher prices for cosmetics as companies invest in research and development to better meet consumer needs. Within this industry, The Body Shop has emerged with a new category of personal care products, offering consumers new products, knowledgeable retail service, and a new philosophy of business that positions its products and services for the socially and environmentally concerned shopper.

Positioning

In addition to attracting the environmentally concerned consumer, The Body Shop further differentiates itself from its competitors through its belief that it is unethical to sell the romance of beauty and youth. Roddick maintains that cosmetics cannot transform skin, but can only cleanse, polish, and protect it. The company prides itself on selling the truth. It simply sells products that will promote healthy skin and hair. These products do not provide magical solutions to the process of aging. Instead, they give consumers what they truly want: wellbeing, health, and self-esteem.

To enhance the credibility of the store's positioning, prices are generally set lower than those of cosmetics in major department stores. Prices are high enough to support the franchise system (startup costs on a U.S. franchise are approximately $300,000) but low enough to provide value to consumers.

The Body Shop appeals to consumers who are tired of traditional cosmetics promotions and expensive department store brands. This new breed of consumer is skeptical of the beauty industry's claims and savvy enough to see through the hype and aggressive selling of everlasting youth and breathtaking beauty. They require more information about the product and how it is made and about the business practices of the companies they support. They are committed to the future and are willing to participate in long-term relationships with companies that can meet their needs.[37]

Retail Stores

Changes in consumer tastes and economic factors (i.e., more women in the workforce) have had a significant impact on the cosmetic industry. More customers are purchasing personal care products at specialty beauty boutiques, one of the fastest-growing segments in the cosmetic industry.[38] The Body Shop was in position to capitalize on this change.

Most of the shops in the company are franchises, and are one of The Body's Shop's most important vehicles for creating and promoting the company's image. Upon entering a store, customers are not bombarded with images of youth and beauty. Instead, they find messages about the company's philosophy and campaigns. These messages are conveyed by huge posters in the shop windows, leaflets and pamphlets placed throughout the stores, and T-shirts worn by the staff.

The company keeps tight control of the materials used and the image conveyed in the stores, including store layouts and merchandising techniques such as gift baskets. This attention to detail is important because the company does not use traditional national advertising campaigns. Storefronts and displays must be consistent and striking to maintain the company's image.[39]

Retail Salesforce

Another important element in maintaining the company's image is the workforce, including the franchise owners. Roddick looks for people who share her passion for global issues and are willing to make a commitment to global causes. Along with other testing procedures, each franchise applicant is required to work within a store, to be evaluated by the store's staff, and to interview extensively with top executives.

Equally important is the selection and training of the salesforce. Employees are not trained to use a hard sell to reach sales goals. Rather, they are empowered with extensive information about the products, their origins, and their uses. The effect of this education is to improve and differentiate the quality of service provided by the shops. Selling is based on information, not persuasion.

Service is enhanced by the enthusiasm created through company campaigns directed at the salesforce as part of the company's educational program. The campaigns, like the Trade Not Aid program, are part of an intensely researched, designed, and executed business strategy. In addition to generating excitement in the shops, the campaigns have resulted in low employee turnover relative to the industry norm. "'It's a way for people to bond to the company,' says Roddick. 'It's a process of learning to be a global citizen and what it produces is a sense of passion you simply won't find in a Bloomingdale's department store.'"[40]

Promotion

The company believes that standard promotional techniques are increasingly ineffective. Consumers can be overwhelmed by the barrage of advertisements and promotions to the point of information overload. The constant assault of claims, promises, and guarantees has also led to consumer cynicism toward marketing efforts.[41] The Body Shop therefore tries to provide integrated and credible information through its philosophy, innovative products, salesforce, packaging, and in-store pamphlets.

Further, each store is given a reference book called *The Product Information Manual* that contains information on all The Body Shop's products. The packaging of the products is very plain; lotions and shampoos are packaged in distinct plastic bottles with black caps and green labels stating clear, factual explanations of ingredients and the best uses for the product. Next to the products are cards with additional information about the ingredients and origin of each particular mixture. Throughout the store, pamphlets are displayed that explain the philosophies behind the products and the company's campaigns (such as Against Animal Testing). In some shops, videotapes are played that detail the company's manufacturing opera tions or its latest campaign.[42]

The Body Shop has achieved its success to date without advertising. Its message is complex and would be difficult to convey in a traditional mass media advertising campaign. In addition, Roddick feels that national advertising campaigns would not reach her customers effectively and therefore would be a waste of money. As Roddick puts it, "I'd be embarrassed to spend a lot of money on ads for deodorant and skin lotion."[43]

Publicity

The Body Shop uses publicity effectively. The company is estimated to generate about $3.5 million worth of free publicity a year from various articles and appearances by Anita Roddick.[44] Her views on the environment are quoted just as often as her views on The Body Shop. Just as important is the support from such influential customers as Princess Diana and Sting, who applaud Roddick's efforts. Free publicity has generated tremendous interest in the company.

MAJOR REASONS FOR SUCCESS

The Body Shop success did not happen overnight. Anita Roddick has invested steadily in her business since 1976, evolving her philosophy and business strategy over time. Pursuing the environmentally concerned consumer, as well as those who simply enjoy exciting and innovative products, has paid off. This consumer has come and gone over time, appeared in different countries of the world at different times, and been concerned about a variety of issues. Nevertheless, Roddick's persistence in developing products for this segment enabled The Body Shop to fulfill their needs related to personal care products and to deliver satisfaction. Using unique products, a focused positioning strategy, effective delivery of information, and strong business principles, Roddick has executed a truly global new product success.

Unusual Global New Products

The base of The Body Shop is its line of innovative cosmetics with ingredients from all parts of the world (and sold to all parts of the world). The development of fair trade with communities in need not only helps stimulate business in those communities, but also provides creative sources of new product ideas and alternative ingredients for current products. New products are developed through a process that is guided by principles requiring natural ingredients, no animal testing, and reusable, refillable, and recyclable packaging. The shape, size, and packaging of each product are also quite different from industry standards.

The products are placed in retail shops with ambiance and an informed sales staff that can explain and otherwise enhance product value. Thus, consumers can learn about and purchase unusual products in a setting very different from the traditional cosmetics counter.

Focused Positioning Strategy

The Body Shop employed what might be referred to as an "un-cola" positioning strategy. Seven-Up soda differentiated itself from common cola drinks through positioning as the un-cola beverage—a clear drink, not a caramel-colored cola. Similarly, everything about The Body Shop positions it against the mainstream cosmetics business. Its products and even its marketing strategy are different in many respects from industry standards.

The famous remark of Charles Revson (of Revlon cosmetics) has been turned on its head: "In the factory we make cosmetics; in the store we sell hope." Roddick would certainly disagree with the notion of selling "hope" in her stores. Instead, she attempts to communicate basic information about her products and the factual truth about what consumers can expect them to do for their hair and skin. Her business clearly shows that a company does not need to follow accepted industry practices to be successful.

Effective Use of Information

Marketing and positioning of The Body Shop through intensive communication of information enables customers to find out anything they care to know about the products and how the company operates. This approach clearly differentiates the company from its major competitors, in some cases creating significant problems for ones that are unable to provide the level of information offered by The Body Shop. Moreover, the immense amount of information humanizes the company. Customers feel they are buying from a company whose values and business practices are not hidden. One outcome of this approach is tremendous consumer loyalty to The Body Shop.

Another outcome of intense communication is active promotion of the company and its products by customers. Favorable word of mouth is a major reason for The Body Shop's tremendous growth. It has enabled a company that does not have a marketing department to succeed in an industry that is as marketing intensive as any.[44]

Strong Business Principles

The Body Shop offers many valuable lessons about how to succeed in a highly competitive environment. Anita Roddick explains these lessons in one of The Body Shop's promotional videos:

> As a result of what we have learned during the last 15 years, we have evolved a simple credo:
>
> - You can run a business different from the way most businesses are run;
> - You can share your prosperity with your employees;
> - You can empower them without being in fear of them;
> - You can rewrite the book in the way a company interacts with the community;
> - You can rewrite the book in terms of third world trade, and global responsibility, on the role of educating the customer, the shareholder, the employee;
> - And still play the game according to the City.
> - You can still raise money, delight the institutions and the banks;
> - You can still have shareholders who get a wondrous return on their investment.
>
> The Body Shop is no more than an experiment, founded on principles, alien to most businesses. I believe The Body Shop is proof that you can become and stay successful and still keep your soul and your sense of fun, and a sense of fun is something I've always wanted to combine with achievement and social consciousness in my life.

CONCLUSION

The success of any new product generates intense competition. By 1990, three significant competitors within the U.S. market had targeted the same niche of customers as The Body Shop. In the late 1980s, Estée Lauder launched its Origins line of products, using its prime counter space and department store locations to appeal to the natural cosmetics consumer. In 1990, The Limited launched a chain of stores called Bath & Body Works and now has more than 200 stores. Kmart has begun to market a line of natural cosmetics called Naturistic that is sold through its 1,800 stores nationwide.

These competing brands have been successful, especially Bath & Body Works and the Origins line, which has sales of approximately $40 million. As a result, the natural cosmetics category now accounts for 4 percent of the $16 billion U.S. cosmetics market and is growing at 12 to 15 percent annually, three times as fast as the industry average.[45]

These emerging competitors pose both a threat and an opportunity. The threat is that they will take away business from The Body Shop. The opportunity is that their marketing activity will stimulate greater numbers of consumers to use natural cosmetics, thus boosting The Body Shop's performance in the market because of its strong market position. Undoubtedly, Anita Roddick would see competition as an opportunity. Few, if any, competitors may be able to create the consumer and employee loyalty and unique new product approach that have led to The Body Shop's success.

France Telecom: Minitel

Thomas K. Billington and Christian Riis-Hansen

The open society, the unrestricted access to knowledge, the unplanned and uninhibited association of men for its furtherance—these are what may make a vast, complex, ever growing, ever changing, ever more specialized and expert technological world, nevertheless a world of human community.

J. Robert Oppenheimer, Science and the Common Understanding, *1953*

France Telecom is the French telecommunication monopoly. In 1991, it posted revenues of more than $15 billion (U.S.) and employed 156,100 people. France Telecom's main business is operating the telephone system in France. It also operates the Teletel system, a videotex telecommunication network launched in 1982 that gives users access to more than 17,000 services through Minitel terminals. The system's enormous success in France surprised U.S. telecommunication companies, which have had mixed results with videotex systems.

The Minitel terminal weighs about 10 pounds and is the size of a nine-inch television set. It has a full alphanumeric keyboard that tucks under or folds up to a screen. The terminals can be used to make plane reservations, purchase appliances, communicate with other people, or search for a used car with exact specifications. These transactions can be performed personally and in complete privacy.

The tremendous success of Minitel is reflected in the total number of terminals, hours used, and services offered during the 1980s. The total number of Minitel terminals grew from 120,000 in December 1983 to six million in December 1991. The total number of hours the Minitels were used increased from 13.5 million in 1985 to 104.9 million in 1991. Finally, the total number of services available on the Teletel system increased from 1,899 in December 1985 to 17,297 in December 1991.[46]

Minitel has redefined the telecommunications industry in France. It helped to transform France Telecom from an out-of-date bureaucracy to a modern, high tech player in the world telecommunications industry. The reach of the Teletel system is impressive. In 1990, 20 percent of the telephone subscribers, 29 percent of the population, and 41 percent of the workforce in France had Minitel.[47]

THE INDUSTRY CHALLENGE

Historically, European telecommunication companies have been state owned. This tradition enabled them to develop projects with high risk and long time horizons, especially ones that would enhance a nation's long-term competitiveness. Projects that might not meet the financial requirements of private firms could be supported by the state to achieve societal objectives. Thus, France Telecom had considerable flexibility in experimenting with telecommunication innovations such as the Minitel. Because of the monopolistic status of France Telecom and its dominance of the nation's telephone lines, competition in French telecommunication services is limited. Any new products France Telecom develops have exclusive marketing opportunities in France.

However, during the 1980s, France was clearly in competition with several countries to build a system that could accommodate a substantial market of electronic transactions across Europe. For example, Bildschirmtext in Germany and Prestel in the United Kingdom were racing with France Telecom to develop videotex systems with very different standards for their respective countries. Each country sought to develop a successful in-country system that could become the European standard. The immediate objective of the race was simply to be first on the market with a major success.

France Telecom was in a good position to compete. It had access to state funds with little pressure to generate a financial return, as well as a strong technological knowledge base and a substantial R&D capability. However, its monopoly status weakened its marketing abilities, its large bureaucratic organizational structure slowed decision processes, and limited new product successes in the past provided few models for the development of a videotex system.

Perhaps the greatest challenge France Telecom faced was the French people. Their image of the telephone company was not very positive. French comedians joked that it was easier to call a suburb of Paris by routing the call through New York than calling direct through France Telecom. Further, a videotex system would require its users to change their behavioral patterns, which could make them reluctant to accept the new technology. Delayed acceptance by French consumers could limit its success and potential for adoption as the European standard. Finally, any perceived threat to the freedom of the French populace, even in the form of a computer-based videotex system, could potentially create a backlash effect.

Before Minitel, consumer needs for information services were being met through a variety of sources. For telephone numbers, consumers could either dial #12 for directory assistance or look up the number in the telephone book. Car rental, theater, and airline information was obtained by calling the respective facilities. Current shopping patterns and commercial advertisers afforded adequate opportunities to meet general consumer information needs. A new service that integrated a variety of information sources on a single computerlike terminal would be a new experience for users and would certainly challenge France Telecom's new product development capabilities.

THE MINITEL DEVELOPMENT PROCESS

The development of a new product or telecommunication service as pervasive in scope as Minitel could not happen overnight.[48] France Telecom had been accumulating knowledge and experience in telecommunication technology over several years. Finally, the time came for this expertise to be focused on an immediate goal: creation of a videotex system that would become the European standard by first becoming a major success in France. The development process for the Minitel began with a remote idea and ended in a comprehensive new telecommunication service.

Evolution of the Minitel Idea

Ironically, the rudimentary idea for the Minitel system originated as the solution to a mathematical, not a telecommunication, problem. Because there were few calculators in France in 1970, engineers thought data could be entered by using the 12 buttons of a telephone, and then the response could be sent back to the user through speech synthesis. From that idea came a prototype that combined a telephone, a computer, and a display screen. A "telephone consultation service" arose, and became the formative idea for Minitel.

The idea for an in-home electronically based telephone directory service was developed further in the early 1970s and grew in popularity at France Telecom for several reasons internal to the organization. One reason was the high cost of producing, printing, and distributing paper telephone books throughout France. A substitute for the telephone book was sought. As paper costs in France were expected to double between 1979 and 1985, the company expected that, at some point, installing an electronic terminal would be less expensive than producing and delivering a free telephone book.

A second reason for pursuing the idea was that the basic French telephone system was antiquated, especially with respect to the length of time it took to reach directory assistance (#12). The directory assistance program in the late 1970s needed to be computerized and eventually expanded to cope with the growing volume of requests. Under consideration was a system (dubbed the "S 3") of computerized work stations for 4,500 operators, to be expanded to 9,000 by 1985. However, France Telecom wanted to consider an alternative system whereby subscribers could personally and electronically request and receive a number.

Organizing the New Concept

The Minitel system, as it is known today, would not exist without Gérard Théry, the new general manager of France Telecom in 1974. He became the product champion of Minitel. With the fervid enthusiasm of an evangelist, Théry tried to keep the videotex product concept simple and rugged; it could become more complex over time. He opposed IBM's substantial presence in France in the areas of computers and telecommunication and its traditionally complex approach to data processing.

Théry also saw the importance of establishing relationships with influential people in government (including eventually Giscard d'Estaing). Many regulatory bodies were involved in decision making that could block the launch of a videotex system throughout France. French politicians and ministers were cautious because another major development project, the Concorde airplane, had yielded mixed results after significant capital investment.

In 1978, after considerable internal study and planning, Théry presented a far-reaching plan to revamp and upgrade the French telecommunication system. He proposed to the government that six ideas be tested: the electronic telephone directory in Ille-et-Vilaine (Brittany), videotex in Vélizy (near Paris), videophone in Biarritz, voice frequency telephone, consumer facsimile, and the Télécom 1 satellite. All but the latter two projects were approved.

Test Markets

In 1980, France Telecom initiated test markets in Vélizy for videotex and in Ille-et-Vilaine for the electronic directory. Vélizy was an attractive test market because it had high telephone concentration and was close to Paris and the National Center for Telecommunications Studies (CNET), where videotex originated. Ille-et-Vilaine in Brittany had the advantage of proximity to a major telecommunications system where problems on the electronic telephone directory could be resolved.

A vicious backlash against videotex occurred in the initial stage of the test marketing process. The replacement of paper by an electronic medium alarmed and angered many French journalists. In addition, many French people resisted the idea of an electronic directory that contained everyone's name, address, and telephone number and offered such a wide variety of other services. As 1984 approached, with the Orwellian specter of Big Brother, one journalist wrote in the October 1979 issue of the journal *Telequal:*[49]

> Whoever controls the telephone is powerful. Whoever controls the telephone and the TV is very powerful. Whoever should one day control the telephone, TV and the computer would be as powerful as God the Father.

Théry anticipated and coped with the backlash in two ways. First, he hired an expert to head the Commercial Affairs Division and handle negative publicity. Second, he tried to work with the newspaper publishers to obtain some cooperation. Complicated negotiations between Teletel, the press, government, and France Telecom ultimately resulted in a lessening of tensions.

Another potential problem was that government-run France Telecom tended to make decisions in private. This privacy angered many key parliamentary legislators, who demanded to be informed. Consequently, an agreement was made that the early Minitel market tests would be confined to a certain small region of France (not beyond Ille-et-Vilaine) until all tests had been evaluated and that France Telecom would continually inform the French Parliament of the test results.

The Vélizy Teletel System Test Market

On July 9, 1981, the test market for Teletel (the name assigned to the videotex system) officially began in Vélizy. The three-year test involved a television-based videotex system rather than a stand-alone terminal. A keyboard was attached to the TV and could be brought out when a person wanted to use the system. The real product being tested, however, was not the hardware but the information services offered, such as electronic mail and transaction services. Furthermore, a very important decision was made early to pursue a quantity over quality approach. The assumption was that offering many services on the system would provide a better test of the system than offering fewer but more sophisticated services.

In 1981, a selected sample of subscribers in the city of Vélizy went on line with a videotex system that included some 80 services that could be accessed during 1982. The samples were constructed of 1,500 typical households and 1,000 people deemed to be heavy users. From the test, France Telecom discovered that people younger than 30 used the system more frequently than people older than 30, that men were the primary users, and that women seldom used the system.

The data from the test helped define users and the system needed to serve them. For example, 30 percent of the households never used the system and 20 percent of the households placed more than 60 percent of the total calls. Four types of services were used most: transaction services, electronic mail services, games (the most popular service for more than half of the subscribers), and information services.

Ille-et-Vilaine Electronic Telephone Directory Test Market

On February 4, 1983, the electronic telephone directory was introduced in Rennes. The test market at Rennes in Ille-et-Vilaine involved many more subscribers (250,000 electronic directory subscribers) than were used in Vélizy (2,500). Rather than being TV-based, the system used stand-alone terminals. They resembled the future Minitel terminal.

Designing an electronic telephone book was not a trivial task. Numerous technical and human ergonomic problems had to be overcome. For example, the user of a telephone book leafs through the pages to find the name of a person or business. Emulating this human activity with an electronic system would be difficult. Instead, a dialog format was developed whereby the user could type inquiries onto a display screen and hope to get correct answers. It took two years to develop this simple dialog between a person and the machine, although the resulting format is considered to be a classic. The size and clarity of the display screen, the keyboard, and even the structure of the database were a few of the other design problems for which the test market was a valuable experience.

Because both test markets showed impressive results, France Telecom decided that demand was sufficient for both electronic directory assistance and the total system of Teletel services. An extensive system would be designed incorporating both services and thereby accelerating France's achievement of competitive advantage in telecommunications. France Telecom decided that a full multiservice system could be targeted at the home user as well as the business segment. The company had funds available to develop a launch marketing program based on the needs of both segments.

The Launch Marketing Program

The most important challenge of the launch was to gain consumer acceptance. Consumers are notoriously resistant to new technologies, although the test marketing programs showed that acceptance was possible. To overcome consumer resistance and attract customers, France Telecom gave Minitel terminals away free at the beginning of 1982. Users had to pay only for using the service. The ensuing publicity and discussion about the free terminals increased awareness and helped customers overcome their reluctance to try the new service during the launch period. The government supported the initial outlay of approximately $165 (U.S.) for each terminal as part of the overall strategy to make France competitive in telecommunications. By the end of 1982, 120,000 terminals had been installed in France, representing an initial outlay of $19.8 million (U.S.) for terminals alone during the launch period.

Information Services Available

Ensuring substantial distribution of the Minitel to households and businesses at launch was necessary to attract suppliers of information services. If consumers found few valuable services on the Teletel system, they would be unlikely to use it. In turn, few information service providers would undertake the investment to develop a new information service without an adequate number of potential users.

The first videotex services available on the Minitel were targeted to the home user segment and were predominantly newspaper services. However, business and professional videotex services soon received top priority in an attempt to increase usage in the business segment. The two first and most significant services offered in the launch period were newspaper services and personal electronic mail and transaction services (largely on the basis of the test market results).

The problem confronting potential information service providers was that offering a new and untested service created substantial uncertainty for the supplying firm. Generally, a leader had to emerge within the supplier firm to champion the development of a particular information service. To support this process, France Telecom fielded consultants with specific industry knowledge who could help these individual product champions to meet the technical requirements and obtain approval and support within their respective organizations.

France Telecom also provided financial incentives in the form of price breaks to spur the development of services. The suppliers negotiated the pricing of their services with France Telecom, which in turn would receive a commission on the total billed amount. During the launch phase, this percentage varied among the services but was kept relatively low.

Communication and Promotion

The communication effort in the launch phase was helped by extensive publicity. For example, the erotic services received considerable attention and therefore helped France Telecom to promote the new videotex product! In addition, newspaper publishers, who were among the first service providers to the system, advertised extensively in their own newspapers. Such publicity resulted in a continued acceleration of awareness and interest for the product. France Telecom also launched extensive advertising campaigns to increase awareness and to educate consumers on the use of the new system.

As further incentive for early adoption, initial pricing to users was kept low because test market results had shown customers to be fairly price sensitive in both the home user and business segments. Such price breaks to both users and information service providers would wreak havoc with the financial structure of most privately owned organizations, but the French government kept the project afloat.

Launch Phase Problems and Need for Revision

One of the problems in the launch stage was the method of payment for services. Few people were willing to subscribe to services at this initial stage of the project. France Telecom therefore implemented a billing system in which it would be responsible for the billing (over current telephone lines) and the customer would be charged at per-minute rates for the time a service was accessed. This approach proved to be more acceptable to users, although billing would always be a problem.

Results of Launch

The most substantial success of the launch was not financial, but the fact that France Telecom was able to stimulate a market for the Minitel and the Teletel service. The launch resulted in an increase in the number of suppliers as well as customers. Because the terminals were distributed free, the first-year distribution was not an accomplishment in itself. Nevertheless, this early market stimulation was followed by eight years of growth for Minitel. The magnitude of Minitel's success can be gauged by the number of terminals, hours used, and services offered.

WHY MINITEL SUCCEEDED

The odds against France Telecom succeeding with a videotex system were very high. No major system had succeeded in the United States, not even by the mid-1990s. At least two major test systems by Knight-Ridder (a newspaper publisher) and Chemical Bank (its Pronto system) had failed. Several major factors can be cited to explain the success of Minitel.

Adequate Resources

The Minitel new product development project was part of a broader strategy by the French government to make France competitive in telecommunications. Because France Telecom was not directly responsible for short-term financial returns, it was able to use almost unlimited resources to promote the product and stimulate the market for the new service. Developing new products is very difficult when resources are constrained. Adequate resources ensure the staffing and budgeting necessary to push a project through difficult periods. However, simply throwing resources at a problem or opportunity does not guarantee success. Other factors must be considered.

Overcoming Market Resistance

France Telecom used its resources wisely to overcome market resistance by two key groups, users and information service providers. The decision to place free Minitel terminals directly in the hands of users, coupled with the curtailment of telephone book delivery, overcame barriers to trial of the online directory and other services. To build a catalog of services to which users would respond, France Telecom offered consulting support to providers, along with introductory low pricing. The test market results showed which services would be well received, and France Telecom emphasized their development. The new system was conveniently available and priced to provide good value (partly government subsidized), but also addressed a broader societal need—the need to communicate with other people in complete privacy on a variety of topics germane to the users' personal lives.

To expand the scope of product acceptance, France Telecom also addressed the business segment's needs for reliability and speed. Business organizations were very receptive to a service that would enable them to speed their business transactions. During the early to mid-1980s, computer e-mail network alternatives were sparse and the national postal service was not always satisfactory. Placing Minitel terminals in the home, at businesses, and eventually in public places made them familiar to the public and accelerated the acceptance of the system over time.

Exhaustive Test Marketing

The decision to invest in test marketing the various telecommunication options turned out to be a wise one. France Telecom had much to learn, not only about the system design and user response to it, but also about how various elements of French society would react. For example, the test market in Vélizy showed the need to counter a negative reaction by the French press. Learning from the test market how local and national politicians would respond to the innovation was also important, enabling France Telecom to minimize their objections when the service was introduced nationally.

Ergonomic Product Design

To gain market acceptance among users, who were largely uncomfortable with computers, France Telecom had to design its entire system to be truly user friendly. The keyboard, the display, the format of dialog between user and machine, the ruggedness and reliability of the system, and the menu of information services offered had to be carefully designed and orchestrated to reduce any problems users might experience. Though parts of the basic system would evolve, the basic design integrity of the hardware and software could sustain the system into the future.

Product Champion

The important role of Gérard Théry as product champion of an electronic directory system and the most extensive multiservice videotex system in the world must be recognized. Through careful planning, he put into place the resources, personnel, and teamwork to bring the new service to fruition. The results made France Telecom first to market with the new service, which set standards in the electronics and telecommunication industries. His actions also helped France Telecom redefine the boundaries of the telecommunication industry. Consequently, France and France Telecom established a good competitive position for the future.

FUTURE PERSPECTIVES ON MINITEL

France Telecom met the challenge of developing a very successful videotex system for its country. When the project started, its objective was to create a system that would become the European standard. Eventually, the prospect of a broader globalization of telecommunication services beyond Europe posed a new challenge. In the global context, the European challenge may become a small part of the strategic fabric of France Telecom.

For example, in December 1993, France Telecom and Deutsche Bundespost Telekom of Germany announced plans for a joint venture.[50] This joint venture, which may involve AT&T of the United States as a third partner, plans to offer global telecommunication services for business organizations operating in multiple countries. In effect, the dynamic and global nature of the telecommunication business environment may alter the strategic value of the product platform created by the Minitel success.

Nevertheless, the model of success provided by Minitel may have given France Telecom the leverage necessary to enter into joint ventures with German and U.S. organizations on a global scale.

France Telecom has had modest success in marketing Minitel outside France. Further, the possibility of a next-generation Minitel may bring about a European standard. Replacing the text-based system with a graphics-based one with icons that span cultural and language differences may help reduce country differences and open the way for a cross-cultural version of the system. However, the European Community is planning various R&D programs to support integration of the latest information technologies, thereby posing a threat to the Minitel. France Telecom must become an active participant in this process if it is to influence the standard-setting process.

Finally, the European Community has expressed a desire to open the entire European market to competition. The result could be a transition from the national, state-owned telecommunication companies to privatized companies with pan-European strategies. In debating such a course, the EC can consider two opposite experiences:

- The world's most successful videotex system was the product of France Telecom, a state-owned telecommunication monopoly!
- In the United States, the telephone monopoly was broken up in favor of open competition. Ironically, despite many attempts, no successful videotex system has emerged as the U.S. standard. Despite many significant yet piecemeal efforts in telecommunication technology, by the mid-1990s politicians and business organizations had only begun to talk about an "information superhighway" for the United States.

Clearly, there will be heated discussions about whether to maintain monopolistic control or to open telecommunication systems to competition.

Whatever happens, France Telecom will be competing in a market that is very different from the one it originally entered with Minitel. Future challenges will prove to be no less daunting than those France Telecom faced in developing the original Minitel system.[51]

5

Motivating the Organization

Organizations are notorious for their reluctance to embrace innovation. Some organizations delay new product development so much that more aggressive competitors seize whatever fleeting market opportunity may have been available. Yet for many of those organizations, new products may be the only means of survival. New products are needed for the future, yet their development is resisted! Why?

This paradoxical situation is somewhat understandable. Organizations are formed to bring stability to usually turbulent business environments so that goals and objectives can be accomplished in a systematic and orderly way. Structure, policies, procedures, and other normalizing rules of behavior are instituted to bring about the needed stability. However, the mere presence of this structure can make change of any kind difficult to absorb. Organization members have jobs to do, and bringing on new problems, tasks, and processes interferes with what has to be done. Hence, in most cases, resisting change is perfectly logical, especially on projects of the magnitude of new product development.

Many other factors also cause organizations and their members to resist change (turf battles, disgruntled employees, lack of expertise, and so on), but recognizing the problem of resistance is the first step toward motivating the organization in the direction of new product development. Overcoming the resistance is the next step. Most theories of organizational change recognize *leadership* as crucial in overcoming resistance to change. If organizational leaders do not want change, it is very difficult for followers to institute.

Leadership involves establishing a clear vision or direction for the organization and the role of new product development within it, putting together a team that understands this vision and can communicate it to other people, and providing incentives for everyone involved to achieve the vision. Although leadership can emerge in many forms in an organization, for new product development it is most successful when top managers appoint a *new product champion.*

The new product champion can succeed if given adequate resources and strong top management support to bring about the necessary changes. The new product champion is responsible for implementing the new product development process. High level cross-functional teams are formed to ensure that all key development functions are included early in the process. Team members from R&D, marketing, production, accounting, sales, and other key areas should be involved at the outset to recognize problems early and make corrections before they become disasters.

Depending on the size of the organization and the complexity of the new product, a variety of subteams can be formed to carry out specific tasks and responsibilities. Coordination, communication, and motivation are as important to the success of these teams as the expertise they apply in performing their tasks. A clear definition of the core product concept is essential. Because engineering, marketing, and production personnel often view the world differently and use different technical languages, a clear and concise statement of the new product vision in a language that all can understand is an absolute must. The concept should be so basic and clear that it communicates well to everyone, even across cultural boundaries when global products are being developed.

The new product success stories in this chapter illustrate three organizations' approaches to new product development and the importance of motivating organizations to overcome their resistance to change. The approaches are different, but they have certain elements in common.

The first new product success is Gannett Company's *USA Today* national newspaper. At a time when newspapers were declining in popularity and television was taking over the national reporting of daily news, Alan Neuharth sustained a vision of a national daily newspaper. Realizing the difficulties of developing such a newspaper in the confines of Gannett's organizational structure, Neuharth took his appointed cross-functional development team of "whiz kids" off site. The story describes how the project evolved from a bungalow in Cocoa Beach, Florida, and how Neuharth managed communication about it during its critical development stages.

The second new product success is Ford Motor Company's Taurus. Ford and other U.S. automobile firms were under intense competitive pressure from Japanese and European automobile manufacturers. American buyers were defecting in droves for better quality and value in foreign cars. After significant losses, Ford finally realized it could no longer make cars in the traditional way. The company had to change because its very survival was in question. A new product champion was appointed and supported with adequate resources to assemble a cross-functional teamwork approach to new product development *within* the organization. With innovative styling, top quality, and effective marketing, the Ford Taurus became very successful. It demonstrated that not only Ford, but also other American car companies, could compete effectively for the car buyer's preferences.

In the third new product success considered in this chapter, a very different approach to new product development in an organization is evident. In this case, innovation is a philosophy of doing business. Canon Inc. and its development of the Canon PC line of personal copiers reveals how innovation can become institutionalized in an organization so that when a market opportunity arises, the organization can respond efficiently and effectively to beat its competitors to the market.

Gannett Company Inc.: *USA Today*

Phillip Ostwalt and Mitchell J. Peyser

> . . . *I relied on common sense. The CEO should have the smarts and instincts to plan ahead, then employ experts to help him figure out "how" to do "what" his vision envisions.*
>
> Alan Neuharth, 1989
> Gannett Company Inc.

In September 1982, Gannett Company Inc., a media company headquartered in Arlington, Virginia, launched a new product that seemed destined for failure. The company's financial officers, industry stock analysts, and newspaper publishers throughout the country believed there was no market for a national daily newspaper. The newspaper industry was in a severe decline, with many prominent local newspapers losing money and ceasing operations. Despite these negative market conditions, Alan Neuharth, Gannett's chairman and CEO, stood by his vision of a national newspaper and launched *USA Today*.

USA Today quickly became Gannett's most recognizable product. Although the newspaper did not report an annual profit in its first 10 years, the Gannett organization firmly supported it because of its contribution to the company's international reputation and stature. The consumer response was clear; *USA Today* became a top-selling newspaper in the United States with an average total circulation of some 1.9 million during 1993.[1] Estimated daily readership, based on assumed multiple readers per copy, is about five million.[2]

The concept of *USA Today* was a radical departure from the traditional newspaper, partially because of the following features.

- Extensive use of color, charts, and graphics
- Daily news stories from all 50 states
- Minimized continuation of stories from one page to another
- Concise writing style
- Extensive coverage of sports and weather
- Sales through distinctive news racks designed to resemble a TV set for the target market of people who grew up with television

Gannett combined these product attributes with the emerging satellite transmission technology to meet the needs of the increasingly mobile and demographically changing American population.

The *USA Today* concept has had a dramatic influence on the entire newspaper industry. In examining media trends in the 1980s, *Advertising Age* noted, "Neuharth's *USA Today* proved there was a market for a colorful, punchy product. The new Gannett paper soon had newspapers across the country mimicking it."[3] *The New York Times* reported that "few of the 1,700 daily newspapers in the United States have avoided copying at least some of the *USA Today* style, if only in the use of color and graphics and more tightly edited stories."[4]

When *USA Today* was launched in 1982, Gannett was the nation's largest newspaper publisher with 86 daily and 33 nondaily newspapers. In addition, the company operated seven television stations, 13 radio stations, and the United States' largest outdoor advertising billboard group. The publicly held corporation consistently reported increasing revenue and income. In 1982, the company reported operating revenues of $1.5 billion and net income of $180 million, up from $1.4 billion and $172 million, respectively, in 1981.[5] Thus *USA Today* emerged from a company that could sustain a lengthy development time if necessary.

THE NEWSPAPER INDUSTRY SETTING

During the 1970s, U.S. daily newspaper circulation increased only 0.2 percent while the U.S. population increased 11.4 percent. Expanding population and flat newspaper sales indicated an industry with limited opportunity. Also during the 1970s, large publishing companies that ran leading daily newspapers in major cities began acquiring small and medium-size local newspapers.

Well-capitalized companies such as Gannett, Knight-Ridder, and the Newhouse Newspapers could achieve economies of scale by owning a chain of newspapers that shared news stories, provided wide advertising coverage, and purchased supplies at low costs. This dramatic shift in the industry caused many locally owned newspapers to exit the business. During 1982 alone, at least 21 dailies folded, including *The Washington Star*, *The Cleveland Press*, and *The Philadelphia Bulletin*.[6]

Advertising Trends

The newspaper industry feared losing both its readership and its advertising revenue, which is estimated to account for at least two-thirds of all newspaper revenue. In the seven-year period leading up to the introduction of *USA Today*, total advertising expenditures in the United States increased 136 percent, from $28.2 billion in 1975 to $66.6 billion in 1982.[7] However, newspapers' share of total advertising expenditures decreased from a 29.3 percent to 26.6 percent.[8] Declining readership contributed to the decline in advertisers and advertising revenues.

Changing Consumer Needs

During the 1970s, Americans' leisure time diminished. The traditional family unit changed from an income-producing husband and a wife who attended to the house and children to a dual-income family with reduced leisure time. No longer could family members unhurriedly read the morning paper or watch the evening news. More than ever before, consumers needed to learn about current events rapidly and conveniently.

Business travel increased during the 1970s. On the road, a person could not have access to a hometown newspaper, or discover how the local sports team had performed in a game the night before. Even local papers failed to provide adequate coverage of the home team's out-of-town games, especially if the paper's press time preceded the end of a late-night game. For example, fans in the major East Coast sports markets of New York, Pittsburgh, and Atlanta would not find results of the previous night's games in their morning papers.

The expanding role of other media in daily life exacerbated the readership decline among the nation's daily newspapers during the late 1970s and early 1980s. Trend forecasters John Naisbitt and Patricia Aburdene noted the increased numbers of media and the record number of new choices within each medium, and wrote that Americans were "drowning in information and starved for knowledge."[9] Given the increasingly changing media environment, they questioned how much information was actually absorbed. The need for a single, reliable source of information in a society overloaded with information was evident. In search of ways to satisfy this need, Americans turned to television, radio, magazines, and weekly specialty newspapers.

Competitive Situation

Cable television news became a formidable competitor in meeting the need for quick news updates. Cable news focused on broad domestic and international issues, with no local coverage. It also offered a variety of innovative news and entertainment alternatives. Networks such as Turner Broadcasting System's (TBS) Cable News Network and ESPN gave viewers quick, up-to-the-minute reporting. Ted Turner, cable television promoter and owner of TBS, predicted in 1981 that "newspapers as we know them today will be gone within the next ten years or certainly [will be] serving a very reduced role. . . . Unfortunately, [newspapers] are becoming very rapidly technologically obsolete."[10] The outlook for a national newspaper was grim.

Some newspapers attempted to fill the need for a single quick and convenient news source. With the exception of *The Wall Street Journal*, these attempts did not fare well. *The New York Times* tried to distribute a national version of its newspaper and was successful in using satellite technology to transmit into other parts of the United States. However, readers were not satisfied with a product that did not include local entertainment listings, sports coverage, and daily features. Dow Jones & Co. folded its weekly *National Observer* in 1977 after it "floundered in search of an identity." *The Washington Post* introduced a *National Weekly Edition*, a "weekly tabloid review of the news," which had a readership of only 50,000 by 1983.[11] This lack of success in the face of a clear market need showed that the design and execution of any new information source would be a very difficult challenge.

THE DEVELOPMENT PROCESS FOR *USA TODAY*

From inception, to design, to the eventual launch of *USA Today*, Alan Neuharth, its founder, conceptualized the product as an easily readable, high quality, national general interest daily newspaper. The core benefit of the paper would be *fast, easy, and convenient access to the news.*

The Emergence of an Idea

The vision for a national newspaper came from Alan Neuharth. "There is the great myth," according to Taylor Buckley, a senior editor at *USA Today*, "that the marketing boys created *USA Today*."[12] However, Neuharth had thought about a national newspaper since becoming CEO of Gannett in 1973. He hoped to satisfy two needs: consumers' need for an easily readable, high quality, national general interest newspaper and Gannett's need to establish a national reputation.

As word about the new national newspaper spread, the media responded with numerous articles and comments on the feasibility of the venture. Most predicted failure. Neuharth, upon hearing that the national newspaper was just his ego trip, responded, "The decision was not glandular, it was aided by research. And we will keep going only as long as we think we will succeed."[13] Throughout the development process, research played an important role in supporting intuition.

Neuharth's concept of a national newspaper was founded on his extensive experience in launching two newspapers and running the Gannett chain of newspapers. Many of the distinguishing features of *USA Today* can be traced back to two newspapers he had developed previously. In November 1952 he had launched *SoDak Sports*, "The COMPLETE Weekly Sports Newspaper for ALL South Dakota." *SoDak Sports* covered all sports across the state in exhaustive detail. Coverage of women's sports was more extensive than in other newspapers, and every small-town team was reported. Although the newspaper failed financially, it originated the concept of broad coverage, spanning a wider region than conventional newspapers.

Florida Today, launched by Neuharth and Gannett Company Inc. in March 1966, tested several features now found in *USA Today*. It had a clearly organized format featuring a page-one left-column summary of the day's news, abundant use of photographs, and expanded weather reporting. Before deciding to study the feasibility of his vision, Neuharth saw three distinct possibilities:

- A stand-alone national sports daily,
- A stand-alone national general interest daily newspaper, and
- A daily and/or Sunday supplement or wraparound section of national news and advertising for Gannett's community newspapers.[14]

Other options included a national magazine, a national weekly newspaper, and purchase of major city newspapers. By late 1979, Neuharth was sure that he wanted to launch the stand-alone daily national newspaper.

Organizational Fit

Although Gannett's financial condition and reputation were at risk, the new product fit well with the organization. The product concept represented an innovation, but the actual product, a newspaper, was consistent with the abilities of an organization already in the newspaper and communications business. The Gannett chain provided the basis for a national printing and distribution network with facilities within a two-hour drive of most metropolitan areas.

Neuharth practiced "intrapreneurship," tapping Gannett's expertise in all facets of the business throughout the organization. Intrapreneurship was crucial to the development of *USA Today*. For example, Neuharth called upon his top reporters and editors from a pool of more than 4,000 to work on *USA Today*. Gannett's significant financial power was also essential to support the risky new venture. One securities analyst stated that "if *USA Today* is a flop, the write-off would not impair Gannett's strong financial position."[15]

Assembling the Team

Neuharth recognized the power of intuition and experience in formulating the idea for *USA Today*. For example, he chose a name that would convey the idea of national scope (*USA*) and quick access to timely news (*Today*). However, he had to test the feasibility of his vision and needed to be sure the organization was capable of delivering it. Consequently, in early 1980, he pulled together a new product development team and a $1.2 million budget.

The team, dubbed the "Whiz Kids," consisted of four young Gannett employees: Larry Sackett, Frank Vega, Tom Curley, and Paul Kessinger. Each would concentrate on a key question related to his own expertise: satellite technology, circulation, marketing research, and advertising sales. The Whiz Kids worked together off site in a small bungalow in Cocoa Beach, Florida. The windows of the bungalow were covered with reflective paper to hide charts and documents from passersby. The team worked in total secrecy for eight months. The bungalow served as a home base for consolidating findings and for meetings with Neuharth.

The team's $1.2 million budget was spent primarily on general market research to discover why people buy newspapers and to answer the following four questions:[16]

- Can we design a daily newspaper that will attract and hold readers around the country?
- Can we generate sufficient advertising support?
- Can we distribute and sell a national newspaper?
- Can we produce and print a national newspaper?

Answering these questions became the focal tasks of the research team.

Preliminary Market Research

Preliminary research indicated room for a national newspaper. From a survey of 8,000 newspaper readers, researchers concluded that people desired more information. Despite the pervasiveness of current media, none apparently satisfied the need to be fully informed quickly and effectively. Further, 23 percent of people surveyed indicated they read at least two different newspapers each week. People often subscribed to home delivery of one newspaper and bought a second newspaper at the newsstand.[17]

According to Taylor Buckley, the original editor of USA Today's Money section, Gannett eventually publicized a desire to become readers' second newspaper to lull competitors into complacency about the new venture.[18] Gannett's true intention, ultimately realized, was to become the primary source of information for a large share of readers. To achieve this goal, the company had to differentiate its product from other newspapers. Tom Curley remembers that one of the key research findings was that people were generally happy with the newspapers they were reading. This finding, says Curley, "caused us to decide we had to be different" from the newspapers people were already reading.[19]

Market research further revealed that the United States was an increasingly mobile society in 1980:[20]

- 850,000 people a day traveled on the airlines,
- 1.75 million people a day stayed in motels or hotels, and
- 100 million people had moved in the past 10 years.

These findings suggested two key design features to appeal to the mobile society: easy-to-read format with short articles and attractive graphics, and broad national coverage enabling readers to find out what is happening in their home states and towns.

To assess demand for advertising, Paul Kessinger, the advertising expert, did research on where national advertisers spent their money. As a national daily newspaper, *USA Today* would be limited in its ability to serve regional advertisers. He found that advertising in *The Wall Street Journal* consisted largely of special interest financial ads. There did not seem to be enough newspaper advertisers to support *USA Today*. Kessinger concluded that *USA Today* would therefore have to target firms that advertised in national magazines. However, to entice those advertisers, Gannett would need to deliver a color capability in the newspaper. Kessinger concluded that he needed a prototype to test the advertising capability of the new venture.

Designing the Prototypes

By late 1980, on the basis of their market research and analyses, the Whiz Kids formulated a tentative recommendation to go ahead with the project. Neuharth began to formulate a clearer image of what *USA Today* would be like:

- Broadsheet format, with 32 to 40 pages,
- Color on every section front,
- Information heavy, with summaries, statistics, and lists,
- Upscale look, and
- Subtle use of red, white, and blue.

Features would include a roundup of the top news from each state, extensive results-oriented sports coverage (including a listing of all scores), and a thorough weather report.

To produce the prototypes, Neuharth borrowed a design team from other Gannett newspapers. The guiding principle at this stage of development was to create something different from current newspapers that would appeal to people looking for a "second read." One of the key decisions was to eliminate "jumps," the continuation of articles from one page to another.

The prototypes provided considerable guidance about the appearance and content of the actual product. The prototypes were also used to gather key data on market response from general readers, opinion leaders, and advertisers. Reactions from opinion leaders and advertisers were largely negative. However, market research on potential readers showed considerable interest in USA Today. In one survey, 21 percent of the respondents said they were "certain" to buy USA Today. This finding was used to project penetration to be 3 percent of the households in each market entered. The same survey indicated strong interest in extensive national sports coverage. Another survey showed that among single-paper buyers, 27 percent would "definitely buy" USA Today.[21]

The prototypes were true to the original core product concept (fast, easy, and convenient access to the news), incorporating editorial and design decisions consistent with that concept. Throughout the process, designers paid special attention to technology, distribution, news rack design, and editorial design.

The Technology

The "national" aspect of the product concept required considerable work to create a network of satellite transmission and printing locations. To facilitate this process, Gannett established the Gannett Satellite Information Network (GANSAT). A satellite transmitting earth station had to be constructed in addition to receiving stations around the country. Larry Sackett, Gannett's satellite expert, investigated the feasibility of a satellite network and found that satellite receiving stations would have to be installed at 12 key locations at a cost of $500,000 each.[22]

Gannett had printing plants in 35 states, most of which produced evening papers and were therefore available in the early morning. In addition, commercial printers would be hired for eight sites. The color printing necessary to attract national advertising would require investment in new offset printing presses. Further, the first-year circulation goal of one million would involve formidable newsprint costs. For example, adding four pages to the newspaper would cost Gannett $2.2 million annually.

Distribution and the USA Today News Rack

Preliminary research indicated potential first-year daily circulation of one million by September 1983 and two million by 1987. In terms of major distribution channels, home delivery, newsstands, and news racks had to be considered. Early estimates showed that USA Today would have to be sold at more than 105,000 sales outlets, primarily news racks. Within the first 16 months of production, 58,000 additional news racks would be needed.[23]

Because the news rack would be the primary outlet for the new product, and because consumers would interact with it, it had to communicate the essence of the product concept. Neuharth insisted on an innovative design that would stand out visually. The rack was eventually designed to draw attention to the newspaper design. The newspaper is displayed higher than in standard racks. Neuharth also insisted on locating the coin slot beside the display rather than on top of the rack as is standard practice. He believed that a coin slot above the newspaper display would draw attention away from the product.

Specifically, Neuharth wanted the machines to display the newspaper so that the publication nameplate (at the top of page one of each issue) would stand out. Perhaps the most significant feature of the news rack design was the intent to appeal to a generation of consumers brought up with television. The final design, resembling a television set, represented a considerable departure from standard newspaper racks. More than a decade after the launch, *USA Today*'s newspaper racks still stand out from others.

Editorial Design and Content

Editorial content also had to adhere to the core concept. Following is an excerpt from a staff guide titled "Writing for *USA Today*."

> TELL THE STORY QUICKLY AND CLEARLY.
> DON'T WASTE WORDS.
>
> Because USA Today has a different mission than most newspapers, so do the reporters and editors. Our readers are upscale, well-informed and looking for a supplement to—not a replacement for—their regular newspaper. So our stories may contain less background on events, more emphasis on what's new . . . .

Editorial content differed from that of standard newspapers by emphasizing the positive aspects of stories. For example, the focus would be on the number of survivors of an airplane crash rather than the number of casualties. Feature-oriented stories would be given preference over hard news.

The Launch

Neuharth kept the Whiz Kids' research data locked up in the Cocoa Beach bungalow, but kept the board informed about the status of the new venture to ensure a continuing flow of resources to research and development. He controlled the information flow in such a way that the board received key information at appropriate times. The board was well aware of the Whiz Kids' efforts. The Whiz Kids presented their findings to the board in October 1980. Ultimately, Neuharth brought the go/no go decision to the board in December 1981. Encouraged by positive public response to the prototypes, the board said "Go."

The market entry plan called for initial launch in the Baltimore and Washington, DC, areas on September 15, 1982. *USA Today* would then expand into Atlanta, Minneapolis–St. Paul, and Pittsburgh by early October. By the first quarter of 1983, *USA Today* was available in Seattle, San Francisco, Houston, Denver, Los Angeles, Miami, Detroit, Chicago, and New York. By April 1983, daily circulation exceeded one million.[24] The New York launch was especially important to the sale of advertising. Because many of the nation's large advertisers and agencies are in New York, the distinct and ubiquitous news racks would provide critical support for the advertising salesforce in visually demonstrating the credibility of their product.

POSTLAUNCH ISSUES

Advertising, editorial content, and capitalizing on opportunities from the brand name equity of *USA Today* posed challenges for Gannett.

Advertising Industry Reluctance

From the beginning, Gannett believed that the circulation and penetration of *USA Today* would establish the newspaper as a legitimate advertising tool. However, the advertising industry was reluctant to accept *USA Today* as an effective advertising medium. Taylor Buckley notes that when large companies advertise in the paper, it is usually at the company's request, not at the recommendation of its advertising agency.[25]

Special niches of advertising have evolved, particularly within the travel and automobile categories, the two top ad categories for *USA Today*.[26] Buckley described one of these niches as "Oh, God!" advertising, appropriately named after the reaction of a company when it sees a competitor's latest surprise promotion in the paper ("Oh, God!"), then combats the promotion with its own advertisement in *USA Today*.[27]

Challenges to Editorial Content

Although the core product remained intact, *USA Today* evolved during its first decade. The paper's news coverage was criticized for being excessively light or superficial. The negative reviews came from both internal sources, including Neuharth, and readers. Accordingly, Gannett has increased the hard news coverage in *USA Today* while remaining true to its original format. For example, Gannett showed its dedication to such coverage by maintaining a staff of 15 reporters in the Middle East during the Persian Gulf War.

By using its technological advances, *USA Today* has implemented other editorial changes to increase readership and profitability. For example, if a major story is applicable primarily to a single region, a unique version of the front page can be developed and sent only to that specific region. This process also enables advertisers to target their sales efforts at a particular region. In an effort to bolster advertising revenues, *USA Today* now provides extended classified sections that can be inserted by region.

Brand Extensions

Because of the broad reader acceptance of *USA Today*, Gannett has made several attempts to leverage the equity it has achieved with the newspaper. Attempts to reach into new media areas with brand extensions have resulted in both failures and successes. One failure was "USA Today: The Television Show." Despite much promotion, it was never fully accepted by viewers. The project was a financial loss.

In contrast, a weekly publication titled *Baseball Weekly* instantly became a financial success. This publication covers all aspects of baseball, providing reports on all professional teams, college baseball, and baseball memorabilia. It has many of the same attributes as the *USA Today* newspaper: abundant statistics, color pictures and graphics, and news capsules.

The *USA Today International Edition* has grown to a circulation of 60,000 a day and is challenging *The Herald Tribune* in overseas markets. The slimmed-down version of the domestic newspaper is transmitted to Asia and Europe for daily distribution. It has yet to show a profit, but the company receives international attention because of the geographic reach of the *USA Today* name.

The latest *USA Today* product introduction is SkyRadio, a live broadcast of news, sports, and talk shows provided to travelers on certain airlines.

The broadcasts are produced from studios in Gannett's Arlington head-quarters and are transmitted by satellite. Passengers can tune in to the broadcasts through standard airplane headsets.

CONCLUSION: KEY NEW PRODUCT LESSONS

Neuharth's position as CEO of Gannett afforded him tremendous power to guide the development of *USA Today*. The importance of his role as the product champion of *USA Today* cannot be overstated. However, his insight in enlisting a new product development team of the right people in the organization to evaluate and develop the vision was critical to success. Furthermore, by selecting an off-site location so as not to interfere with daily organizational operations and by managing the flow of project status information into the organization, he minimized organizational resistance.

The success of *USA Today* illustrates the importance of a clearly articulated core product concept that benefits consumers. In the early 1980s, with the newspaper industry in decline, Alan Neuharth had a vision for a new kind of newspaper that would appeal to the public. He stuck by his original idea for an easily readable national newspaper despite criticism by journalists and other opinion leaders. *USA Today* was not meant to appeal to journalists; it was designed for readers.

Although most companies measure success in terms of profits, success can be measured in other ways. *USA Today*'s rapid and successful circulation growth made it a top daily newspaper in the United States. Profitability eluded Gannett for *USA Today* during the 10 or so years after its launch, but the newspaper has increased Gannett's visibility, influenced newspaper design, and become a standard part of American culture. Only a company with adequate resources, including significant cash flow, high profitability, and capable people, could have undertaken and sustained a venture of the magnitude and risk of *USA Today*. The national newspaper project fit well with Gannett's core competencies and with Gannett's overall desire to achieve national presence.

Ford Motor Company: The Taurus

Mary E. Griffith and John W. Judge

*Businessmen go down with their businesses because they like the old
way so well they cannot bring themselves to change.*

Henry Ford, My Life and Work, 1922

In early 1979, Japanese automobile manufacturers had less than a 14 percent share of the U.S. car market and an oversupply of their small economical vehicles. However, during that year, the fall of the Shah of Iran and the fear of oil shortages triggered a memorable gasoline crisis in the United States that changed their fortunes. The long lines that formed at gas stations made a significant impression on U.S. car buyers.

By the end of 1979, 22.7 percent of Americans were purchasing more economical imported cars. During the year, the Ford Motor Company lost three market share points in the total U.S. automobile market and more than $199 million. The following year, the company lost a staggering $1.5 billion.[28] This consumer defection was not limited to Ford automobiles. American consumers who initially turned to imports because they provided better economy discovered quality and design features that were not available in most American automobiles. Not only were in-car features more consumer oriented, but the imported cars spent less time in the service bay. The Japanese system of total quality management was a devastating competitive advantage in marketing to increasingly value-conscious consumers.

Initially, Ford seemed uncertain about how to handle the increasing loss of customers to competitors. Ford executives could not understand why Americans would want to buy an import, and hence made few changes to

143

current designs. As a consequence, Ford sales continued to plummet and the company had losses of more than $1 billion annually in the early 1980s. By the first quarter of 1986, however, Ford had managed to turn its $1 billion annual loss into a gain of $728 million. In addition, Ford was starting to be hailed as a leader in American car design.

The beginning of Ford's reversal of fortune can be attributed to one car: the Taurus. In a relatively short period of time, it changed consumer perceptions of Ford, and also showed other American automobile manufacturers that success was possible in an industry known for its failures. In 1987, Taurus sales contributed significantly to the company's record earnings of $4.6 billion, which enabled Ford to surpass General Motors in earnings for the first time ever. By 1988, Ford was selling 374,000 Taurus models annually and the Taurus was the best-selling car in America. Moreover, the Taurus eventually gained top spot in sales, overtaking the number one Honda Accord.

THE DEVELOPMENT OF TAURUS

The Ford Taurus was a triumph of planning and design, a true new product development success story. Lewis Veraldi, head of the product planning and research division, had become increasingly frustrated during the late 1970s by top managers' lack of support for the new models his team developed. Veraldi's team had created many unique new designs, including an early predecessor of the minivan, but Ford's top managers felt the new designs would be too costly. By 1979, however, the company was reeling from the 1978 OPEC oil price increase, consumer support of fuel-efficient imports, and General Motors' success with its new models. Although Ford's strategy had been to redesign its line of boxy midsize cars to be more fuel efficient, the public resoundingly rejected all of Ford's reworked designs. Moreover, the quality of Ford cars was at an all-time low. Even new cars were unsatisfactory to consumers in performance and reliability.

Clearly, something had to be done if Ford was to catch up to its foreign and domestic competitors. In 1980, Veraldi was approached by Ford top managers and told that he would have their complete support in designing a "world-class car"—as long as it met certain requirements. His early record with the very successful European Ford Fiesta apparently gave them confidence in his abilities. Ford officials wanted Veraldi to design a car that answered two important questions: "What don't people have in their present car that they would want in this one?" and "Why should I bother to cross the road from another dealer's lot to buy this car?"[29] At last Ford's top managers had recognized that to succeed they needed to take a fresh approach.

Veraldi turned out to be the right person for the job, and the Taurus might not have been as successful without his presence. Veraldi was a true product champion in every sense. He provided leadership by clarifying the vision set down by top managers and motivating people to make that vision a reality. Veraldi brought unique credentials to the project. He was one of the few people at Ford who had worked on teams in both design engineering and manufacturing. The development of the Taurus was unique to Ford in many ways because of the product development process instituted by Veraldi.

The Taurus was born as Project Sigma, a design project that Veraldi's group had undertaken to replace the current midsize line. Once Veraldi was given the go-ahead to develop the design, he initiated a product development process that was unique to Ford. It involved *simultaneous* or *concurrent engineering*. Ford termed the process "Concept to Customer," and for the first time emphasized customer needs and manufacturability through every aspect of the process. Cross-functional teamwork would be central to the development project:

> Veraldi decided that everyone involved with Sigma would be in on the project from the beginning. Regular meetings would be held between all areas of the production process, so that every discipline would understand how the car was taking shape and what the problems in the process were. Each division would elect an individual to represent that discipline at meetings.[30]

The end result was a team that Veraldi likened to a symphony. Under his role as conductor, all members worked together in productive harmony: "Component engineering, manufacturing, service, dealer organizations, public relations, design, safety, all these people were the cellos, trumpets and tubas."[31]

This new team concept was not immediately well received and, in Veraldi's symphonic analogy, was often discordant. Veraldi believed that one of the most important aspects of the team process was having an exclusive commitment from each worker for the duration of the project. However, many Ford supervisors were reluctant to let their best people go for so long. In many instances, Veraldi had to work out compromises.

As might be expected, conflicts arose among team members who were not used to working together and working under different types of managers and deadlines. However, as the team began to see how their efforts could have positive results, differences were gradually set aside to allow the Taurus project to evolve.

The benefits of the process became evident in comparison to Ford's traditional *sequential* new product design, whereby one part of a project would be completed by one department, then passed on to another department for the next part of the project, and so on. In a sequential process, an undetected early-stage design problem that affects downstream production can be resolved only by sending the product back to design (if quality is a goal). The design area must then correct the problem and pass the product on to the next department for its revisions, and so on back to production. However, when the entire team works together at the outset, many of the downstream problems can be anticipated and resolved early in the process.

The Team Taurus approach resulted in several important achievements for Ford. First, it greatly reduced product development time. The Taurus took only four years from product conception to launch, a time comparable with that of Japanese automakers and two years shorter than average. Second, it increased manufacturability of the car. Traditionally, manufacturing engineers did not see the designs until just months before production was to start. In Team Taurus, they were involved from the beginning and were able to guarantee the manufacturability of any particular design element. The savings were tremendous. Typically design changes for a new car entering the production phase cost $150 million; for the Taurus, they cost only $35 million!

Third, the team decisions were not made just by executives; line and assembly workers were asked for their input about many of the car's design elements. Two new programs at Ford empowered workers. The *employee involvement program* gave hourly workers the opportunity to make changes in how they performed their jobs. Workers were allowed to make design suggestions on how to improve efficiency in the plant, and their suggestions were actually listened to and often acted upon. Workers were also educated about the importance of improving quality at Ford and were empowered to go so far as to stop the production line if they detected any faults.

This program was a major change at Ford, where previously fast production was given priority at the expense of all else. The employee involvement program resulted not only in better cars for customers and a more efficient production process, but also in higher levels of employee satisfaction and increased morale. Similar results were achieved through the second program, *participative management,* which enabled low level managers to make decisions without the approval of higher managers.

THE CORE PRODUCT CONCEPT

The team approach was not the only unique element of the Taurus project. The core product concept incorporated two key aspects that redefined design and styling in American cars. First, Jack Telnack, the chief design executive, incorporated a slick aero styling into Taurus plans. The breakthrough design not only caught the car buyer's attention, but also delivered the message that the car represented a new start for Ford. Visually and logically, the aero design conveyed the idea of fuel efficiency to buyers.

Ford's major design and styling decisions are typically made as far up in the company as the board of directors. Even Lewis Veraldi's influence as product champion would not have been enough to get the Taurus concept approved without the enthusiastic backing of the new Ford president, Don Peterson. Peterson wanted a break from the past and thought the aero design provided it. He has commented, "We had made so many mistakes in the past by following this or that trend, this or that competitor. Finally we realized that we should not be driven by other people's choices but by our customers."[32]

The second key aspect of the core product concept was the notion of "best in class." It was implemented through benchmarking, a process of seeking the best of thousands of product features of the top-selling cars in the world. No product feature was overlooked. Ford developed an inventory of more than 400 features ranging from door handles to the sound system to glove compartment size. Veraldi felt that the car should represent the best of all possible cars. The resulting product is a car that could almost be considered the perfect automobile. By putting the drivers' needs first, Ford gave Taurus owners many appealing extras, such as a net in the trunk to hold grocery sacks upright and color-coded service pointers under the hood.

This aspect of the core product concept would not have been possible without the extensive market research that was conducted for the Taurus. With five years of both quantitative and qualitative studies, the Taurus was the subject of more market research than any other Ford automobile. The company surveyed owners of both Ford and competitive brands to learn what problems they were experiencing. In solving these problems, Veraldi and his team members helped refine the "best-in-class" aspect of the product concept.

THE MARKETING PROGRAM

The innovative aero design reminiscent of European styling, coupled with best-in-class product features linked to Japanese product quality, provided an attractive product for potential buyers. Competitive pricing (about $10,000) in relation to popular imports at the time enabled young professional consumers with families to realize considerable value in the car. An extensive promotional program that targeted dealers and other stakeholders as well as consumers generated excitement about the car's launch.

One element of the car resulted from chance. Veraldi and a colleague were brainstorming names for the new product when the conversation turned to astrology. The two men discovered that their wives were both born under the sign Taurus, and realized that "Taurus" would be a strong name for the project until research could come up with a better one. Ironically, when a list of names was presented in a consumer survey, "Taurus" scored highest and became the product name.

Positioning flexibility was built into the Taurus design because of the time lag between development and market entry. Despite the fact that Team Taurus was able to cut two years off development time, concept planning for the Taurus still had to take future market conditions into account. For example, the positioning might depend on economic conditions and gasoline prices as the launch date approached. (Some Ford economists had projected that the cost of fuel would be as high as $3.00 a gallon by the time the car was developed.) The Ford Taurus could be positioned as a small, fuel-efficient luxury automobile or as a midsize family car. In fact, six positioning statements were tested, and the one selected focused on the car's two design principles: reason plus beauty.

Ford asked its advertising agencies to start promoting the car several months before the launch. Prelaunch promotion was directed at suppliers, production workers, dealers, the media, and customers. Ford held a Hollywood-style movie premier for 400 influential members of the press 10 months before the car was scheduled to be available. Some $100 million was allocated to advertising, including major television, magazine, and newspaper campaigns.

With more than 200,000 employees and numerous suppliers across the nation, Ford realized that word of mouth could be an important promotional tool. To take advantage of it, Ford sent a heavily promoted caravan of Taurus and Sable models across the United States. Press conferences and rallies were held in 110 cities. Another caravan was sent out to keep the momentum going when the production schedule was delayed for two months. Ford's emphasis on advertising and promotion clearly paid off. The promotional buildup generated more than 150,000 advance orders for the Ford Taurus!

DIAGNOSING THE SUCCESS

Even at a total investment of about $2.88 billion, the Taurus project was a huge sales and financial success for Ford. Equally important is the fact that it helped reestablish Ford as a desirable brand among potential automobile buyers. The Ford Taurus was recognized by consumers and the industry with numerous awards, and was *Motor Trend*'s 1986 Car of the Year.

The success of the Ford Taurus project was clearly the result of decisions and actions within the organization. Only the Ford organization itself could implement a turnaround. The decision by top managers to entrust resources and direction to a new product champion (Lewis Veraldi) was the first critical event. The second was the product champion's action to assemble cross-functional teams and motivate them to carry out the critical development tasks. The third was the sustainment of the process to its completion by involving Ford employees at every level of the organization to truly focus on satisfying customers, both before and after their purchase of the car.

Another key success factor was the emphasis on total quality management. Through an emphasis on quality, Ford added value in a way most American car manufacturers had ignored. The Taurus was designed to be as perfect a car as possible, and engineers tried to build quality into the design. However, despite their efforts, the car had numerous problems. Rather than risk having these problems damage the Taurus reputation, Ford engineers went back to the drawing board to correct them and incorporated the changes into the manufacturing process. Engineering teams were sent out to production plants to diagnose and correct the problems. This effort was consistent with the basic tenets of total quality management, which emphasizes continual process improvements.

A third key success factor was offering the Taurus, with its innovative aero design and top quality, at a competitive price. This value-based positioning appealed to a segment of customers that was demographically different from the average buyer of a midsize car, who had an average age of 59 and an average income of $28,000. The Taurus buyer has an average age of 47 and an average income of $38,000. The Taurus buyer is also better educated; 43 percent of Taurus buyers have college degrees in comparison to only 29 percent of buyers of midsize Ford cars. Ford was able to please this difficult new segment by a commitment to customer satisfaction. Through hotlines, constant attention to buyer problems, and year-to-year improvements in the basic Taurus production process, problems were eliminated.

CONCLUSIONS

The Ford Taurus success continues. Many of the car's features, such as the aero design, have been used in several other models. Many people at Ford give the Taurus credit for turning the company around and making it successful. From 1986 to 1989, Ford gained 4.1 percentage points of market share; in 1987, Ford out-earned General Motors for the first time. Although Ford's performance in the truck market also contributed to its financial results, the Taurus stands as an important symbol of success for the company.

Despite Ford's success with Taurus, especially in adapting the basic styling to its family of products, the company has not succeeded in copying the new product development process throughout the organization. Ford failed to institutionalize the team approach used in the Taurus project. The company has been very conservative in its design choices since the launch of the Taurus. Ford president Philip Benton said, "I was there at the design committee meetings in 1987 and 1988, and I think we said, 'Hey we bit off a lot. Now let's capitalize on what we've got.'"[33]

Some new product development projects at Ford have resulted in budget overruns and overweight cars. The worst example is the 1988 Ford Thunderbird, which was $1,000 over budget per vehicle. Since early 1990, Ford CEO Red Poling has attempted to restore discipline to the product development process. Unfortunately, this effort has only increased the conservatism in design choices. Money-saving measures such as farming out development of some models has deprived Ford of the engineering and manufacturing know-how that made the Taurus a success. However, the revolution continues. In April 1994, Ford undertook a major reorganization to improve efficiency and market response. Reportedly, it is "shaking up its once all-powerful finance staff, subordinating much of it to the operating executives who are trying to remove bureaucratic obstacles to faster new-vehicle development."[34]

The new 1994 Ford Mustang provides further evidence that the process has not taken hold companywide, and may have even triggered the reorganization.[35] The once wildly successful Mustang (in the 1960s and 1970s) ran into hard times during the 1980s. The line would have been dropped had it not been for a "skunk works" effort within Ford by a group of Mustang loyalists. The Mustang product champion was able to persuade key executives to support a cross-functional team-based development project that strongly resembled the Taurus success. To everyone's surprise, a completely revamped Mustang was developed in three years at a development cost of about $700 million. Ford had accomplished the fastest and lowest cost development project in its recent history. The Mustang was priced competitively, named *Motor Trend* Car of the Year, and garnered advance orders for about 53,000 cars. Ford had to expand production to meet the expected demand for the new Mustang.

The development of the Taurus helped turn Ford around. Success was possible in the automobile industry, but the organization needed commitment and motivation to achieve it. Whether top managers can achieve this kind of success organizationwide and on a consistent basis, rather than on a project-by-project basis, remains a challenge not only for Ford, but for any organization.

Canon Inc.: Personal Copiers

Subhash Agrawal and Toshiyuki Ikuma

When a crew and a captain understand each other to the core,
It takes a gale and more than a gale to put their ship ashore.

Rudyard Kipling, Together, *1904*

Canon, the worldwide camera and copier company, introduced two revo-
lutionary new products in 1982, the PC-10 and the PC-20 maintenance-
free personal copiers. Designed to be smaller, simpler, less expensive, and
more reliable than the nearest competitor, they were the world's first truly
"personal" copiers. They were designed for use in small offices or at home
by professionals and self-employed individuals. The PC copiers were
rapidly accepted by these potential buyers, resulting in a major success
for Canon.[36]

Through the success of the PC copiers, Canon achieved market performance, market expansion, technological benefits, and organizational
renewal. Within a few months of their market introduction, sales had
reached a point at which Canon's manufacturing facilities were operating
near capacity. By the end of 1987, the PC copiers had become the most-
sold copiers in the world. They served the needs of a previously ignored
market segment (small offices and home offices), one that Canon has since
dominated.

Overall, Canon's market share in plain paper copiers increased dramatically, almost doubling in the United States from 1982 to 1991. The development of the PC copiers also enabled Canon to acquire major technological
know-how and patent rights. The company leveraged this technology

through many new and successful products, including the laser and bubble-jet copiers. Consequently, Canon's worldwide sales of business equipment more than tripled from 1982 to 1991, and during that time Canon became the world's largest copier company in units sold. This success was not only financially rewarding, but also energized the Canon organization.

THE CANON ORGANIZATION

Canon started in Japan in 1937 as a small camera manufacturing company. It grew rapidly after World War II. Although it was the world's largest camera company in 1982, less than half of its revenues came from cameras and more than a quarter of its revenues came from large copiers. Canon had diversified into many areas in the 1950s and 1960s, including office micrographic equipment in 1959, copiers in 1962, and electronic calculators in 1964. It had also expanded globally during that period, with Japan, the United States, and Europe each accounting for roughly one third of its business.

Canon's main business strengths were its commitment to technology and an aggressive, entrepreneurial, and risk-taking corporate culture. In every sense, R&D drives Canon's strategic direction and business, but success could not be achieved without its flexible organizational structure that allows for collaboration, creativity, and synergy between different functional and business areas. Over the years, this structure has resulted in numerous R&D accomplishments. For example, among other feats, Canon introduced its New Process (NP) copier technology in 1968, the first acceptable alternative to the xerographic process. It also developed the world's first electronic camera, the Canon AE-1. Both of these developments became major commercial successes.

Since the 1960s, Canon has also been one of the world's leading companies in patent ownership. For example, Canon acquired more than 500 patents each for the NP and the AE-1 electronic camera technologies. These patents enabled the company to preempt its competitors by establishing strong entry barriers, earn revenues by licensing technology, and build a reputation in the market as an innovator.

Canon's entrepreneurial culture facilitated a steady stream of new ideas, product development, entry into foreign markets, and bold strategic alliances with competitors (such as the one in which Canon licensed its technology to, and manufactured products for, Eastman Kodak).

Canon's corporate culture deviated from the traditional Japanese management style. Canon openly recruited engineers from other Japanese companies, and often paid its employees not simply on seniority but also on performance. Its corporate philosophy showed tremendous respect for the individual to stimulate and reward the energy and creativity necessary for innovation.

Canon's main weaknesses were poor marketing and inadequate protection of its technology, which resulted in market failures and missed opportunities. For example, its pocket calculator failed because of late entry in an already saturated market. Its NP series of copiers took a long time to become successful because the company was slow to convey the real benefits of the technology to users. Also, Canon may have licensed too soon its "liquid dry" system of copier technology to more than 20 competitors, thereby forfeiting the financial benefits of a proprietary sales position.

On balance, if Canon could develop technology that squarely met and satisfied a market need, it would have tremendous potential for success, especially if it could better manage its marketing capabilities. It had achieved success with the marketing program for its innovative electronic camera (the AE-1), but the copier division had not had a major marketing success despite significant technology breakthroughs. At issue was Canon's new product development and marketing response to copier market opportunities.

COPIER MARKET BACKGROUND

Prior to the introduction of the Canon PC copiers in 1982, the world copier industry was characterized by rapid market growth, major advances in technology, and increasing competition. The direction of the technology and the market favored plain paper copiers over coated paper copiers. In 1981, revenue in the world copier industry was more than three times greater and unit sales were almost five times greater than the 1976 levels. This growth had occurred uniformly across the United States, Europe, and Japan. By 1981, the copier industry had worldwide revenues of about $19.5 billion, with about 45 percent in the U.S., 30 percent in Europe, and the remainder split about evenly between Japan and the rest of the world.

Before PC copiers became available in 1982, copying was done on a departmental basis within companies and through commercial copy centers. Copy centers served a range of copying needs, from small copying jobs to large, high speed/high volume projects involving document preparation. Satisfaction of copying needs depended on a copier's price, quality, performance, features, maintenance, and after-sales support. Those factors became the bases for defining various market segments.

For example, one part of the market could be characterized by low usage (no more than 5,000 copies per month), a need for clear copies and simple features such as enlargement and reduction, moderate price sensitivity, and minimal need for after-sales support from the vendor. Another segment of the market might be characterized by high usage (more than 25,000 copies a month), a need for high resolution copies and complete document preparation, high price sensitivity, use of numerous copying features, and an extensive vendor maintenance requirement.

Most copier companies sought to meet the market needs of the segments that had large usage requirements. Because of its patented process, Xerox was the world market leader in satisfying the needs of high volume users. However, many Japanese firms such as Canon, Ricoh, Toshiba, and Minolta successfully developed alternate technologies, initially to serve the Japanese market, but subsequently to penetrate the U.S. market with high quality products at competitive prices.

As competition for the large users increased, growth opportunities became available in other market segments with different needs. For example, convenience copying at commercial centers increased more rapidly than the entire world copier market. Although these centers themselves presented opportunities for sales of large and midsize copiers, the needs of *their* users, usually small offices and home offices, represented a hidden market opportunity.

For small offices and the growing number of home offices, taking a large job to the local copy center was reasonable, but going to the copy center to make just a few copies was a nuisance. High value would be placed on a relatively inexpensive copy machine that could make satisfactory individual copies and perform routine copying projects. Larger copying projects could still be taken to local copy centers. The opportunity for an easy-to-use, durable, low priced, and maintenance-free small copier awaited innovation. Canon was one of several competitors that recognized this opportunity, and all were racing to build the best machine possible and be the first to market.

THE CANON PC COPIER DEVELOPMENT PROCESS

Because of the strong support of new ideas in the Canon organization, the idea and vision for a personal copier developed readily. Such a copier had been discussed a few years previously and not regarded as feasible, but senior managers at Canon seized upon the idea during the late 1970s. However, the barriers to success were high. At the time the lowest copier prices were more than $2,000, and the machines required substantial maintenance. Nevertheless, spurred on by the success of the AE-1 camera, top managers were keen to develop a similarly unique product for the copier market.

Canon conducted market surveys in both Japan and the United States to understand the nature of the copier market and to confirm that the small office/home office market segment was an attractive one. The company also solicited informal feedback from its salesforce. Both the formal and informal studies indicated a growing opportunity in the market segment consisting of small offices with fewer than five employees and home offices of self-employed professionals.

By the end of 1979, Hiroshi Tanaka, the director of the copier division, received the go-ahead from top managers to develop a new line of copiers to meet the needs of the targeted segment. A staged new product development process ensued, which involved concept development, engineering feasibility studies, prototyping, engineering model development, and trial mass production.

A small team was formed and the core concept was developed around several clearly defined key benefits:

- Being the world's lightest and most compact copier (under 45 pounds);
- A price of about $1,000;
- Ease of use; and
- Maintenance-free operation.

These benefits were the basis on which an engineering taskforce examined the feasibility of the concept. The engineering team had to evaluate disposable cartridges, instant toner fusers, and other components to reduce current copier price by a factor of 50 percent and increase current copier reliability by a factor of 10.

By September 1980, a companywide taskforce parallel to the engineering taskforce was formed. It was headed by Tanaka, who had become the product champion. This taskforce consisted of more than 200 people working in more than 23 groups drawn from many horizontal functional and business lines at Canon: marketing, production, engineering, design, optics, cameras, copiers, quality, costs, and even legal. To generate enthusiasm among the taskforce and mobilize the entire company behind the development process, Tanaka used the slogan, "Let's make the AE-1 of copiers."[37]

This taskforce, the second largest ever assembled at Canon, was divided into subgroups and smaller teams. A development and design group was divided into seven teams (such as the toner development team) and a production group was divided into 10 teams (such as the plastic molding team). Six other teams were also included in supporting roles: a steering committee, a cost team, a quality team, a patents team, a marketing team, and a user application software team. Clearly, effective communication among the various teams was essential for success.

If feasible, the smaller teams worked in parallel with each other. For instance, while the design team was working on the functional aspects of the new product, another team was investigating the feasibility of new materials and components. Because the small, informal subteams interacted frequently, many issues were resolved before they became problems. For instance, in its effort to design a global product, Canon faced the dilemma of whether to use the A4 paper size (used in the United States and Europe) or the B4 paper size (used in Japan). An innovative, yet low cost, compromise solution was eventually reached that promised to make the new product globally appealing: the copier would use A4 paper size, but would also have a special facility to copy business cards, which are used in large numbers in Japan.

The taskforce faced two major hurdles: (1) providing reliability within tight cost/price limits and (2) circumventing the "Xerox wall," or Xerox's tight patent protection on many aspects of copier technology. Xerox also had a strong hold on dealerships and salesforces. Because Canon wanted to sell the personal copiers in all markets, large and small, it would need to station service staff over a large geographic region. Because of the low volume of copying in the target segment, absorbing this service cost would be difficult for Canon. Therefore, an absolute requirement for the new copier was high reliability, with no breakdowns and no need for service. Similarly, it was absolutely necessary for Canon to develop its own proprietary technology.

These issues led to the process of "inverted thinking," which Canon managers defined as planning from scratch when left with no options. For example, studying the causes of copier troubles, Canon discovered that 90 percent of them involve the drum. This finding led to a major concept change and the genesis of the disposable cartridge. With disposability, the problem-causing part would be discarded after a certain number of copies, thus making the copier essentially maintenance free. Similarly,

Canon realized that it could neutralize Xerox's distribution strength by selling the new copiers through totally different channels: office product retailers and mail-order catalogs.

Although the actual development process was much more detailed and comprehensive than described here, its major features included:

- A product champion supported by top managers;
- An integrated taskforce, using interpersonal communication as a means of technology transfer;
- The use of parallel development wherever possible;
- Deliberate attempts to create energy and enthusiasm;
- Quality and cost goals incorporated in the earliest stages and used as key criteria in the major go/no-go decisions at each phase of development;
- Extensive prototype development; and
- Extensive product testing.

The outcome was a new personal copier that met all of its design criteria and top management expectations.

The PC copiers were "new" products in many respects: features, performance, physical characteristics, and technology. Two models were developed, both plain paper copiers capable of producing up to eight copies a minute. The PC-10 was the base model, priced at $995, and the PC-20 was an advanced model with automatic paper feeding (but identical to the PC-10 in every other way), priced at $1,295. Smaller than an electric typewriter and weighing less than 45 pounds, the Canon PC copiers became the most compact, lightweight, and inexpensive copiers in the world. Not only had Canon achieved its goals, but with its new product development process beat all major competitors into the personal copier market.

MARKET ENTRY

The taskforce delivered the PC copiers within a three-year development time. Canon introduced them into the market by the end of 1982. They were launched first in Japan, and then a month later in the United States and Europe. Prior to the launch, Canon organized two major conferences for its salesforce and retailers to educate them about the product.

Canon supported its launch of the PC copiers with a high profile media campaign, especially in the United States. Taking as a model the communications strategy used in the successful launch of the AE-1, the company spent almost $15 million in the United States and $1.5 million in Japan during 1983 for television advertising. Television was selected because the target markets of professionals and small-office personnel were not concentrated in geographic location or media usage habits. In fact, during 1983 Canon became the single largest TV advertiser in the United States. In Europe, television was not used as extensively because of the lower penetration rate of TV sets and the relatively high cost of advertising.

Print advertisements were used extensively in three major global market areas (United States, Europe, and Japan), primarily in business, general, and lifestyle publications such as *Fortune, Business Week, The Economist,* and *Time.* Canon also advertised in many in-flight airline magazines. Across all of these linguistically and culturally different media environments, Canon attempted to develop a clear and common communication strategy: it emphasized the *personal, simple, reliable, affordable,* and *fun* nature of the PC-10 and PC-20 copiers.

REASONS FOR SUCCESS

The success of the Canon PC copiers was swift and long lasting. The most obvious reasons for their resounding success are that Canon:

- Recognized a growing market opportunity;
- Set clear objectives and goals;
- Capitalized on its entrepreneurial corporate culture and flexible organizational structure to facilitate the flow of ideas, resource sharing, and a quick response to the external environment;
- Developed and exploited its technological strengths; and
- Recognized a weakness in its marketing area and overcame it through experience learned from its AE-1 new product success.

However, underlying these reasons is Canon's fundamental attitude toward innovation.

Many organizations, for a variety of apparently logical reasons, are resistant to new product development projects. Not Canon. Its personnel are stimulated to rise to new challenges, especially those presented to them by leadership. The espoused "three-J's" corporate philosophy builds on respect for the individual and emphasizes *ji-hatsu* (self-motivation), *ji-kaku* (self-awareness), and *ji-chi* (self-reliance). This guiding philosophy has been clearly communicated to each employee and is engraved on the facade of corporate headquarters. Consequently, when given a challenge to develop a personal copier with certain characteristics, everyone worked cooperatively to meet it.

Cooperation involved the formation of many teams on all aspects of the project, some working in parallel and some depending on the work of others. Parallel development teams can accelerate a development process because one group does not have to wait for another to finish its work. If the groups communicate effectively, they can expedite the identification and resolution of difficult development problems.

A product champion was instrumental in effectively communicating top managers' vision of the new product concept to all teams. He continually motivated and inspired participants to achieve clearly stated goals and objectives. He also included as many young people as possible in the various task groups, especially at the early stages of development, to stimulate creativity and new ideas to solve difficult problems.

The clarity and integrity of the new product concept were instrumental in maintaining effective communication among various groups that were approaching the problem from different functional perspectives. Marketing personnel would see the problem in different terms than R&D engineers; both would see the problem in different terms than production managers; and so on. A clear product concept that can be understood by all participants tremendously improves communication.

CONCLUSION: LONG-TERM SIGNIFICANCE OF THE PC COPIERS

The launch of the PC copiers was a major milestone for Canon. Not only were these products successful, but the know-how obtained during the course of their development helped Canon establish a technology platform on which to build other new products in the future. The success of the PC copiers enabled Canon to dominate the small office/home office market segment for many years. Strategically, these products helped Canon lessen its dependency on its camera business, and helped it to become a truly global company. For example, to reduce costs and maintain adequate margins in the personal copier business in an increasingly competitive environment, Canon moved many of its production and sourcing activities overseas (to Germany, France, the United States, and Taiwan).

Finally, the success of products such as the PC copiers and the AE-1 cameras demonstrates to employees that Canon's special philosophy of doing business with the individual in mind can work well and provide benefits to all. The result is high employee morale, willingness to work together on future projects (i.e., less resistance to innovation), and evidence that new product development can be an important part of the organization's continuous process of renewal.

6

Creating New
Product Ideas

A new product idea is generally an abstraction of a new product, usually presented as a brief oral or written statement. It can come from any number of sources and, as noted in Chapter 1, on average about 11 new product ideas may be needed to yield one successful new product. The continuous funneling of ideas into an organization's new product development process is therefore critical for ongoing success.

Because rough product ideas come from many sources, they are often subjected to initial creative filtering by someone in the organization who shapes them into clearer conceptualizations and interpretations. This process is especially important for startup organizations that depend on their first product for success. The new organization will need creativity to transform the idea for its first product into reality.

Creativity in the ideation process is instrumental in moving an idea beyond an abstraction into a realizable product concept. How organizations find creativity, support it, and otherwise manage it as a valuable resource not only affects the initial qualification and shape of the idea, but also the subsequent development process. In this chapter, three success stories involving creativity illustrate its central role in new product development.

The first story recounts the emergence of an idea for a new sailboat, the Laser. The need for a new type of sailboat that could be transported on the top of a car was expressed by a large sporting goods manufacturer. The initial idea for the sailboat was created by yacht designer Bruce Kirby during a telephone call to him about the need. By the end of the day, he had produced a sketch for what would eventually become a new class of sailboats. However, the idea was rejected by the sporting goods manufacturer in favor of alternatives that were less racy in design. The story describes how the idea was resurrected and turned into a major success.

In the second story, a new product idea was inspired by a common problem: What do parents who want to go running, jogging, or walking do with their children? When runner and cyclist Phil Baechler had that problem, he began tinkering in his garage to devise a way to bring his infant son along on his runs. By combining bicycle and traditional baby stroller parts in a creative way, Baechler came up with a very different kind of stroller, one that was stable over a variety of terrain, highly maneuverable, and comfortable for his baby. The story shows how creativity goes beyond just coming up with an idea. Creativity is an ongoing necessity to solve the myriad problems that occur throughout new product design. Baechler's new product revolutionized the baby stroller market and became the core product for a successful new business.

The third story shows that managing the ongoing process for creating new product ideas can be as important as the ideas themselves. Software designer Doug Carlston recognized a need for educational software that is fun for children to use. The result was the very successful software program *Where in the World Is Carmen Sandiego?* It was well received by children and adopted for use in schools and homes. How Carlston built the team to design the original software is not as important as how he fostered creativity within the organization to develop a continuing stream of new ideas and products based on the original game software, and new software as well.

Sunfish/Laser, Inc.: The Laser

Georgia Feldmann and Morris H. Hadley

For you are such a smart little craft—
Such a neat little, sweet little craft,
Such a bright little, tight little
Slight little, light little
Trim little, prim little craft!

William S. Gilbert, Ruddigore, *1887*

Designing the Laser sailboat was an inherently creative process.[1] From inception, no comprehensive marketing or formal testing program was used. The designers and marketers called the boat's success an "absolute stroke of luck." Yet, the expertise of the company founders, combined with a market that depended on lead users, ensured a rigorous interactive testing and development process that led to success.

The Laser is a mono-top sailboat that weighs approximately 127 pounds (57.7 kilograms) and is 13 feet, 9 inches (4.19 meters) long. Its sail is large in relation to the size of the hull. The craft comes in three sizes. It is a sprightly, sporty little boat that, in 1971, incorporated the latest designs and materials. Bruce Kirby, the designer, explained that he had used the same S-curve for the bow that he had used on his previous 14 designs. He related that "experienced sailors can always recognize my work by looking at the bow." Built of fiberglass, the boat was designed to be light but sturdy enough to withstand the knocks of being carried around and loaded on and off car tops.

By almost any measure, the Laser is a very successful boat design. It comprises the largest number of so-called "one-design" craft afloat, with more than 155,000 currently sailing. The boat's appeal derives from its manageability, its commitment to a fixed, unchanging design, and its status as the premier racing-class boat worldwide. Laser-class races are held in more than 85 countries. In November 1992, the Laser received its ultimate accolade by being selected as an official racing sailboat class for the 1996 Olympics.

THE SAILBOAT MARKET

The sailboat market was traditionally associated with large craft for up-scale buyers who could afford them. Even a purely cruising boat requires considerable maintenance and upkeep. Boat owners must pay for mooring space and, in cold climates, dry-docking during the winter. The market for large sailboats was influenced by sailboat racing, a sport that demands a large investment in both time and money. Sailboat racers were constantly looking for technical advantage, which in turn would be adopted by weekend and leisure sailors who wanted to have the latest equipment and designs.

Skill and experience afford a powerful advantage in sailboat racing, but one that can be offset, to a large degree, by improved equipment. For example, the only U.S. America's Cup loss was due largely to the technical advantage of the Australians, who introduced a super-secret "winged keel" innovation. Subsequently, a similarly equipped American boat regained the Cup. Despite the skill of the skipper and crew, if all other factors are equal, a slight technological advantage is usually enough to ensure victory.

The strong American economy and the corresponding growth in consumers' discretionary income drove a booming sailboat market throughout the 1960s and 1970s, a "golden age" of sailing that no one expects to see again. The image of a youthful President John Kennedy sailing off Hyannis Port just after 1960 buoyed the image of sailing. The sport of sailing seemed reachable and desirable to many people, and the industry had the advantage of a growing market.

The Small Sailboat Segment

For the majority of consumers who thought they might enjoy sailing but could not afford it, the Sunfish was a welcome new product in the 1950s. The Sunfish is a 160-pound open-hull boat designed for the novice who is looking for fun in a small boat that is very reasonably priced. The phenomenal success of the Sunfish established the equivalent of a mass market in small sailboats.

With lower sailboat prices, increasing numbers of young people were becoming involved in the sport. Boats that could be used for training as well as racing were in demand. Further, once involved in the sport, sailors were likely to trade up to larger craft as their living standard improved. To meet these new needs, sailboat manufacturers produced more and different variants of boats, as well as continually upgrading and offering new equipment for current boat designs. Gordon Clayton, a former Laser marketing executive, observed that sailing had become an "armaments race."

The One-Design Sailboat

Although large sailboats were selling strongly and the popularity of the Sunfish was growing steadily during the 1960s and 1970s, no small, inexpensive, high performance sailboats were available. The Sunfish is an excellent small boat, but its dinghy hull design limits its sailing performance.

Meanwhile, many sailors were becoming frustrated with the increasing amount of regatta time being spent on checking compliance with class specifications. "You spent half the time [at a regatta] measuring boats," remarked Bruce Kirby, the designer of the Laser. A "one-design" class of racing boats that would not change much would expedite enforcement of classification rules at races.

The costs of improving a sailboat's performance were also a concern to sailors. New upgrades cost significant amounts of money, yet the actual increase in performance could be realized only by the experienced sailors. Certain technical improvements were of value only if a sailor already had a high degree of skill. Many sailors were looking for a small, inexpensive boat that was responsive and fun to sail. They also wanted a boat that would be part of a class that truly would not change. Such a class would not only ensure fairness in competitions, but also limit rising costs associated with new technologies. Technology would be secondary to nautical skill. The basic idea was a boat that would be easy to sail but have the inherent performance capability to test a seasoned sailor without the need for upgrades.

Pursuing this idea of a one-design boat had risks, however. If someone wants to race a boat, other people must have boats in its class to race against it. Consequently, the manufacturer has an incentive to get many copies of a new class of boats out to the market as soon as possible. Success would depend on producing and selling, as quickly as possible, enough boats for the formation of clubs and the organization of regattas.

The Market Opportunity

The small sailboat market was served by a large number of geographically dispersed manufacturers, few building more than one size of boat. A single producer usually built one class of boat in a specific geographic region. Clayton remembered that "we didn't know what was going on 500 miles away [from Toronto, Canada], much less what was going on at the West Coast."

The market was also highly fragmented in terms of distribution. No manufacturer owned a distribution and sales network. Many of the distributors were former sailors who bought and sold boats on the basis of their own preferences and experiences. Clayton described the distribution network as "lots of order takers but not a lot of high powered salespeople." Advertising and marketing experience was minimal among both the distributors and the manufacturers. As a result, sales were often based on word-of-mouth recommendations. Expert opinion, especially on the latest technology, was very important to a potential buyer, either directly or through specialty sailing magazines.

Potential buyers who might be interested in a one-design boat would most likely be the many young sailors who had entered the market in the 1960s and 1970s. They were typically between the ages of 20 and 30 years and were interested in performance, though cost was a consideration. Many of these potential buyers could not afford the mooring and dry-docking costs of large boats, not to mention equipment costs. Further, many people in this target group did not live by the water; they had to transport their boats. A boat that could be carried on the top of a car would clearly reduce the cost of sailing.

DEVELOPMENT OF THE LASER

Hudson Bay Company, a large Canadian sporting goods manufacturing company, was planning to introduce a complete new line of camping equipment in 1969 and wanted to include a portable folding sailboat. Ian Bruce, a Canadian entrepreneur, was involved in the sailboat project and in October 1969 called his friend Bruce Kirby, an American boat designer, to explore a possible design. Kirby had more than seven produced boat designs to his credit. He was then editor of an American sailing magazine, *Yacht Racing*, and in close touch with sailing developments on the U.S. East Coast.

The Original Idea

During the initial telephone conversation with Ian Bruce, Kirby began doodling and made a sketch. For the rest of the day, he expanded on the idea in the sketch. Because he was basically given complete freedom in designing the boat, he pursued this original idea.

However, because Hudson Bay was looking for a small, inexpensive folding boat to be part of a line of camping equipment, it did not respond favorably to Kirby's design. Describing the boat he designed, Kirby said, "I gave Ian [Bruce] more boat" than was asked for initially. The proposed design was a "hot little boat."

Pursuing the Concept with Design Principles

Even though Hudson Bay decided not to use the design, Bruce and Kirby did not forget the boat. Bruce recruited sail designer Hans Vogt, and the three-person team worked out the basic concept of the boat. All three were members of the tightly knit global community of former Olympic sailors (Kirby had sailed for the United States, Bruce for Canada, and Vogt for Denmark) and were heavily involved in the sailing industry. They stipulated the following design principles for the new boat concept:

- Simplicity, or reduce sailing to the essentials: The boat would ensure that the pure skill of a sailor would be pitted against that of another sailor, as well as against nature, without technological intrusion. The most advanced materials and methods available in 1969 were to be used, but the goal was to produce an enduring, classic design.
- One fixed design: The boat would remain true to the one-design concept. It would not change over time under any circumstances.
- Maximum performance/speed: Given the design constraints, as much performance and speed capability would be built into the boat as possible.
- Transportability: The new boat would be transportable on the top of a car and easily stored.

- Durability: A mono-top design would be used to make the new boat extremely sturdy, able to handle the shocks of transport and the sea. Also, sails would be durable and easy to rig. Launch from the beach would be easy.
- Low cost: The boat would be an affordable out-of-pocket purchase. Bruce wanted to price the boat so that the potential buyer's choice could be between "a wild weekend or a new boat."

Kirby viewed the whole design process as an artistic endeavor. He did not feel "constrained by experience." Further, because it was an entrepreneurial venture, constraints were imposed on the designers. The principle of simplicity was deemed especially important to the design. Kirby had been involved in developing large, complicated boats. He intentionally kept the new concept simple. The kind of classic design sought would be very difficult to achieve. One of the new boat's possible competitors, the Fin, had "lot's of string," as Kirby put it, so he made certain that the rigging had "minimal clutter."

From Design to Launch

The design principles implied a new class of boat, which meant risk of market nonacceptance. The barriers to new entrants, even in the small boat class, were significant. The design and testing of a new boat and the time that would elapse before enough boats were bought to generate clubs and regattas meant high capital commitment over an extended time period before any profit could be realized. The team recognized these risks, but believed the only alternative was to go ahead with new product development. Because of the boom in the sailboat market, and their collective experience and confidence in the design, the team decided to proceed with the boat without any formal market research.

To maintain the integrity of the one-design class, Kirby and his colleagues were committed to carefully controlling the design and manufacturing process. Each craft manufactured would be licensed and numbered through a plaque installed on the boat. Thus, when other manufacturers were licensed, they would have to adhere to a technical manual of manufacturing procedures to ensure that each unit met standards. At a regatta, a boat with the appropriate plaque would not need to be measured for class specifications.

The three designers spent most of 1970 developing a prototype. They originally wanted two prototypes, but were able to complete only one.

Yacht Racing magazine's regatta at Lake Geneva, Canada, in the summer of 1971 provided a perfect opportunity to test the boat's performance. Industry experts, regulators, and many other people involved in sailing were in attendance. Ostensibly the races were just for fun, but they enabled all classes of sailors to test their skills against each other. Kirby recalls that the competition confirmed the designers' "gut feelings" about the new boat. Nevertheless, the three spent the winter fine-tuning the design, continuing to elicit response from leading sailors and other people involved in the sailboat business.

Once the boat was refined, its creators decided to launch their product at the 1972 New York Boat Show. Boat shows were very important to the market launch of a new craft; both consumers and dealers attended. In addition, a print advertisement announcing the new boat was placed in the early spring 1971 issue of *Yacht Racing* magazine. With the design fixed and the price set in a reasonable range ($695 was the initial target price), the new boat needed only an appropriate name.

Before the name "Laser" was selected for the new boat, several other names had been considered, "The Grasshopper" and "The Week-Ender" being a few of many ideas. At the celebration following the *Yacht Racing* magazine regatta, a young McGill University student suggested the name "Laser." Kirby was at the other end of the table and did not hear the exchange, but the name stuck and afterward the team agreed that it was a good name. Although the name "Laser," with its connotation of high technology and rapid change, did not seem to match the proposed concept of an unchanging classic design, it was consistent with the connotation of speed and performance. Kirby felt that the laser image would appeal to young, performance-oriented sailors, the initial target market.

When the boat was introduced at the 1972 New York Boat Show, 144 copies were sold right off the showroom floor, an "unofficial record" according to Kirby. Soon the new craft became the talk of the sailing community, and sales climbed rapidly. Throughout the 1970s and the early 1980s, an average of 24 Lasers a day were produced. Sales peaked in 1984 and, after a downturn, began a resurgence in the early 1990s.

WHAT DROVE THE LASER'S SUCCESS?

The creators of the Laser used no formal studies of market opportunity, no formal marketing research or concept testing, nor any systematic testing of advertising or marketing response for the new sailboat. What began as an idea became a success without the help of formal business analysis. The new product evolved from creativity, interaction with the market, and a design commitment that bonded the product to the market.

Enhancing Creativity

The way in which the three designers worked together was a key element in the success. Cooperation among creative people is often problematic, but such was not the case for the Laser. Although the design originated with Ian Bruce's telephone call and basic idea for a new sailboat, Bruce Kirby was given free reign in creating the new design. He also retained a great degree of control over the project, which proved to be very important in maintaining the team's focus. Proceeding from Kirby's rough sketch to the actual prototype required the concentration of all three designers. This challenge was met in large part by adherence to the agreed-upon design principles.

Several other factors also contributed to the team's keen interest in the successful development of the Laser. First, the opportunity to be part of a groundbreaking new design project was very attractive. Second, all three designers had experience in World Cup racing, which may have provided a shared set of values and sense of professionalism that defined their relationship. Third, the potential financial reward of a major success would have been an incentive for cooperation.

Interacting with Lead Users

Creativity and design integrity were important for the new craft, but so was ongoing feedback from key members of the sailing community. The sport of sailing is led by a group of world-class racing experts whose equipment and practices are emulated by less expert sailors who keep track of the latest changes through the sailing magazines. Obtaining reactions from the elite group of sailors provided excellent points of reference throughout the design process. Combining the advice of lead users and their own expertise, the designers were able to create a new boat that ultimately established a new class of sailing.

Forging a Bond with the Market

A segment of the market was clearly interested in a sailboat class with an unchanging design that would emphasize sailing skill over the latest gadget or design twist. Gordon Clayton said that once it became clear that the Laser company intended to maintain a constant design, the "class took care of itself." Clayton also remembered that consumers helped maintain and reinforce the Laser design. Clearly, a strong bond had been forged with the market, a tremendous advantage for a new product.

The company further reinforced the permanence of the design by using production techniques that deterred unauthorized modification. For example, small ultrasonic dots printed along the leading edges of the sails made altering the sails very difficult. The classic design assured consumers that they would not eventually have an outdated boat. As Kirby explained, the buyer purchased the complete boat up front, and would never need to change or upgrade anything. This consistency was one of the Laser's strongest selling points.

EPILOGUE

Unfortunately, the company founded by Ian Bruce, Performance Sailcraft Corporation, eventually went out of business. To continue selling the Laser, large discounts had been given to dealers. Sales were strong and acceptance was good, but the company could not overcome poor margin and cash flow levels. Also, according to Bruce Kirby, expansion had been too rapid. The company simply ran out of money after several years. The successful Laser design carried on, however. Pearson Yachts bought the design and continued marketing it. Margins were brought under control and the Laser was profitable, but the company's other boat lines did poorly and Pearson declared bankruptcy in 1991.

North Sails then bought both the Laser and the Sunfish and formed a new company called Laser/Sunfish, Inc., led by Peter Johnstone. At the age of 26, he became part of a new entrepreneurial team dedicated to expanding Laser/Sunfish sales and producing the "next" Laser. Laser/Sunfish, Inc. entered the 1990s performing well. With the selection of the Laser as one of the sailboat classes for the 1996 Olympics, the company should reap additional sales benefits. In any case, the boat is assured a place in nautical history.

Racing Strollers Inc.: Baby Jogger

Kathryn J. Cancro and Jeffrey O. Teach

The dynamic principle of fantasy is play, which belongs to the child, and as such it appears to be inconsistent with the principle of serious work. But without this playing with fantasy no creative work has ever yet come to birth. The debt we owe to the play of the imagination is incalculable.

Carl G. Jung, Psychological Types, *1923*

Born of the imagination and motivation of Phil Baechler in 1982, the Baby Jogger redefined the worldwide stroller market.[2] The Baby Jogger is a lightweight, durable, and versatile stroller that enables an active family to spend time together without sacrificing personal freedom. The stroller was designed to carry a child as the parent runs behind. Baechler created the first rough prototype so that he could spend time with his infant son while training for a marathon.

Subsequently, Baechler and his wife Mary formed Racing Strollers Inc. to fill the ever-increasing demand for their product. In seven years, Racing Strollers Inc. grew into a profitable and successful company serving both domestic and foreign markets. Most of its strollers are still sold in the United States, but international demand continues to grow. With total annual sales of less than $10 million, Racing Strollers Inc. is a small company by most standards. Nevertheless, its success shows how a new product idea can go from the garage to the world market.

GENESIS OF THE BABY JOGGER IDEA

Phil Baechler was training for a marathon after the birth of his son. Because he worked as the night-shift copy editor for a local newspaper in Yakima, Washington, the only time he could train for the race and be with his new son was during the day. To meet both needs, he thought of ways in which he could safely take his infant son along on runs. The idea to build some sort of lightweight stroller came from his observation that cyclists occasionally pulled their children in small trailers behind their bikes.

Baechler, a cyclist as well as runner, purchased a used stroller and built a prototype in his garage to implement his idea. Using a variety of bicycle and other parts, he assembled something that resembled a small rickshaw with three bicycle wheels mounted on an aluminum frame. The baby seat was attached to the frame over the two rear wheels. The single front wheel was mounted far enough forward on the frame to stabilize and balance the stroller. With a handle high enough to accommodate an adult, the new stroller steered and glided effortlessly, easily traversing small obstacles and rough terrain.

Baechler put his six-month-old son in the prototype stroller and took him on a 10-kilometer race. The first public appearance of the aptly named "Baby Jogger" prompted mixed reactions from the crowd. Some people looked on in bewilderment and others asked where they could buy one. After the race, Baechler realized that he had developed a product that could be of interest to other people.

FROM IDEA TO PRODUCT

Creating a finished, manufacturable product from the first prototype presented several obstacles. Supply and design problems plagued early attempts to create a truly marketable product. For example, framing tubes for the original models came from pieces obtained at a nearby aircraft plant. Baechler first experimented with both steel and aluminum tubing. Steel, which welded well, was too heavy. Aluminum tubing was lighter, but was difficult to connect to provide structural integrity to the frame. Crimping the ends to connect the parts caused aluminum to lose its malleability and strength.

The solution to the tubing problem came during a random trip with a friend to a boating supply store. A plastic hardware connector used for boat railings formed a strong yet flexible joint that was perfect for connecting aluminum tubing. This discovery made possible a lightweight, rugged stroller design. Baechler began designing his own connecting pieces using custom plastic molds. Eventually, the molds contributed to the first Baby Jogger patent. Similar creative problem solving was necessary throughout the development process.

The manufactured Baby Jogger, similar in design to the first prototype, consists of a frame of aluminum tubing with 20-inch pneumatic bicycle wheels and a nylon canvas seat. Although parts are bought from suppliers, the basic assembly process, including tube-bending, is done on a just-in-time assembly line. The specially designed plastic joints facilitate this assembly process. The Baby Jogger has a seatbelt to hold the child safely in position. Its sturdy, rugged construction enables it to operate on such formidable terrain as snow, sand, grass, and gravel, all of which are off limits to the traditional stroller.

BUILDING THE ENTREPRENEURIAL ORGANIZATION

The Baby Jogger addressed unmet needs for many runners. It provided a bridge between pursuing athletic activity and spending time with their children. To meet these needs, Baechler followed a typical entrepreneurial approach to launching a product. For the first few years, he and his wife kept their regular jobs, made custom strollers in their garage, and kept the books on the kitchen table.

Partly because of the couple's lack of business experience, the company made no money in the first few years. Baechler recalled, "We didn't even understand the concept of overhead. We just set the price based on our materials costs."[3] As the company grew, the Baechlers hired consultants to help with organizational development. "It's like we're getting our MBAs on the job," remarked Phil.

Like any entrepreneurial endeavor, the young company had limited access to capital. The Baechlers' $8,000 nestegg went quickly, and finding outside investors proved difficult for an untested product. Without funds to build a parts and equipment inventory, the Baechlers could construct a new stroller only after receiving payment from the preceding delivery. Sales were slow but steady in the first years. Finally, in 1984, Baechler received a patent for his design. He then incorporated the company.

Racing Strollers Inc. finally secured an operating line of credit, then a $241,000 development loan from the Small Business Administration in 1988.

This funding enabled the Baechlers to expand from a rented 4,000-square-foot garage into a 12,000-square-foot all-purpose facility.[4] The Baechlers finally seemed to have a solid foundation and were ready to pursue active corporate growth.

Phil Baechler concentrates on design and development and Mary remains the problem-solving manager for Racing Strollers. She states that the credo of the company, "doing the right thing by a person,"[5] applies to all of Racing Stroller Inc.'s employee, distributor, and customer relations. The company pushes customer commitment to the limit by providing lifetime guarantees on all its products. The company will go so far as to replace a previously purchased stroller if the company comes out with a feature or design that the customer prefers.

MARKETING THE BABY JOGGER

In many ways, Racing Strollers Inc. brought the stroller industry out of the "dark ages" by recognizing an unmet market need and meeting that need with a superior quality product.[6] For years the market had been filled with cumbersome, rickety strollers that were only good for walks in the park or strolls through the shopping mall. New product development was minimal in the industry, with trite accessories and upgrades the norm.

A typical pram-type stroller costs between $100 and $200. Although it weighs about two-thirds as much as the Baby Jogger, its wheel diameter of four to five inches precludes speed and smooth riding. The traditional stroller is useful only in limited-movement environments. Child-size backpacks are another way to carry children, but are generally uncomfortable and difficult to manage in active sports such as running.

Exceptional quality and versatility set the Baby Jogger apart in the stroller market. At an introductory price of about $240, it defined a new premium segment among similar product offerings. It is an all-purpose, versatile stroller with uses far beyond the traditional "strolling." Although taking a child jogging or rollerblading may be the most common use for the Baby Jogger, the fact that it has become part of everyday life for many parents adds value to its basic purpose.

Racing Strollers Inc. depends primarily on word of mouth to promote its product. Through customer usage, the product makes regular appearances before its target audience. Its bright colors and unusual design attract attention. The company cannot afford extensive national advertising, but has consistently run modest advertisements in magazines such as *Runner's World* and *Parents*. Nevertheless, most sales have been to people who heard about the product from friends or saw one on the street. Finally, the uniqueness of the product has made it a newsworthy item and the Baechlers have capitalized on publicity whenever possible.

The company originally relied on mail order to distribute Baby Joggers. Once it expanded production facilities, it began product introduction to the trade through sporting goods and children's products trade shows. Attendance at these events was beneficial in many ways, especially in introducing the product to global retail trade outlets. To maintain control of the Baby Jogger quality image, the company made the product available only through a carefully selected distribution network of some 3,000 outlets in the United States, Europe, Japan, and Australia.

CAPITALIZING ON SUCCESS

The sales performance of the Baby Jogger clearly demonstrates the success of this entrepreneurial new product. In 1987, sales were $500,000. They almost doubled in 1989 to just under $1 million and reached $5 million by 1992! In that year, the Yakima, Washington, plant employed 35 people dedicated to the production and distribution of the Baby Jogger product line. The original Baby Jogger accounts for about 60 percent of sales, but sales have been growing through product line expansion.

The original Baby Jogger model was a platform from which numerous derivative products were created; each derivative filled a particular market niche. The Baechlers listened carefully to customers and used the feedback to develop product line extensions. For example, many parents wrote to the company praising the Baby Jogger's role in raising their first child, but saying that the arrival of a second child precluded family outings. In response, Phil Baechler designed the Twinner, a double-occupancy model of the Baby Jogger.

This response to customer requests continued with further line extensions: the Zipper, the Super Jogger, and the Special Needs stroller models. The most affordable of the models, the Zipper, resulted from repeated requests by city dwellers for a smaller version that could fit easily in the urban environment. The Zipper has 12-inch wheels, collapses for storing, and easily maneuvers in and out of elevators, apartments, and small city stores.

The Super Jogger deluxe model was designed for people who requested an even sturdier model that could operate on snow or rocky mountain paths and carry larger children. The Special Needs model was designed for the handicapped child. It was not intended to replace the conventional wheelchair, but to enable the child to explore places that otherwise would be inaccessible. Because of its durable and sturdy design, a handicapped child can be included in a picnic at the beach or a walk in the woods without the limitations of a conventional wheelchair.

REASONS FOR THE BABY JOGGER SUCCESS

Although Phil Baechler may not have considered what would drive the success of the Baby Jogger during his efforts to create it, three factors are apparent in hindsight: (1) creativity and persistence, (2) social, demographic, and economic trends, and (3) consumer needs.

Creativity and Persistence

Ideas for new products probably occur to millions of people every day in response to their own needs and problems. Sometimes people act on those ideas, but generally they do not. Phil Baechler acted on his idea, which emerged from his own basic needs to pursue running and to be with his infant son. Other runners with the same needs (and apparently there were many, who eventually bought Baby Joggers) may have thought of the idea before Baechler, but only he was motivated enough to go out to the garage and tinker with parts to see what he could create.

In this case, the creativity was not so much in coming up with the idea as in bringing the idea to reality. Clearly, part of the creative process was the persistent problem solving that was necessary to realize the idea. Whether in putting together the first prototype of the Baby Jogger, or in trying to keep the business afloat when cash flow became a problem, or in persuading dealers, creative persistence paid off for the Baechlers' entrepreneurial venture.

Social, Demographic, and Economic Trends

Although Phil Baechler may not have formally studied the market for the Baby Jogger before or during its development, he surely had a sense of his surrounding environment and whether other people would be interested in purchasing such a product. He certainly recognized from his own situation that people like himself were concerned about their health and family, as well as the economic times that confronted them.

Throughout the 1970s and into the 1980s, people began to recognize the personal benefits of regular exercise. Jogging and other aerobic exercises became a national pastime, and people became psychologically addicted to the positive feelings associated with routine exercise. However, the time available for running and other strenuous activities was limited because of other increasing demands on time.

The number of double-income families increased dramatically during the 1970s and 1980s. The so-called "baby boomers" reached marriage age. In many cases, both spouses worked, not only for economic reasons but also to satisfy career goals. When these couples began having children, they found it increasingly difficult to balance personal and family time. Exercise routines established before the children were born as an essential part of life became impossible to maintain. The attempt to allocate scarce personal time between family activities and personal exercise routines raised concern about basic personal needs and parental responsibilities.

The Underlying Needs

Thrust into a situation of conflict between personal and family goals and activities, many individuals who lead an active personal and professional life feel a certain loss of control and guilt associated with the parenting role. A helpless child's needs must be met or its life and development will be threatened. Parents may worry that they are not doing everything possible to ensure that the child develops normally and has every benefit of life. Even employing a babysitter is not satisfactory for many parents. Relatedly, ensuring that the child gets adequate sensory stimulation, enjoys an active life, and experiences the outdoors as often as possible not only satisfies a parental need, but is helpful to the child as well.

In effect, the Baby Jogger helps to ease the transition from couple to family and to fill a void between parent and child. With the Baby Jogger, parents no longer have to feel guilty about taking their daily jog in lieu of spending time with their children. A parent's adult activity can be combined with a family-oriented excursion. Additionally, a parent who does not have to sacrifice a valued activity does not feel resentment toward the child. The Baby Jogger enables parents to work the child into their program without ceding completely to the child. They can preserve their freedom and spontaneity. Hiring a babysitter is unnecessary for many situations. Whether the parent wants to go shopping, to the beach, or for a walk through the woods, the versatile Baby Jogger will safely transport the child. It gives parents the freedom to continue exploring and maintaining an active lifestyle.

The Baby Jogger benefits the child as well. First, children benefit from quality family time. Rather than staying behind with a babysitter, the child can be included in the parents' activity, which contributes to family bonding. Second, the Baby Jogger introduces the child to the rhythm of exercise during formative years, a pattern that can become beneficial in adulthood when exercise is even more important. Third, the motion of the Baby Jogger has a calming effect on the child, similar to the gentle swaying of a rocker or a ride in the car. Fourth, the ride provides sensory stimulation for the child; the child sits higher up in the Baby Jogger than in traditional strollers and experiences more of the changing sights and sounds of the world as it whisks by.

MAINTAINING THE EDGE

Although the Baby Jogger design received a legal patent in 1984, imitation running strollers were quick to enter the market. Competitors such as Huffy have introduced similarly designed products priced below the Baby Jogger. The Baechlers believe that imitation is the best compliment, and although they retained patent attorneys, they recognize the benefits of competition to consumers.[7] They believe by continuing to improve the quality of their product consumers will be better satisfied and Racing Strollers will remain the market leader.

To maintain its edge as market leader, Racing Strollers Inc. will undoubtedly have to adjust its corporate and managerial structure as it grows, without damaging the creative and responsive spirit so valuable to the company. Competition often forces continuous product improvement, more analytical approaches to marketing, global expansion, acquisition of capital, and dedication to the customer. Perhaps the last area will be what carries the organization into its future with continued success. As Mary Baechler says in commenting on the effects of Tom Peters' *In Search of Excellence* on her business:

> Anyone in our company can stop production if he thinks there's a flaw. Any employee can send a stroller that's on order Fed Ex (at $87 a pop) if he feels

we have not met our delivery commitments. Beyond our lifetime guarantee for frames and one year guarantee on the wheels, our customer service people can do whatever it takes, up to $300 per customer, to make things right for the customer. . . . We stay in contact after each repair, and the customer gets a postcard to send that comes directly to me and lets me know if we took care of matters to the customer's satisfaction.[8]

CONCLUSION

New product development, even in mature markets, can succeed if one is willing to think beyond what is given. By exploring unmet needs and taking advantage of changing trends, any company can design a product that can fill a gap. Phil Baechler, in meeting his own need to spend more time with his new son, hit upon a hidden need among many of his peers. By pursuing a creatively driven problem-solving process to realize his idea, he achieved success. This process is one that any company can use to continuously evaluate its market and discover hidden opportunities.

Attention to customer input and feedback sustains the success of the Baechlers and Racing Strollers Inc. By listening to customers' requests and demands, the company continually refines its current products and develops new ones that meet specific customer needs. To maintain market share, any company must remain attuned to its customers' demands and develop products that consistently fit into their ever-changing lifestyles.

Marketing often becomes the main focus of survival for an entrepreneurial company. However, financial support and proper managerial policies must be in place for the company to succeed. The lean years of Racing Strollers Inc. show that even a great idea can have difficulty without adequate financial support. Not until the company became a structured enterprise with adequate cash flow did it finally begin to realize a return on its efforts.

Creativity in concept formation and implementation was fundamental to Racing Strollers Inc. Phil Baechler could have easily kept his invention as a toy for himself and his son. Fortunately, he recognized that he had discovered a need that was common among his peers. His championing of the product and constant drive paid off in the development of a true new product success.

Broderbund Software, Inc.: *Where in the World Is Carmen Sandiego?*

Brian J. Giblin and Michael R. Levy

Behold, I show you a mystery; We shall not all sleep, but we shall be changed.

1 Corinthians, 15:51

Back in the mid-1980s, Doug Carlston, founder and chief executive officer of Broderbund Software, Inc., observed the market for children's software and saw a need that his competitors ignored: educational programs that are fun for children. Broderbund's launch of *Where in the World Is Carmen Sandiego?* in 1985 implemented Carlston's vision and helped transform Broderbund from a software publisher and distributor into an acclaimed software development company.

Where in the World Is Carmen Sandiego? (*Carmen*) was motivated by a game that Carlston had played with his brother as a child. *Carmen* quickly caught the imagination of children and has grown in popularity since it was released. By 1993, the *Carmen* series had sold more than three million copies since its 1985 launch and had led to spinoff books, clothing, a PBS game show, and other licensing projects.[9] Each version led to increased sales of previous versions in the line, and each year sales exceeded those of the previous year.

WHAT IS THE GAME?

Carmen was designed as a fun program for children between the ages of eight and thirteen. The player is a detective for the Acme Detective Agency who must find and arrest members of Carmen Sandiego's gang. At the beginning of each game, a historic treasure is stolen (such as Galileo's telescope or the Brandenburg Gate) and the player is assigned the job of identifying, tracking, and arresting the criminal so that the treasure can be returned.

The game operates as a global treasure hunt with geographic clues. The player must question witnesses and decipher the clues to determine who the criminal is and where the perpetrator currently resides. For example, the detective will be told that a blond-haired criminal was seen changing his money into rupees. The child must then determine which country uses rupees as currency. A reference book is supplied to help interpret the clues. The original version of *Carmen* included a copy of *The World Almanac*. Other versions have included an atlas, a desk encyclopedia, and a travel guide.

Carmen is an enigmatic figure. She wears a trench coat and a hat that covers most of her face. Furthermore, she maintains an elusive aura by rarely appearing directly within the games. The players are after Carmen, but told little about who she really is. According to the User's Manual, Carmen Sandiego is a former spy for the Intelligence Service of Monaco. Her police dossier contains the following miscellaneous information:

> Carmen Sandiego (known to the inner circle as "Buffy") is reported to be an agent, double agent, triple agent and quadruple agent for so many countries that even she has forgotten which one she is working for. The auburn-haired founder of the Villains' International Legion of Evil (V.I.L.E.) has recruited the most cunning and resourceful band of thieves in history. During her years as a Monacan secret agent, she generally posed as a tennis pro and always traveled to and from the matches in her 1939 Packard convertible. Carmen has a fondness for tacos and never appears in public without her famous ruby necklace "The Moon of Moldavia."[10]

Each game is different and challenging. The clues, criminals, cities, and stolen treasures change each time the player begins a mystery. Players sign on in their own names, enabling the game to keep track of their experience levels. Periodically, the player is promoted and begins to receive more difficult clues; thus, as the player becomes more proficient, the clues become more complex. Further, *Carmen* targets neither boys nor girls; it has equal numbers of male and female villains. The game is also nonviolent. For example, when a criminal is caught, a character simply yells "Stop, Thief" and the criminal is arrested. Carmen Sandiego is mysterious and evil, and the game is fun to play despite being educational!

WHAT IS BRODERBUND?

Broderbund Software, Inc. was founded by a pair of brothers, Douglas and Gary Carlston. The company name is a multilingual composite of "brotherhood." Douglas, a Harvard law school graduate, decided he could earn more money programming his personal computer than practicing law. At the outset, the Carlstons began publishing and distributing software for other programmers rather than developing their own.

An early constraint on Broderbund's growth was its capitalization. A failed public offering in 1987 and a canceled merger kept Broderbund from going public until November 1991.[11] The lack of capital forced Broderbund to stay within its niche (not always a bad thing). Nevertheless, the company performed well financially. In 1992, it had sales of about $75 million, with $9.7 million in profit. Although Broderbund is a leader in its market segment, it remains a small company with only 3 percent of the sales volume of Microsoft.[12] Its products are highly regarded and it has earned numerous software publishing and educational awards, including a Parent's Choice Gold Medal.[13] Broderbund is estimated to control a 25 percent market share in the educational software market.[14]

WHAT IS THE EDUCATIONAL SOFTWARE MARKET?

Educational software has traditionally been ignored by the major software companies. Tim Bajarin, a consultant for Creative Strategies, Inc., argues that Broderbund has "prospered by going after the home market when most of the industry says it doesn't exist. Given the limitations they've had to work under, they've done a marvelous job."[15] Although one of the claimed benefits of home computing was its educational value, there was little evidence in the early 1980s that educational software would deliver that benefit.

In the school market, most of the educational software was computerized "skills and drills." One teacher described the problems with early educational software:

Kids know the difference. They know that Football Spelling has nothing to do with football and everything to do with spelling. And by and large they don't want that much to do with it.[16]

Surprisingly, a large proportion of schools ordered computers for student use during the 1980s, but teachers were as guilty as software developers in failing to use or stimulate demand for innovative software. Perhaps Broderbund's major contribution was simply recognizing that educational software was not meeting the needs of children, and developing products accordingly.

Whether at home or at school, parents were surely perplexed by the lack of computer software that could motivate their children. One of the great promises of the personal computer for home use was that it would enable parents to improve their children's education. The expectation that a computer would aid a child's intellectual development prompted many parents to purchase one. Unfortunately, many computers became simply word processors.

Meanwhile, children were hammering away at their Nintendo games and watching television. They knew the difference between fun and learning. In effect, a large potential market opportunity was lying dormant in homes and schools around the world. Only a product affording a creative blend of fun and education would be able to seize this opportunity.

HOW WAS *CARMEN SANDIEGO* CREATED?

In 1984, the dearth of educational software for children to use on computers at home and at school became apparent to Doug Carlston. He had the idea of developing software based on an impromptu game he had played as a child with his brother, a game of trying to identify a city by its longitude and latitude.[17] He championed the new idea and put together a team of employees that included programmers, designers, and marketing personnel.

The first concept the team generated from Carlston's idea was called "Six Crowns of Henry VIII." Somewhere during the development process, the name evolved into "Carmen Sandiego." Programmer Dane Bigham came up with the concept of Carmen Sandiego and Cricket Bird wrote the first script.[18] Carlston suggested that the game include a reference book.[19] Factual data could be woven into the clues and location descriptions to encourage use of the reference book.

After the first *Carmen* game was launched, a large part of the success of the series was attributable to the talents of Lauren Elliot and Gene Portwood—two talented designers. Portwood had developed his understanding of children and of the creative process as an animator at Disney Studios. Elliot had trained as an architect.[20] *The Los Angeles Times* described the team as a "Mutt and Jeff" couple who:

> . . . share a passion for wrist watches, all manner of toys, Monty Python movies, Captain America comic books, and, of course, Carmen. At work they share a generous toy- and gadget-filled office. Off hours, they and their wives are close friends.[21]

Portwood and Elliot produced storyboards and initial graphics, and staff produced the finished software. To maintain product quality and consistency, Broderbund maintains a *Carmen* "bible" that describes Carmen and her gang's characteristics in detail. It ensures that newly hired artists do not deviate from the running story. Typical design teams consist of eight to 10 individuals.[22]

Portwood and Elliot have a simple rule for testing concepts: if they lose interest in a concept in less than a week, it is discarded.[23] Concepts that move forward in the design process are play-tested in schools before release. Children of employees often play-test the games. Focus groups are also used in testing product concepts. The goals of this form of use testing are to identify problems in the program and observe player response to the game. Adjustments are made as needed.

HOW WAS *CARMEN SANDIEGO* MARKETED?

Because Broderbund had been heavily involved in distributing and marketing software developed by other programmers, its launch of *Carmen* followed its usual patterns of marketing. Editorial coverage in influential industry magazines, availability on retailer shelves, and selected promotions helped to build awareness of the product. The launch price of $38 put the software in a reasonable range for cost-constrained educators and parents.

Because of the dearth of entertaining software with an educational capability, the product became popular in schools and children started requesting the game from their parents.[24] This demand created a pull-through effect on the distribution chain for the product. Broderbund had used a clever positioning strategy. Because children are very wary of educational products and resist any attempts at force-fed education, the product had to be positioned in the child's mind as fun. Broderbund repeatedly emphasized that the product is a *game* and is intended to be fun.

To accomplish a fun positioning, Broderbund labeled its products as "explorations." When children hear "exploration," they think of adventure and explorers, such as Marco Polo. When parents and teachers hear "exploration," they think of information and learning. The idea of exploration was also part of the product. The game enables children to learn on their own through an adventure that they control. The child becomes an "explorer" in the game and knows more about the world after the adventure. Knowledge empowers children. Elliot observed, "It turns out that kids love knowing things that their parents don't."[25]

To market upgrades and new products for the *Carmen* line (an important source of sustained revenue for a software firm), Broderbund developed an in-house direct mail capability. A database is compiled from the returned customer response cards included in the software packages. According to Karen Ford, corporate projects manager, "We had tremendous success using direct mail to sell upgrades of The Printshop and the four additional volumes for Where is Carmen. The database marketing approach is a big winner for us with these two programs; it pulls like you wouldn't believe."[26] Broderbund has become more sophisticated in its usage of customer response cards:

> We originally created our warranty cards to collect the basic information, but as time went on we decided we wanted to do some low-level demographics so we added more questions. Now we have three different cards, one for productivity, one for education, and one for entertainment software, and each has 50 little boxes to check off if they apply. In addition, there is also a fill-in space for the buyer to add ideas for products they would like to see Broderbund develop.[27]

This direct mail capability has helped Broderbund grow and maintain its product line over its seven-year history.

WHY DID *CARMEN SANDIEGO* SUCCEED?

The obvious reason for *Carmen*'s success is that it filled a need for educational software that was fun for children to use on computers at home and school. Much of the credit for the success of *Carmen* should therefore go to Doug Carlston, who recognized the market opportunity and was the original visionary and product champion of the game. A less obvious but perhaps equally important reason is the *management of creativity* within the organization to sustain the original success. All too often software firms fail after their first success because they do not build an organizational capability that supports creativity, a must for success in the software industry. Finally, almost by chance, Broderbund discovered a small but growing market segment and concentrated on serving that segment.

Carmen Satisfies Needs of Children, Parents, and Educators

The game delivers on its promise of being fun, which children require, and simultaneously fulfills the needs of teachers and parents. First and foremost, however, *Carmen* makes the child the center of the purchase process. By understanding how children think and how they respond to computers and games, Broderbund was able to offer a product that related to children on their own level.

Broderbund understood that children need to be challenged and entertained, and to have their basic curiosity aroused. Most arcade games can entertain and, for a time, even challenge a child; but once the game is mastered, the child loses interest. In contrast, *Carmen* perpetually raises curiosity by asking, "Where in the world is Carmen Sandiego?" The game evolves through the fantasy of traveling all over the world looking for clues. Further, *Carmen* empowers children by making them detectives. The game conjures up the archetype of the eternal battle of good versus evil, where the player becomes the "good guy" chasing "evil thugs."

The game fulfills parents' need to feel that they are doing a good job of parenting. Part of being a "good" parent is educating the children and giving them a happy childhood. Because *Carmen* delivers education *and* fun, it helps parents meet these basic requirements. Rather than resenting and resisting their parents' educational efforts, children may express appreciation and affection because they actually like to play the game. Also, by keeping children productively occupied, the game gives parents some peace and quiet. While children are playing/learning on the computer, they are not watching television, complaining, fighting, or doing other things that upset parents. In sum, the game meets parents' needs, and they become a positive influence in the purchase process.

Educators can recommend the game because children learn geography, history, analytical skills, and the use of reference books as they play. This benefit helps to justify the heavy investment many schools have made in personal computers. As it does at home, *Carmen* keeps children occupied and under control at school. Because children like the game, they may like the teacher. Finally, parents express approval of teachers who use the game in the classroom and gratitude to teachers who recommend use of *Carmen* at home. Consequently, teachers become a positive influence in the purchase process.

By continually developing creative new versions of *Carmen*, Broderbund feeds the cycle of learning and need satisfaction among children, parents, and educators. However, the challenge is to maintain the creativity necessary to sustain interest among these key buying influencers.

Broderbund Manages Creativity Well

Managing creativity is a difficult task. Broderbund accomplishes it by opening horizons for the generation of new ideas. The firm engages in practical and informal *environmental scanning*. It tracks social, demographic, and other trends to identify ideas. Although the company will consider any idea from any source, an idea must conform to its internal development process. This process puts the idea under the control of creative teams that evaluate it. Such empowerment, albeit within reasonable bounds, is extremely important to creative people who value their freedom.

The evaluation is based on such factors as *Carmen Sandiego*'s history and the idea's conformance to the design integrity of the *Carmen* environment. Programming is the responsibility of the creative people. It is done through Broderbund's in-house developmental software, which eliminates dependency on outside programmers who may not have the same values as the creative team. Thus, the evaluation and execution of ideas is influenced by the shared values of the organization.

The creative atmosphere at Broderbund is decidedly on the childish side! It is not unusual for employees to engage frivolous pursuits:

> In one department, a blowup shark in a tie, inflatable crayons, and a mock-up of the Starship Enterprise hang from the ceiling. For inspiration, the animation group goes on field trips to see "Aladdin" and "The Little Mermaid." The company cafeteria serves sushi, and a yoga class is offered twice a week.[28]

The resulting products are much more sophisticated and realistic than the ones most competitors offer to children in the educational software market. The attention to detail is appreciated by children. According to *Carmen* codesigner Gene Portwood, "I learned at Disney to sweat the details. To us, Carmen is very real."[29] To illustrate, fellow designer Lauren Elliot describes a setting in *Carmen:*

> In the Acme Detective Agency, there's a coffee machine. Sometimes you put in a quarter and get a cup. Sometimes you only get half a cup. And sometimes the cup tips over and you lose your quarter. We want to show the real world."[30]

Broderbund Found a Market Segment and Grew with It

In what at first seemed a cruel twist of fate, Broderbund could not raise the capital to expand into the lucrative markets for business software. In the 1980s, when software firms were growing rapidly by selling spreadsheets, word-processing programs, and databases to business organizations, Broderbund was forced to focus on a much smaller segment of the consumer market. The company was in the educational software market by choice, but was aware of the relative success of such software firms as Microsoft, Lotus, WordPerfect, Borland, and others.

To fund entrance into the larger business software markets, the company attempted to go public in 1987, but failed because earnings did not materialize. An attempt to expand through a merger also failed. The company decided to stay in its market niche and become good at what it did. It took control of its design and development process (rather than using outside programmers and software) and developed its competency through the *Carmen Sandiego* software. Fortuitously, because the market segment was small, the large software companies had little interest in developing educational software. Broderbund occupied a niche that competitors ignored and was able to build its core competencies in product development. Once the company realized that its products met the needs of a rapidly growing market segment, it was poised to be the market leader. By Christmas of 1992, Broderbund had five of the 10 top-selling educational software titles![31]

WHAT IN THE WORLD IS
CARMEN SANDIEGO'S FUTURE?

The growing home and educational software market became so large that Microsoft and other large software companies began to explore its opportunities. Personal computer hardware became relatively inexpensive and CD-ROM players began to show up on home computers equipped for "multimedia" software applications (sound, visual imagery, animation, and text). Broderbund realizes it does not have the resources to continue alone against a giant like Microsoft. It may seek strategic alliances with other firms that complement its talents, or it may be swallowed by one of the giants.[32]

Continuation of the Broderbund name into the future may be questionable as acquisitions and mergers occur in the educational software market. In any case, it is clear that the creative organization behind *Carmen* and the brand franchise will live on. The managed creativity necessary to develop other *Carmen*-like educational products for all age groups is in place. Further, Carmen Sandiego is the first major character to cross over from software programs to mass merchandising. The potential brand equity in the name may be leveraged in extension products for some time to come.

The *Carmen* line now consists of five titles (*World, USA, Europe, Time,* and *America's Past*). Two of these titles (*World* and *USA*) have been made into deluxe versions with high resolution graphics, "talking characters," 60 animations, more difficult clues, and more cities. In February 1992, Broderbund introduced a CD-ROM version containing 150 digitized traditional and folk music clips, 150 digitized photographs, 3,200 clues including 500 foreign language clues, hundreds of animations, and a sound score.

The owner of the *Carmen* name is likely to continue a careful licensing policy to avoid saturating the market. Examples of *Carmen* licensed products are a daily public television show, feature film rights, storybooks, board games, videogame versions (Sega Genesis), albums, and T-shirts and sweatshirts.[33] A Saturday morning cartoon series has been rejected in the fear that older children would lose interest in *Carmen* if they saw their younger siblings watching the cartoon.

Eventually children will outgrow *Carmen Sandiego,* but the organization that is marketing the concept can be assured that in the next generation, parents who grew up with and learned from *Carmen* will want it for their children. The mystery will continue!

7

Designing New Products from Concepts

Whereas a new product *idea* is an abstraction, usually presented as a brief oral or written statement, a new product *concept* is a more structured interpretation of the product. More specifically, a new product concept should include the major consumer benefits and features that will define the product and satisfy a market need. Like an idea, a concept can be a written description of the new product, albeit in much greater detail; but it can also be an artistic rendering, a real or simulated model, or any other representation that facilitates comprehension of the new product.

A clear new product concept is necessary for two reasons. First, it provides an integrated basis for communicating the essence of the new product to all stakeholders, especially different departments in an organization. Because engineering, production, and marketing personnel may all speak different professional languages, it is essential to have a clearly stated *core product concept* that everyone agrees characterizes the new product. Product design cannot proceed efficiently and effectively without a core product concept that is linked to a basic market need. A "bar soap that moisturizes, deodorizes, and improves the health of skin" characterizes in simple terms a desired product outcome. Although this concept may vary somewhat in definition during the development process, it should maintain its core integrity to focus attention on the satisfaction of consumer needs and concerns.

The second reason for having a clear new product concept is to establish a basis for testing the proposed product's merits before substantial investment in a prototype or a real working model. Often, financial risk can be reduced if a systematic design to go ahead with a new product (or not) is based on a tested concept. Building a new airplane, a new hotel, or a new piece of software would certainly pose less risk if a clear new product concept passed certain financial, marketing, operational, organizational, and other tests before the commitment of substantial resources.

Formal methods of testing are not always used in designing new products from their concepts. The reason is that products differ, as do new product situations and managerial risk-taking abilities. For example, when new product development is under time pressure to beat competitors to market and the organizational culture supports accelerated development, managers may be willing to design the new product from a concept without significant testing.

Such is the case in the first new product success story in this chapter. The idea for MCI Friends and Family was created within one month by the company's newly formed marketing team and the product was launched six weeks later without significant market testing. Although MCI's downside risk for the new product may have been perceived as low from a competitive standpoint, its failure could have jeopardized MCI's market share and quest for respectability. However, Friends and Family was a resounding success, and the story considers how and why.

Other organizations and managers are less willing to take risks in turning their concepts into new product designs. In these cases, a considerable amount of market research may be necessary to make the design features more specific and to persuade managers of the value of the new product. Recall from Chapter 5 that organizations are often reluctant to take chances on new product concepts that may be significantly different from current organizational formulas for success.

The creation of Courtyard by Marriott, described in the second story, epitomizes a well-researched concept development and evaluation process. Sophisticated marketing research approaches were used by acknowledged experts in the field. They carefully measured consumer preferences to specify design features, estimated cannibalization of the company's other business, and placed a financial value on the entire effort that could be used as the basis for decision making. Such effort was justified by the organizational difficulties of betting the Marriott name, associated with upscale business hotels, on a relatively new line of less expensive hotels.

As a new product concept becomes more specific and more research is done on it, the risk of losing creativity in the design process increases. Maintaining creativity is essential to ensure that the benefits identified through research are embodied in the product and communicated effectively to potential buyers. The third story in this chapter tells how Lever Brothers used careful research on the bar soap market to identify what benefits were wanted most in a new bar soap by a large and growing segment of consumers. They wanted softer skin (moisturizing), they wanted to prevent body odor (deodorizing), and they wanted clean and healthy skin (antibacterial efficacy), all by means of one soap—a product that did not yet exist!

Lever's research and development took about two years to combine these benefits in one effective bar soap, benefits that previously could be found only in separate products. The company then took another two years to test market the new product and solve problems in its distribution and marketing. During that time, Lever managers became focused on the major technology breakthrough they had achieved with the new soap and based their positioning and communication strategies on the image of the year 2000 to represent their progressive new product. However, the advertising agency resisted and effectively argued that an emphasis on "human touch," the "family," and "2,000 body parts" would be more effective. Both ideas were used creatively to communicate the new product to consumers.

MCI Communications Corporation: Friends and Family

Jennifer L. Givens and James Kyle Lynch

*When you meet your friend on the roadside or in the market place, let
the spirit in you move your lips and direct your tongue
Let the voice within your voice speak to the ear of his ear;
For his soul will keep the truth of your heart as the taste of the wine is
remembered
When the colour is forgotten and the vessel is no more.*

Kahlil Gibran, The Prophet, *"On Talking,"* 1923

MCI Communications Corporation created the idea for a new residential
long distance service in January 1991. Through a rapid new product development process, this new service, called "Friends and Family," was designed and launched by March 18 of the same year. The new service was
so successful that in 18 months after launch, more than eight million
customers subscribed. By January 1993, the service had 10 million subscribers.[1] Seventy-six percent of Americans were aware of Friends and
Family, an awareness level higher than that of MCI itself![2]

MCI's Friends and Family was launched as a special long distance service offering a 20 percent discount on calls made by MCI customers to other
MCI customers in their "circle" of up to 20 friends and family members.
Customers also receive the discount on their own number and one international number. The Friends and Family discounts are calculated at corporate headquarters, then the bills are sent to local telephone companies

for printing and mailing.[3] Friends and Family customers receive one simple bill that shows clearly which calls are discounted and the total monthly savings.

A person who subscribes to Friends and Family first starts a calling circle by giving MCI an initial list of circle members' names, addresses, telephone numbers, and relationships. MCI then contacts the individuals listed and invites them to participate in Friends and Family. The subscriber starts saving 20 percent on calls to a circle member as soon as that person joins Friends and Family. If that person is already an MCI customer, the subscriber begins saving immediately. Circle members also save 20 percent when they call the subscriber. Finally, MCI offers to establish a circle for each circle member.

The subscriber can continue to build the circle, adding new members at any time, and can call 1-800-FRIENDS to ask questions about the circle. MCI also sends updates by mail. The subscriber can let MCI know if a circle member moves. The subscriber incurs no cost in starting the program and has the opportunity to talk longer with family and friends without spending more money.[4] The story of how this highly successful new product concept was designed and implemented begins with the business environment in which MCI was operating.

THE BUSINESS ENVIRONMENT

Before the historic legal decision to break up the Bell System in 1982, the long distance telephone business was a monopoly dominated by AT&T. The outcome of a lawsuit brought by MCI was that consumers gained the right to choose a long distance carrier. Subsequently, the long distance telephone market became increasingly attractive, with growth rates in the teens and an estimated $65 billion in total revenue by 1993.[5]

About 46 percent of the long distance market was basic long distance service, with most growth coming from other long distance services such as 800 and 900 numbers.[6] By 1990 the industry had sifted out many upstarts, and three companies dominated: AT&T, the incumbent, held about two-thirds of the market, MCI held about 13 percent, and Sprint and other companies held the rest.

Prior to the introduction of Friends and Family, each competitor positioned its product differently. AT&T was the market leader and industry giant, and spent 10 times what MCI spent to position its service as the reliable choice. AT&T hoped people would pay a premium for its perceived superiority. Sprint positioned its service as the leader in fiber-optic technology, implying that Sprint's long distance reception was clearer than MCI's or AT&T's. Sprint ads showed people "hearing a pin drop" over the phone. MCI positioned itself as the low cost leader.

The importance of information technology increased in the industry in the 1980s. Each competitor was trying to gain an edge with computers. They used the following strategies:[7]

- AT&T spent heavily to pull together the variety of computerized billing and service systems that had been used before the Bell System breakup in 1984.
- MCI spent more than $300 million to upgrade its computer systems to provide flexibility and innovation in residential calling services.
- Sprint installed a new billing system that was a great improvement, but the version for large customers was repeatedly postponed.

The race for technology improvement in the 1980s was necessary to cope with growth, but it also set the stage for the development of new customer services that would become the basis for future battles for market share.

MCI—The Company

In 1990, MCI provided a full range of services to almost all segments of the telecommunication industry in the United States and internationally. The company was publicly traded and, despite a recession and increased competitive pressures, was financially successful. Company revenues were $7.68 billion in 1990, up 19 percent from 1989, but earnings per share had dropped after a three-year increase.[8] Achieving profitable market share growth against a large, well-funded competitor (AT&T) would be an uphill battle.

MCI's competitive advantage was its youthful, entrepreneurial corporate culture in addition to its advanced computer system. MCI's relative newness in the industry enabled the company to avoid organizational blocks and respond quickly to consumer needs and technological developments. However, the company had difficulty persuading customers that its newness was an advantage, and MCI's cost leader strategy proved difficult against Sprint and AT&T, both adroit competitors. A low price strategy has limitations among consumers who might perceive quality as an important purchase criterion. Consequently, MCI hoped that its bold investment in advanced billing and database information technology would provide a technology platform for the development of a variety of new services that other carriers could not easily or quickly match.[9]

The Customer

Beginning in the 1960s and 1970s, contemporary American society became increasingly mobile as people sought better climates and living conditions and better employment opportunities. Increasing numbers of young people left home for out-of-state colleges and often took jobs in distant cities. People who lived on farms and in rural communities began to move to cities as family farming gave way to large and concentrated agribusiness. People found themselves far from family and friends, but still had a basic human need for a sense of belonging. Calling long distance became an increasingly popular way to keep in touch with friends and family members.

To meet the needs of residential consumers, long distance companies had to offer good customer service, convenience, flexibility, reliability, and low cost. Consumers wanted clear, instantaneous transmission and 24-hour operator service to address problems. They also wanted the convenience of collect calling, third-party calling, person-to-person calling, and easy-to-understand billing.

The flexibility to call whoever, whenever, wherever, and however without restriction came to be expected by most consumers (whatever technological difficulties may be involved), almost as a right. Americans have grown accustomed to having such service whenever they pick up the phone and at a reasonable cost. Most residential consumers have a finite budget and they enjoy the feeling of getting a bargain.

Although the competitors positioned their products differently, they offered the same basic service of efficiently connecting two parties over long distance. By 1990, long distance carriers had dramatically increased advertising to gain market share.[10] Some residential customers began to see long distance service as a commodity and switched to low priced MCI. Others were concerned about reliability and were reluctant to switch from tried-and-true AT&T service.

THE DEVELOPMENT OF FRIENDS AND FAMILY

MCI's aggressive move into the residential market began in 1990 with the establishment of a consumer markets division. This action had been strategically planned for some time, but required intensive capital investment in technology and infrastructure to ensure a strong platform for development. Coincidentally, pressure for performance had been mounting from Wall Street and from an increasingly hostile competitive environment. Mud-slinging advertising wars in the late 1980s had done little to improve market share, but a lot to damage bottom lines.

As a publicly traded company, MCI had an urgent need to shore up revenues and earnings. Lowering price further and/or escalating the advertising war would not accomplish that goal. New products and services clearly held the most promise for improving financial results if they could be developed and launched in a timely way.

The Friends and Family Idea

Early in 1991, the marketing team was behind schedule in developing new products. They had begun generating ideas for 1991 products in January. The preliminary idea for Friends and Family was conceived by the end of the month. The original idea was simply to offer residential consumers some type of savings plan for 1991. The marketing team envisioned a plan called "MCI to MCI" that would give customers savings on calls to three other MCI customers. Customers would pay a five-dollar annual fee for the savings.

An independent consultant suggested modifications to the plan and it eventually evolved into Friends and Family. The brilliance of Friends and Family was that it not only offered current customers a discount, but also enabled MCI to expand its customer base. Rather than asking customers for the names of other customers, MCI offered to contact all of their friends and family members. Each new Friends and Family customer generated up to 12 new leads for MCI.

Internally, the project was kept secret and was given the code name "Gemini." Employees were forbidden to use the Friends and Family name. The intention was to catch AT&T by surprise in the market. Because MCI wanted to launch early in the year, it had no time for test markets or prototypes. In February the company placed "teaser" ads to alert people that something new was on the way. Tara Clyne, an MCI marketing manager, described the process:

> We had teaser ads on TV February 15, we didn't even know how it worked but we wanted to get ads out there fast. We didn't even have a system in place to do it. We had no order system. We had nothing, but we wanted it on

TV saying "Coming Soon Coming Soon." We didn't give any details because we didn't know what any of the details were.[11]

Thus, the marketing team believed so strongly in the new service that they were willing to begin teaser ads for it within two weeks of hatching the idea and to launch the service on March 15, a month later!

Part of the reason for their confidence in the new concept was its foundation on solid assumptions about human behavior. The system would make staying close to family and friends easy and economical. Not only would the original customer save 20 percent, but that person's friends and family members would also receive the discount when they called that customer. The cost savings would enable people to talk longer and the reciprocal savings would enable people to feel good about the program.

Setting Up Cross-Functional Teams

Bringing the new service idea to life in the consumer's mind required parallel efforts in marketing and systems development. Therefore, Friends and Family "launch centers" were established for each of those two major areas. Each team consisted of employees from the marketing, sales, software development, billing, and telemarketing departments. For the six weeks prior to launch, the two teams held meetings at the end of each day to draw up massive lists of things to be done and to prioritize work assignments. In addition, MCI had to work closely with the Bell companies that would be integrating the Friends and Family billing into their statements.

MCI empowered the launch teams by giving them full autonomy. Only decisions that would radically change the product or its billing structure had to be passed up to higher managers. No such modifications were made. The cross-functional team approach was crucial to the six-week development time. People "lived" in the launch centers for six weeks, but they got the product out and AT&T had no time to prepare a counterattack.[12]

Integrating the New Service within the Organization

For Friends and Family to be launched in such a short time required many areas of the company to work closely and efficiently together. The billing system necessitated a complete overhaul of MCI's computer system. The hardware was in place, but most of the software for Friends and Family had to be created. Further, the telemarketers had to adapt their selling techniques to the new product. Privacy issues were at stake and the company had to refine its sales message to ensure that the product's image was not tarnished from the start. For example, telemarketers are careful *not* to say things like "we will *get* your friends and family to join." MCI asked customers to *nominate* family and friends, whom MCI would call and *invite* to join on the customer's behalf.

Product Testing—The One-Day Test!

Once MCI knew its computer system would correctly calculate the Friends and Family discounts, it believed the launch could continue even though the entire billing system was not yet in place. The company did not test the system with customers, but simulated the computations on its computers one day before the launch. Just before the launch MCI also tested and modified the telemarketing scripts. Once ads went out announcing the new service, the telemarketers had to be prepared for handling the calls.

Launch and Timing

The Friends and Family team launched the new service with an intensive media effort involving network television, direct mail, and billboard advertising. After the teaser ads in February, the company began describing the program on network TV on March 1.[13] Initially Friends and Family was launched with a "nostalgic" campaign that focused on staying close with friends and family. MCI provided an 800 number to call for details about the program. At that time, 19 days before the formal launch, MCI had a basic idea of what the product would be but was still working on the necessary software.

The telemarketing campaign was implemented as responses were received. MCI still had no way for telemarketers to access the database directly. Names of subscribers and their circles were taken down by hand, sometimes on scraps of paper. Then they were faxed each evening to the computer programmers to be uploaded into the system.[14]

Finally, MCI used an intensive direct mail campaign to explain the new program. Within two weeks, regardless of whether they signed up through the 800 number or by mail, subscribers received a mail update on the status of their calling circle. Eight weeks after the initial signup, subscribers received a final status report of their circle. Because of its national database capability, MCI was able to give each new subscriber a personalized list and explanation of the family members and friends who had joined, and those who had declined to join, the circle.

MCI spent more than $30 million on network advertising to launch Friends and Family.[15] The general time pressures on the launch and the official March 18, 1991, launch date were driven by financial and competitive concerns. The goal was to get the basic product out as quickly as possible, assess response, and then spend the rest of the year refining both the system and the product. An aggressive launch eliminated the need for continued project secrecy, would catch AT&T off guard, and would define a new level of competition in the market.

In-Market Refinement of Friends and Family

At the outset, the Friends and Family service launched in March was planned to be a basic product for which refinements and add-on products would follow. A Friends and Family calling card was offered soon after the launch, an 800 number service was included in August 1991, and international calling was offered in November 1991.[16] These additional services addressed consumer needs other than price. Also, managers discovered that some customers' circles were filled, so the original 12-member circles were expanded to 20 in January 1992. These "add-ons" sustained customers' feeling that they were getting a bargain and continued the excitement. For example, the company's Friends and Family "Free Speech" promotion announced in May 1992 gave 10 minutes of free long distance calling a month to one designated person in the calling circle.

In addition, MCI changed the telemarketing approach to Friends and Family. After the launch, MCI found that people gave information about relatives much more freely than information about friends. Perhaps consumers thought relatives would be tolerant and would accept them no matter what they did, but did not want to offend their friends. Tara Clyne says:

> We [now] have a special group of telemarketers that only call family members . . . family is the highest close rate, the easiest sale. Friends are a little bit tougher and require a little different scripting. It is working better that way now that we have split it up.[17]

Customers readily accepted the new promotions and new add-on services. Both approaches helped to generate new customers and to retain current customers.

Just as MCI used its advanced billing and database capabilities as a platform to launch Friends and Family, it used the success of Friends and Family as a platform to launch Friends of the Firm, which offers similar billing and cost advantages to small businesses.

THE SUCCESS OF FRIENDS AND FAMILY

The launch of Friends and Family was not without risk. To the investment world, the enormous advertising and marketing expenditures on a virtually untested new service idea may have seemed foolhardy. According to MCI chairman and CEO Bert C. Roberts, "We had a difficult time, especially in the beginning. . . . It was a real balancing act, but we stuck to our game plan and we proved that advertising translated directly into results."[18] Although determining whether market share changes were directly associated with the new program was difficult during the initial months after launch, AT&T's reaction suggested that the program was going to be a success.

Rather than responding with its own new product (which would have been difficult), AT&T countered with negative advertising. It claimed that Friends and Family savings were not substantial; however, consumers did perceive 20 percent to be a significant saving. Even AT&T's large cash incentives (up to $75) for anyone who had joined MCI but wanted to return could not slow the exodus to Friends and Family.

AT&T also mounted a privacy-based ad campaign showing people upset as MCI's telemarketers hassled them to switch. In the ads, the solicited individuals accused their family and friends of inflicting unwanted sales calls on them. With its powerful advertising budget, AT&T drew widespread attention to the privacy issue among consumers, making it difficult for MCI's telemarketers to offer a rebuttal. (Even in 1994, three years after the launch, AT&T was running television ads showing an MCI sales caller interrupting a wedding!) However, because MCI followed a strict protocol in its practices, which it believed did not compromise privacy, the telemarketers could handle the situation on a one-customer-at-a-time basis. To AT&T's dismay, MCI's market share and database continued to grow.

At the six-month mark, market share improvements could be traced to the new program. In 1991, MCI gained in revenue (9.8 percent increase), customers (market share up to 17 percent), and traffic (up 15 percent) from 1990 levels as people joined the new service.[19] MCI has acquired a large database of customers and prospective customers, which it uses with the incentive of the 20 percent discount to entice people to switch from AT&T. The company now has customer information that competitors do not have. In addition to being an effective tool for MCI's telemarketers, this database can be used to market future MCI services. Finally, the sheer innovativeness of the new service won many industry awards for MCI.

WHY WAS THE NEW SERVICE SUCCESSFUL?

MCI's Friends and Family was successful for many reasons, but three stand out: swift concept execution, product design with an attacker's advantage, and a novel product concept that subtly fit an array of consumer needs.

Swift Concept Execution

The ability to proceed from an idea to a multimillion-dollar new product launch in six weeks with no formal concept testing procedures suggests a highly flexible organizational structure and a culture that clearly supports risk taking and creativity. As Roberts indicates, "The MCI culture dictated by Mr. [William] McGowan [MCI's founder] is that you never assume you can't do something. Just because no one's doing it doesn't mean it can't be done."[20] Such an attitude, coupled with an emphasis on teamwork and delegation of responsibility, enables an organization to move quickly in response to new product ideas, market needs, or competitive actions.

Quickness of response was part of MCI's culture, but the company had been *planning* for an aggressive consumer marketing program with new product development as the main driver. This program required a flexible computer and network technology to track and bill calls and otherwise deliver the promised services. Without long-range planning for new technology, the Friends and Family concept would not have been possible.

MCI's Attacker Advantage

When facing a well-entrenched and dominant competitor that has significant resources, a smaller competitor must learn how to attack effectively or struggle for life. MCI, with a competitive positioning based on low price, was at a disadvantage in a long, slow advertising war with a powerful competitor. All but a relatively small segment of highly price-sensitive consumers were reluctant to switch from their current telephone service provider.

Heavy advertising and low prices could not lead to profitability without rapid growth in the subscriber base. Success came with the simple yet effective design of Friends and Family, which gave MCI a devastating competitive advantage. AT&T found it very difficult to respond with a competitive service because of its large market share (still 60 percent even after the Friends and Family market entry). Even if AT&T had equivalent flexible technology, offering a 20 percent discount on its calls would not increase its new customers (or prevent loss of current ones) enough to offset the loss in revenue! MCI had much more to gain than to lose relative to AT&T in taking the risk with its new service.

MCI's technology investment also provided a competitive advantage over AT&T in terms of a national billing capability that AT&T did not have. AT&T still depended on the local telephone companies to calculate, print, and send its bills. Moreover, MCI was able to solicit new customers more successfully by using the information acquired from the calling circles. While AT&T and U.S. Sprint were making cold calls, MCI could call "on behalf of your family and friends." The closing rate of Friends and Family calls was three times greater than that of cold calls, and MCI's customer base increased rapidly.

Novel Product Design for Consumer Needs

The novel aspect of the new service was the way in which its design capitalized on an array of interactive consumer needs. First, the service was clear and easy for potential subscribers to understand, and telemarketing afforded convenience in obtaining information and signing up. Second, the service appealed directly to consumers' need to economize. Low cost alone, however, was not enough to encourage switching from AT&T. Linking the 20 percent discount to social needs based on interpersonal relationships (friends and family) created a snowball effect that rapidly increased the number of subscribers.

Third, and perhaps most important, although the 20 percent discount was a prime motivator, some of the risk of switching from AT&T or Sprint was alleviated by the social aspect of the service design. That is, the risk of switching from AT&T could be shared among friends and family if something went wrong. The worst that could happen would be that circle members would return to AT&T if they did not like the service (even before knowing that AT&T would eventually offer cash incentives for them to return). Individuals could feel confident about trying MCI because their social network was also involved.

Finally, once a network of social relationships was established, subscribers were reluctant to switch to another carrier because everyone with whom a subscriber communicated would also lose their discounts on calls to the subscriber. Thus, the design of the service reinforces membership and makes it difficult for someone to switch. AT&T's difficulty in winning people back, even with cash incentives, is a testimony to the effectiveness of the service design.

CONCLUSION

The development of Friends and Family in six weeks (from idea to launch) positioned MCI as an aggressive and credible leader in the long distance telephone market. It also changed the strategy in that highly competitive business from reliance on advertising and price to new product development. MCI's entrepreneurial organization, with its cross-functional teams, proved that its new product development process was sufficiently flexible to give it a strong competitive advantage. Its subsequent launch of Friends and Family II and the first discount collect calling service (1-800-COLLECT) showed that it was not going to cede any ground to AT&T, but would maintain an aggressive posture through new product development.

As MCI's customer base grows, its challenge will be to keep the computer network flexible for continued support of innovative product extensions and improvements. Further, as MCI's share grows, AT&T will eventually find it profitable to respond with its own aggressive discounting program that could make MCI's program less profitable. In any case, the historic legal decision to open the long distance telephone market to competition has certainly led to lower long distance telephone costs and has provided a new way for friends and family to bond together.

Marriott International Inc.: Courtyard by Marriott

Thomas A. Rogers and Bradley Tirpak

Whoe'er has travel'd life's dull round,
Whate'er his various tour has been,
May sigh to think how oft he found
His warmest welcome at an inn.

> William Shenstone (1714–1763),
> written on a window at an inn at Henley.

In 1983, Marriott unveiled a moderately priced hotel chain called Courtyard by Marriott (Courtyard). Since then, Marriott has opened more than 200 Courtyard hotels, and the chain's occupancy rates have easily exceeded the industry average for the moderate price segment. Courtyard's financial success has been coupled with high customer satisfaction and top ratings from travel magazines. However, the possibility that launching a moderately priced hotel concept under the Marriott name could threaten the upscale image of traditional Marriott hotels had caused considerable concern within the organization.

From the early 1960s through the early 1980s, Marriott Corporation's earnings grew an average of 20 percent a year as its lodging and food service businesses expanded.[21] By 1980, though, senior managers in the planning department of the company's hotel division foresaw problems in maintaining this growth level. Marriott's full-service, upscale hotels were drawing increased competition from such companies as Holiday Inn.

Likewise, the planning department realized that the market for large urban hotels would reach saturation by the mid-1980s, leaving few desirable locations for new Marriott hotels.[22] In short, Marriott would soon run out of places to build its traditional hotels.

Bill Marriott, the chief executive officer, and Frederick Malek, the executive vice-president of Marriott Hotels, believed that the company would have to search for new products or services that would enable it to maintain its goal of a 20 percent annual sales growth rate. "We've got to leverage our name," said Marriott back in 1984, "We've got a good name going."[23] Choosing not to diversify out of the hospitality industry, the Marriott Corporation decided to stick to what it did best: building and managing hotels.

However, Marriott was unaccustomed to developing new hotel concepts. Since the opening of its first motel in Arlington, Virginia, in 1957, the core concept of a Marriott hotel had gradually evolved. By 1980, "Marriott" meant a 350-room, full-service, high quality hotel located either downtown or near an airport. The changes since 1957 had been incremental and opportunistic, with Marriott gradually increasing its hotels' size, quality, and amenities. During those years, the company had little formal customer-driven focus, but rather relied on its expertise in operations for its business.[24] Courtyard would mark a new approach.

DEVELOPMENT OF COURTYARD

Being unfamiliar with formal new product development processes, the company may have been tempted to put its name on a hastily created, scaled-down, limited-service version of its upscale hotels. Instead, Marriott chose to design a hotel from scratch by undertaking a methodical customer-based research and development approach similar to that used by consumer products companies. The project began in 1980 and followed a rigid, sequential design process to uncover the attributes customers wanted and were willing to pay for in a midprice hotel. Development and test marketing cost more than $2 million and took almost five years to complete.

The Development Team

The first step of the process was the creation of a small cross-functional team to oversee and champion the project. The team consisted of six people with expertise in such areas as marketing research, strategic planning, and finance:[25]

- Don Washburn, vice-president of planning for the Marriott Hotels division, was instrumental in selling the concept within Marriott.
- Tom Curren, senior vice-president of planning for Marriott Corporation, along with Washburn, was the other true champion of the project.
- Jim Durbin, president of the Marriott Hotels division, was less directly involved with the details of the development and more involved in providing advice on broader issues.
- Bruce Robertson, finance director for the Marriott Hotels division, did all the financial calculations for the project.
- Doug Shifflet, vice-president of marketing research for the Marriott Corporation, directed all marketing research and worked closely with outside marketing research firms.
- Marsha Scarbrough, manager of marketing research for the Marriott Corporation, managed the marketing research for the project.

Washburn, Curren, and Robertson dedicated all of their time to the project, and Shifflet and Scarbrough were able to devote more than 80 percent of their time to it. Durbin spent less time in his oversight role.

Market Opportunity Analysis

The team's first task was to analyze the industry and the competition. At the time Marriott estimated that moderately priced rooms (about $35 to $60) represented approximately 45 percent of all U.S. hotel rooms. The main competitors were the Holiday Inn, Ramada Inn, and Howard Johnson chains. These chains generally received low marks for customer satisfaction because they operated older, franchised facilities that were not providing consistent service at all locations. Convinced of the opportunity in this part of the lodging market, the team focused on creating a midprice hotel concept. The next step was to analyze consumers and segment the market.

Focus Groups and the Segmentation Study

In 1980, Marriott conducted 20 focus groups to learn about buyer behavior and undertook a segmentation study to identify different types of customers. This research alone lasted one year and cost $300,000. The segmentation study revealed two types of travelers who were not being served well by midprice lodgings in the United States: "security seekers" and "functional roomers." The security seekers wanted well-lit hallways, safe entrances, secure rooms, and fire safety features. Functional roomers were looking for rooms suitable for both lodging and business. They wanted stand-alone desks, alarm clocks, and functional telephones. In essence, they wanted a room in which they would not have to sit on the bed to work, read, or even view TV.[26]

Measuring Preferences: Conjoint Analysis[27]

From the focus groups, the researchers identified seven major "facets" of a hotel, other than price, that affect a traveler's purchase decision: external surroundings, room, food, lounge, services, leisure activities, and security. Within these facets, 50 specific attributes of a hotel were represented, each with multiple levels. For example, the service facet had 12 attributes, one of which was "reservations," which had two levels, "call the hotel directly" and "call an 800 reservation number." A new hotel concept could be designed as a profile along the 50 attributes, and consumer preferences for the new hotel could be obtained.

Because of the enormous number of possible concepts that could be tested, hybrid conjoint analysis was used. This approach breaks the preference measurement problem into a series of data collection subtasks, and the analysis provides estimates of each respondent's "utility function" for the attributes. These individual utility values can then be used in additional analyses for purposes of market segmentation, choice simulations, and product optimization.[28]

To implement the preference measurement approach, a marketing research firm conducted a survey of 601 travelers. Respondents were contacted randomly, screened, and invited to central interviewing facilities in three major cities. The following major data collection tasks were the basis for hybrid conjoint analysis.

- The researchers gave every participant a fictional $35 with which to "build" a hotel. Each participant was given seven cards, one at a time, for each facet. On each card were all the attributes and levels used to describe that facet, along with a dollar amount for each level (Marriott's cost accounting department had allocated relative prices for each feature on a card). The participants read the cards and selected the specific features they wanted in a hotel. A participant who selected too many features and went over the $35 budget had to eliminate some features or choose ones that were less expensive.

Thus, participants were forced to make realistic tradeoffs. Other preference measures were also taken, including the attributes and levels that characterized the participant's current hotel, its acceptability on each level, and the ranked importance of each attribute.

- Participants then were asked for their preferences for 50 "complete" hotel offerings. Hotel profiles were created by systematic selection of all possible combinations of concepts from the seven facets, each with five levels. The levels were selected by the Marriott new product development team. By accepted experiment-design techniques, the subset of 50 profiles was selected from all possible hotel concepts to reduce bias, yet allow estimation of utilities for each facet and level. The researchers gave participants five cards, each of which represented one of the 50 concepts. The participants indicated their likelihood of staying in each of the hotels.

- Data for another conjoint analysis were collected specifically on room design. Participants in this study were asked to rank the various room designs on the basis of such factors as room size, decor, heating and cooling, bathroom size, bathroom features, and other amenities.

The results of these conjoint analyses would help managers determine what mix of features would best meet travelers' needs. For example, if a certain new hotel concept were offered against competing concepts, what share of choices would the new one receive? Clearly, with assumptions about how travelers make their choices (such as maximizing their utility), managers could use a computer search to find the hotel concept (and all its features) that produced the greatest share of choices.

Other Research: Price, Location, Name, and Positioning

The researchers used other data collection procedures and models to test the price elasticities of various hotel concepts. Respondents were given five cards describing the hotels in terms of features and price. Each card listed four present hotels and two new hotel concepts, and the participants were asked how likely they were to stay at each hotel at the given price. From this model, the researchers learned the expected market share for each of the concepts tested. This information enabled Marriott to judge which combination of price and features would fare best against its competitors.

Optimal locations for the hotel were determined by asking participants to allocate 100 points among a set of locations. The locations were defined in terms of closeness to business, shopping, sightseeing, nightlife, theaters, airport, and highways. Marriott also tested possible hotel names, and respondents selected "Courtyard by Marriott" over 10 other choices.

To help with the positioning of the new hotel, the marketing researchers recorded participants' reactions to a variety of statements, such as "gives a complete break from the usual routine" or "gives a safe and secure feeling." Also, participants were asked their impressions of such descriptions such as "a casual feeling in a hotel with understated elegance" and "a good, no frills, basic hotel." From this research, Marriott chose the positioning statement: "A special little hotel at a very comfortable price."[29]

Refining the Core Product Concept

Using the results of the research, the project team developed a core concept for the product by the middle of 1981. The hotel would be relatively small, about 150 rooms, and would provide limited service. Amenities such as a doorman and room service would not be provided. Similarly, the hotel's restaurant and lounge would seat only 100 customers and would serve a limited menu. The design of the hotel would incorporate the residential features of a garden apartment complex: low buildings, well-landscaped exteriors, small meeting rooms, and no large lobby.

Security features were also incorporated in Courtyard's concept. An enclosed courtyard, which was central in the design of the hotels, would shield the pool and outdoor public area from the outside world. Improved door locks and limited, key-only entry into the hotel after 11:00 P.M. would increase the sense of security. To make individual rooms functional, the concept included such features as a large free-standing desk, a king-size bed, an AM/FM radio alarm clock, and a separate seating area with a couch.[30]

In addition, rooms would be slightly larger than those of competing lodgings but would cost less. Rates were set between $40 to $60 a night, depending on whether a customer wanted a single room, double room, or suite. Courtyard would be able to offer this low price because the research indicated that Marriott could reduce costs by limiting the service and public space that price-sensitive travelers did not want. Finally, the hotels would be built in suburban areas, near business parks if possible, to attract business travelers and limit competition with other Marriott hotels.

In short, the concept was designed to deliver the core benefits of value, functionality, and security that the "functional roomers" and "security seekers" sought from a midprice hotel.

Prototype

Early in 1982, Marriott constructed a prototype room with three possible designs at its hotel in Gaithersburg, Maryland. The prototype had moveable walls that were used to test several hundred customers' opinions on room layout and size. The study found that people did not mind rooms that were smaller than the intended design, as long as the rooms were shorter and not narrower. That discovery enabled Marriott to decrease the depth of the rooms, which was expected to save the company $80,000 in construction costs on each hotel.[31]

Test Market

Marriott chose Atlanta, Georgia, as its test market and opened its first Courtyard there in October 1983. The project team picked Atlanta as the test market for the following reasons.[32]

- Atlanta was demographically favorable because it attracted many business travelers.
- Marriott had four hotels in Atlanta, so cannibalization of sales could be measured.
- Atlanta had plenty of Holiday Inns and Ramada Inns for Courtyard to compete against.
- Construction could begin soon, because building permits and zoning approvals were easily attainable in Atlanta.
- Atlanta was far enough away from corporate headquarters to prevent daily interference.

The results of the test market were favorable. Occupancy rates during the first six months were 90 percent, and research found no signs of cannibalization of other Marriott properties. Courtyard received high marks from guests, even when compared with higher priced competitors. The test market lasted two years and eventually included five Courtyard hotels. Over that period, occupancy rates exceeded 85 percent. Feedback from the test market led to a few changes in room design prior to launch: rooms were made a bit smaller and closet doors were installed.[33] The price and the core features were left unchanged.

THE LAUNCH OF COURTYARD

Encouraged by the test market results, Marriott began a nationwide launch at the end of 1985, with the goal of opening 30 to 40 new Courtyards a year into the 1990s. Initially, hotels were constructed in seven major and seven secondary markets.

The marketing program for the launch relied heavily on public relations and direct mail. Limited use was made of billboards and newspaper advertisements. The direct mail campaign targeted business travelers, with the belief that those lead users would try Courtyard and create positive word-of-mouth advertising. The limited advertising that supported the launch reinforced the messages of the direct mail campaign. Print advertisements touted Courtyard as "A Hotel You'll Be Proud To Recommend," and listed residential and functional features of the basic Courtyard concept.

Courtyard hotels were built in clusters (i.e., eight to 10 Courtyards in a metropolitan area) with a centralized local office responsible for accounting, reservations, and other administrative tasks. This cost-cutting measure later became unnecessary as improvements in personal computers allowed more administrative tasks to be performed at corporate headquarters in Bethesda, Maryland.[34]

ORGANIZATIONAL ISSUES IN THE DEVELOPMENT OF COURTYARD

As might be expected, skepticism and resistance arose within the Marriott organization toward the idea of a midprice hotel bearing the Marriott name. The company had fought since 1957 to build an image of high quality, full-service hotels. Some managers feared that attaching the Marriott name to a moderately priced hotel would do irreparable damage to that image. Image management was indeed an important corporate strategic issue.

Courtyard overcame the resistance because of a strong product champion who had the full support of the CEO.[35] In addition, the thoroughness and soundness of the research gave the project team sufficient evidence to sell the concept effectively to the doubters within the company. The team did not simply create an inexpensive brand extension; instead, it went to great lengths to design a hotel concept that would be moderately priced *and* maintain the high level of quality expected of a Marriott property.

A good example of the kind of internal selling that was done by the product champion occurred when Don Washburn flew out to Marriott's Camelback resort in Arizona. There he spent a week with the company's founder, the elder J. W. Marriott, explaining and touting the Courtyard concept and reassuring him that the Marriott brand name would not be tarnished.

Likewise, prior to the test market, Washburn and Bill Marriott flew to Atlanta to attend a luncheon for all of the local Marriott hotel managers. Their intent was to create enthusiasm for Courtyard and to allay some of the concerns of managers who worried that Courtyard would hurt their own revenues. At this luncheon, Washburn explained the Courtyard concept, answered questions, and reassured the regional managers that little cannibalization was expected.[36]

In fact, the fear of cannibalization was a major cause of resistance, because many managers thought Courtyard would compete with the Marriott Hotels. Here again, the thoroughness of the marketing research helped the project overcome organizational resistance. Because the research involved simulations that specifically measured cannibalization and found it to be low, the team had hard evidence that the Courtyard concept was distinct enough to draw a different set of travelers than the typical Marriott hotel.[37]

To help manage the organizational issues, a separate administrative division was formed when Courtyard was launched nationally. As the division grew, its management positions were filled with employees from the Marriott Hotels division. Marriott, a company with a tradition of promoting from within, also took the rare step of hiring some outsiders to help manage the division. The culture at Courtyard was less policy driven than that at Marriott Hotels; a more "hands-on" approach was expected.

According to Craig Lambert, Courtyard's vice-president of marketing, many longtime Marriott Hotels employees who came to Courtyard in its early days had difficulty adjusting to its culture, and they often transferred back to the Marriott Hotels division. Those who were able to succeed at Courtyard were the "quasi-mavericks" and the newer employees who were not firmly entrenched in the traditional Marriott Hotels way of doing things. In fact, Lambert stated that Courtyard "sought people who enjoyed being different."[38]

THE CONTINUING COURTYARD SUCCESS

Courtyard was well received by travelers. Since its launch in 1986, Courtyard has scored high in customer satisfaction surveys. Furthermore,

Courtyard has been rated the top moderately priced hotel by *Zagat U.S. Travel Guide* and *Business Travel News*.

One of the best measures of financial success in the lodging industry is a hotel's occupancy rate. According to Lambert, the breakeven occupancy rate for a Courtyard hotel was about 65 percent.[39] Since its introduction in 1983, the Courtyard chain has surpassed this breakeven point, averaging occupancy rates above 70 percent. Likewise, Courtyard's occupancy rates have always been well above the industry average for limited-service, upper class hotels. The absolute magnitude of the success is shown by Courtyard's 1991 revenue of almost $457 million.

Courtyard's success was one reason Marriott was able to maintain high sales growth in the late 1980s. In 1984, Marriott operated 147 hotels with close to 66,000 rooms, and its lodging revenue was $1.6 billion.[40] From 1986 to 1991, Marriott opened 185 Courtyards, adding more than 27,000 rooms to the Marriott portfolio. More important, Courtyard was the first step in Marriott's strategy to segment the lodging industry. By 1991, Marriott was operating 698 properties in various segments and its lodging revenue was almost $4.4 billion.[41]

The Successful Role of Market Research

The market-research-driven development process was also a success in terms of hotel design. Since 1986, no "core" changes have been made to the Courtyard concept. The only changes have been subtle, such as the mix of rooms. For example, to attract more weekend pleasure travelers, Courtyard now offers more rooms with double beds instead of king-size beds. Also, Courtyard has taken further steps to customize its hotels for business travelers, adding such amenities as facsimile machines, modems, and voice mail. The chain's 1992 advertising implied the role of market research with its message: "Courtyard: the hotel designed by business travelers."

The modifications were based on information gathered through customer research. Marriott has taken customer satisfaction surveys continuously since 1984. In addition, every several years Courtyard does broader surveys on the image of the Courtyard brand and its overall position. An example of one of these "pulse checks" is the conjoint analysis Courtyard did in 1989, which confirmed that Courtyard's core concept and features were still consistent with customers' needs.[42] Courtyard spent between $500,000 and $1 million a year on such research throughout the middle and late 1980s.[43]

Success in Leading the Competition

The Holiday Inn, Ramada Inn, and Howard Johnson lodging chains initially reacted to Courtyard by renovating their moderately priced facilities, many of which were 20 to 30 years old. These competitors also reduced their room rates to make them more in line with Courtyard's. Nevertheless, Courtyard continued to gain share in the midprice market. Only after the success of Courtyard was apparent did other chains attempt to duplicate the Courtyard concept. A prime example is Holiday Inn's midprice, limited-service Holiday Inn Express. Nevertheless, Marriott's first-strike advantage proved to be a lasting one.

Success with Courtyard Spinoff Projects

The development of Fairfield Inn followed the Courtyard project. The hotel division's planning department assembled a Fairfield project team and took advantage of the lessons learned from the Courtyard project, duplicating the steps used to design a new lodging concept. Partly because it was able to use the "core piece of research" gained from the development of Courtyard, the project team developed the Fairfield Inn concept in less than two years. Test marketing began in 1987 and Marriott launched the concept in 1988. By 1991, 93 Fairfield Inns were in operation.[44]

CONCLUSIONS

In 1980, Marriott had been in the hotel business 23 years, yet it had the foresight not to assume that it knew what travelers really wanted in moderately priced lodgings. The Courtyard by Marriott concept was successful because Marriott went to consumers and asked them to define their needs and decide which lodging features met them best. This approach was new for Marriott and the lodging industry because, in essence, Marriott let consumers develop the concept and design the facilities.

Marriott spent a long time and a large amount of money developing Courtyard. However, given Marriott's competitive situation and lack of new product development experience, the six-year process was appropriate. Because Marriott did not expect the upscale market to become saturated until the mid-1980s, launching Courtyard before 1986 was not imperative. The project team had time to take the methodical, thorough approach that was necessary to overcome resistance to a midprice hotel concept within Marriott. Also, Marriott was willing to proceed slowly and spend millions of dollars because it appreciated the possible damage that could be done to its valuable brand name if Courtyard was not well received.

Marriott's strategy to segment the lodging industry has enabled it to maintain its high growth goals. Marriott's lodging revenues grew 175 percent from 1984 to 1991 as the corporation began offering economy hotels, midprice hotels, extended-stay hotels, and all-suite hotels. However, this expansion was not without problems. By 1990, Marriott was heavily burdened by debt and having difficulty selling many of its properties in a slow real estate market. Marriott therefore underwent a major downsizing of its administrative staff in 1990, divided into two different corporations, and began restructuring operations. The financial problems were not brought on by Courtyard, which continues to be a steady performer for Marriott.[45]

Lever Brothers Company: Lever 2000

Hidehisa Aoki and Mahan T. Tavakoli

Skin. The outermost covering of body tissue, which protects the internal organs from the environment. The skin is the largest organ in the body. Its cells are continually being replaced as they are lost by wear and tear.

American Medical Association, Encyclopedia of Medicine, *1989*

In 1991, Lever Brothers Company (Lever) launched a new bar soap called "Lever 2000."[46] The soap was designed to offer three major benefits in one bar: moisturizing, deodorizing, and antibacterial efficacy. Building on these three benefits, the company successfully differentiated Lever 2000 from its competitors through a family appeal communicated by the slogan: "Healthy skin care for the whole family." This new focus helped Lever 2000 become the third-best-selling soap in the United States only one year after its national launch.

In that short period of time after launch, Lever 2000 attained a market share of 8.5 percent in dollar volume and 7 percent in unit volume. Another measure of Lever 2000's success was its 40 percent rate of repeat sales, which was high for a new soap introduction. Through its success, Lever 2000 helped Lever achieve the highest share (32.4 percent) of dollar volume in the U.S. bar soap market in 1992. Lever's share had been just 19.5 percent in 1982.

THE SITUATION BEFORE LEVER 2000

Lever Brothers Company is the wholly owned U.S. subsidiary of Unilever, a large London-based Anglo-Dutch multinational organization. During the 1970s, Lever became notoriously complacent and unprofitable in the United States and required attention from its parent organization. Brands such as Surf, Wisk, Dove, Caress, Lux, Shield, and Lifebuoy had difficulties or became also-rans to aggressive U.S. competitors. In 1979, Michael Angus was made regional director of Lever. Rather than operating from his London office, as had been the tradition, Angus moved to New York and became actively involved in transforming Lever Brothers.

In an aggressive string of actions during the 1980s, Angus began to restructure the company, buying and selling businesses and rejuvenating ones that were kept. In the process, manufacturing was redefined and a new form of competitive marketing, led by new product development, was put into place. For example, in 1985, Lever launched a new fabric softener called "Snuggle" into a highly competitive market. By all accounts it should have failed as a new brand because it lacked name equity from a current brand. However, because of attention to product development and aggressive marketing, it held a 21 percent market share after four years, behind only Procter & Gamble's Downy in the market.

In 1986, Angus became chairman of Unilever and focused on global marketing and manufacturing. He placed strong emphasis on upgrading current brands and developing new products to improve competitiveness and profitability. Part of his challenge was overcoming Unilever's large global bureaucracy, which slowed new product introduction. Since World War II, Unilever had followed the traditional multinational strategies of vertical integration and geographic decentralization. Angus believed *global* product management teams would facilitate product design and manufacturing, provide economies of scale, and encourage bottom-line responsibility. Local country managers would no longer be able to create fiefdoms, incur excessive costs, or make decisions without accountability.

Angus further increased his focus on the U.S. market to fight the ever-strengthening threat of Procter & Gamble (P&G). Unilever's plans were to counter P&G's global efforts by attacking P&G's home base. Forcing P&G to spend more of its resources to maintain market share in the United States would hamper its efforts to expand overseas. Through its new commitment to the U.S. market, Unilever increased its market share to a high of 25 percent for U.S. household products in 1989, up from 15 percent in

1980, but still substantially less than P&G's share. Despite this tremendous progress, the fact that P&G was still number one in many categories of products caused some dissatisfaction for Unilever and Lever Brothers' managers.

OPPORTUNITY IN A MATURE BAR SOAP MARKET?

In the large but mature bar soap market, estimated to be some $1.5 billion in sales, Lever Brothers' Dove was the number two product with a 14 percent market share, following the long-established leader, Dial. Caress, another Lever Brothers' soap, had a 6 percent market share. Lever's other soaps had not achieved any significant gains in the market. The market for bar soap was essentially flat, with little growth other than that associated with very small population changes.

The maturity of the bar soap market made it highly competitive. Gaining share and defending a position would be possible only by tracking whatever changes could be identified in the attitudes and behavior of the population. The bar soap market had three broad product categories: deodorant bar soaps, complexion bar soaps, and other soaps. The latter category included a variety of hypo-allergenic, heavily perfumed, and abrasive (Lava) soaps and ones with other dominant special characteristics.

The deodorant soaps were the largest category in the bar soap market. Their appeal was based on the real or perceived possibility that a person's body odor might offend other people. For example, the market leader, Dial, used slogans such as "round the clock protection." The complexion soaps or "beauty" bars were claimed to prevent dryness and preserve skin. These beauty bars were usually more heavily scented than deodorant soaps and had a more creamy texture. They included Lever Brothers' Dove and Caress and P&G's Camay. However, a "pure soap" subcategory was also important, dominated largely by P&G's Ivory. Deodorant soaps were more popular among men and complexion soaps were more popular among women.

Despite the maturity of the bar soap market, competitors had to keep track of any significant trends. For example, by the late 1980s, consumers were using less deodorant soap. The market share of deodorant soaps dropped from a stable 50 percent during the 1970s to 43 percent by 1986. Many factors might explain this decline, including concern about purity, allergic reactions, and a growing preference for skin protection among men. A perhaps more important trend was the aging of the baby-boom population, who were becoming more concerned about health matters, including skin care. Fear of wrinkling and aging too quickly, combined with continuing concern about body odor, influenced their choice of soaps. Such subtle trend changes can go unnoticed unless a specific effort is made to track them and determine whether they afford a market opportunity for a new product.

THE DEVELOPMENT OF LEVER 2000

Through research on the soap market, Lever Brothers found that consumers were dissatisfied with the choices available to them. Soaps either deodorized or moisturized, but no soap was positioned to do both. The managers decided to address this gap in the market through the introduction of a totally new soap rather than repositioning a current one.

Lever managers pushed the research and development team at Lever to try to combine the moisturizing ingredients used in soaps such as Dove with the deodorizing ingredients used in soaps such as Dial. Although consumers are not generally familiar with the technology behind everyday products such as bar soap, chemically combining ingredients to produce desired effects is often a challenge. Texture, smell, creaminess, durability, shape, residue, and other tactile factors are a function of numerous ingredients that must be combined to produce a stable bar of soap that is pleasing to all major senses.

The research team eventually developed and patented a process that combined moisturizing and deodorizing properties in one soap, along with antibacterial agents. This technological development enabled Lever to launch the first product in the soap market to provide the three major benefits of moisturizing, deodorizing, and antibacterial efficacy.

The positioning and naming of the soap became the next important step in the development process. Many names were considered, but the "2000" name kept emerging. For example, "Nova 2000" was a popular contender. Eventually the president of Lever Brothers, Jack Cookson, decided on the name "Lever 2000." The reason for the 2000 in the name was to give consumers a futuristic image of the soap. Managers felt that they could advertise a "technological breakthrough" associated with their new formulation combining moisturizing, deodorizing, and antibacterial ingredients in one soap. This positioning also seemed to fit into the "high tech" promise of society as it moved toward the new century.

Although the high technology positioning associated with the year 2000 was communicated to the ad agency, it persuaded Lever Brothers to change the focus to "2,000 body parts." The advertisers felt that technology of the year 2000 would not sell something as personal as soap, which touches the body. They also felt that technology was not important to soap consumers, but that they would respond to a "high touch" emphasis. The differences were resolved with a "high tech/high touch" positioning that presented a comfortable *contrast*. Advertisers often use contrast to capture consumer attention in a cluttered market. The product name, benefits, and its packaging would reflect the technological advantages of Lever 2000, and the advertising strategy and the actual soap would emphasize the high touch benefits.

After selection of the name and positioning, a very distinctive package design was created that would communicate and reinforce the positioning at the point of purchase and at home. The packaging reflected the high tech counterpoint to the high touch of the "2,000 body parts" ad campaign. The box design was simple and modern. The Lever name was printed in dark blue boldface capital letters across the face of a silver box with a grid of fine horizontal lines. The "2000" was in a less bold font directly below the Lever name. The launch box had "NEW" in the top left corner with a green background. Below the 2000 line was the slogan: "It's better for your skin."

The soap itself was designed to be very touchable. Each bar was rectangular, but with softly curving oval sides and tapered all around to fit the hand. The soap was white with a "LEVER 2000" imprint on the rectangular face. The soap and its package were in many ways part of the high tech/high touch contrast that enhanced the basic positioning strategy.

In mid-1987, the company began a test market in Atlanta that lasted for two years. During that time, it fine-tuned the Lever 2000 marketing program and achieved an 8 percent market share, along with other favorable test market results. This information added to the conviction of Lever Brothers managers that they had a winning product. They passed the information to Unilever, which then gave Lever the go-ahead for a national launch. The goal was to have the new soap in stores nationwide by September 1991.

Lever emphasized a promotional program that would stimulate consumers to try and buy the new Lever 2000. First, the product was launched with heavy sampling to induce trial. Lever mailed samples of the new product to almost half of all U.S. households. Second, Lever engaged in heavy couponing to further stimulate trial and repeat purchase. Although the new product was launched at a price averaging about $1.69 at retail for two five-ounce bars, coupons enabled consumers to buy the two bars for just under one dollar. Third, Lever employed a heavy launch advertising campaign costing about $25 million.

Lever allowed its advertising agency considerable freedom to coordinate and change the advertising campaign if necessary. This action led to the now famous "2,000 body parts" campaign. In whimsical good taste, but with attention-getting images, the campaign showed the naked body parts of various family members and how the new soap would address their skin concerns. The new ad campaign rapidly built awareness of the new Lever 2000 bar soap concept. Print ads were placed in magazines such as *Time, Rolling Stone*, and *Good Housekeeping.*

The advertising and promotion helped Lever educate and persuade consumers about the logic of buying the one brand of soap that had all of the benefits formerly obtainable only by buying two or three varieties of soap. The following outline of one of Lever's five-by-seven-inch 12-page coupon brochures mailed to households illustrates the logic of its positioning approach.

Page 1: Healthy skin care for the whole family (photos of family body parts)

Pages 2 and 3: Your remarkable skin
- Three layers of skin
- The problem: Soaps

Pages 4 and 5: What you should know about the mildest antibacterial soap ever created
- Proof of superior mildness
- Proof of superior antibacterial effectiveness
- Deodorant effectiveness, too

Pages 6 and 7: Skin care needs vary with age
- Children
- Teens
- Adults

Pages 8 and 9: Helpful hints on skin care for your whole family (lists five hints based on whether skin is normal, dry, or oily—limit bathing to once a day, avoid rubbing or scrubbing the skin with a sponge or brush, etc.)

Pages 10 and 11: Other ways to ensure healthy skin for the whole family
- Nutrition
- Water
- Sleep
- Exercise

Page 12: 30-cent coupon on two bars of Lever 2000

Distribution of some soaps is restricted to certain retail outlets, but Lever chose to make Lever 2000 available in a large variety of stores. Although about 70 percent of bar soap is sold in food stores, Lever also distributed intensively to drugstores, mass merchandisers, and wholesale price clubs. With heavy promotion and intensive distribution, Lever was able to generate a rapid buildup in sales volume, as evidenced by its substantial first year success.

REASONS FOR THE SUCCESS

Designing new products from ideas and concepts often follows market research, as in the case of Lever 2000. Although market research can give a clear sense of the benefits consumers want in products—such as deodorizing, moisturizing, antibacterial, and so on—it cannot guarantee success. Translation of these benefits into a clear and attention-getting positioning strategy is also necessary, which requires creativity and testing as well as attention to research results. For example, a major reason for Lever 2000's success was its high tech/high touch positioning, a theme that did not emerge until the development of the creative advertising part of the marketing program.

The contrast between high tech and high touch served to attract consumer attention and gave consumers a logical argument for trying the new soap. Once they tried the new soap, a relatively large portion of consumers repeated their purchases, indicating satisfaction that the product's promise was met. The success of the positioning depended on the working relationship between the advertising agency and the client (Lever). The creativity of the agency combined with strategy-driven marketing research and technical product development by the client led to the successful positioning approach. (Recall that Lever was originally headed in the direction of a strictly high tech approach.)

A second major reason for the success of Lever 2000 was a product design that was superior to any available in the market. By technically combining deodorizing and moisturizing capabilities, Lever was able to bring a truly new soap into the market. Consumers could get the ingredients of at least two soaps in one. The product not only was differentiated from its competitors, but also met consumer needs.

A third major reason for success was related to consumer behavior. Prior to Lever 2000, a family may have needed two or three different bar soaps to meet all the needs of husband, wife, and children. By combining multiple benefits into one soap in a believable and effective way, Lever enabled a family to simplify its purchasing of bar soap. Consider the following points:

- The same bar could be shared by all members of the family. "Family sharing" in an otherwise fragmenting society may have been an important social psychological benefit to consumers.
- For families that share a single shower and/or bath, and have different soap preferences, the physical placement of multiple bars on a single soap dish would be difficult. A single bar that everyone could use eliminated that problem.
- To the extent that men were beginning to prefer less harsh soaps but still wanted the deodorant benefit, Lever 2000 represented a perfect compromise. Also, with greater convergence of attitudes between the sexes, men's strict association of moisturizers with femininity may have relaxed by the early 1990s.

Clearly, family needs represented an opportunity for a company that had the technological capability of combining multiple ingredients to produce an effective soap offering a human touch for the family.

A fourth reason for the success of Lever 2000 was its highly integrated marketing program. The positioning of Lever 2000 as "healthy skin care for the whole family" was delivered through a technically superior product design, the "2,000 body parts" advertising campaign, an effectively designed high tech package, a bar design that was soft and rounded to the touch, heavy sampling to induce trial, heavy couponing to offer value and build repeat purchase, and intensive distribution. The marketing program produced the desired consumer response and led to market success.

Finally, managers' commitment to the product cannot be overlooked as an important success factor. In a stagnant and mature market, Lever's managers provided time and resources for R&D to develop the new product, supported the brand with ample marketing and advertising budgets, and signaled a clear direction for the bar soap team without imposing rigidity. Flexibility was built into the process to give Lever 2000 the greatest chance for success. By allowing the ad agency creative freedom and by test marketing the innovative product, Lever Brothers showed the flexibility and commitment to success that are necessary for risky new ventures.

CONCLUSIONS

A clear sign of success for a breakthrough new product, even something as mundane as bar soap, is its effect on competitors. The launch of Lever 2000 literally changed the structure of the once sluggish bar soap market. For example, in 1992 Dial launched a new bar soap called "Spirit," which offered the same three benefits as Lever 2000, as well as several versions of original Dial for various skin conditions. P&G repositioned its Safeguard brand with a Lever 2000 type of slogan: "Mild enough for the whole family." It also launched a new bar soap under its Oil of Olay brand name at a reasonable price to compete directly with Lever 2000.

Whether Lever 2000 will be able to sustain its market position under competitive threat will be determined over time. However, top managers' commitment of time, energy, and resources that resulted in the initial success is likely to keep Lever competitive in the market. For example, to meet competitive threats, Lever began launching extensions of its Dove brand and of its new Lever 2000 brand (an unscented version). With the 1991 launch of Lever 2000, the bar soap wars began!

8

Refining the
New Product

For many new products, success depends on *getting it right*. An idea may be excellent and consumers may respond favorably to a concept description of it, but unless it really delivers the promised benefits, its value may never be realized. Substantial *product refinement* may be necessary as the product concept is defined into a prototype and subsequently revised. Such refinement typically involves a variety of testing to ensure that the product works as potential buyers expect, that quality is built into it, and that it can be manufactured effectively and efficiently.

Product testing and refinement usually are done by the design team, who work closely with lead users, regular users, industry experts, and other people involved in the product's usage and performance. Testing generally takes four general forms: *alpha, beta, gamma,* and *delta* tests. Alpha tests on a prototype or a rough version of the product are conducted with potential users *within* the organization. The goal is to eliminate as many problems as possible before the product is released for additional testing outside the organization. Beta tests are conducted with *primary users* of the product, preferably under actual usage circumstances. Software manufacturers rely heavily on alpha and beta testing to identify design problems as soon as possible. Gamma tests are conducted among the *stakeholders* for a new product, individuals or organizations other than potential buyers that might be key barriers to or facilitators of new product development (regulators, industry media, politicians, and so on). Delta tests occur some time after product launch. A small sample of products are repurchased from consumers to carefully evaluate wear and tear of the product under actual usage circumstances. Usage and other performance problems are identified for product improvement.

The new product can also be tested further in the broader context of its launch marketing program (pricing, promotion, distribution, and so on), usually by *simulated, controlled*, and *conventional* test marketing. These approaches vary in the degree to which they represent realistic purchasing situations. Simulated test markets are done with panels of consumers or purchase laboratories; at the other extreme, conventional test marketing consists of actual new product launch in one or more geographic locations under real market conditions. By obtaining consumer, trade, and other stakeholder responses, the manufacturer can refine the product and its entire marketing program.

Most forms of product refinement take time, a resource that many firms find scarce in fast-moving and highly competitive markets. Consequently, new product developers always face the challenge of trying to accelerate the development process without compromising quality. The ideal goal is to accelerate the product design process and improve quality simultaneously.

Accelerating new product development is as much a function of leadership and organizational design as it is of expertise. Leadership with a clear vision helps focus the new product development effort and increases the chance that the expertise will follow. For example, in the first story in this chapter, the project to develop Huggies Pull-Ups, a new disposable training pant, was nearly abandoned. Designers could not find a satisfactory material for the waistband (the pants would not pull up without tearing). The solution was found relatively quickly when the project leader searched within the company and found a suitable material that had been developed for another use.

The Pull-Ups experience exemplifies the value of cross-functional input, which is especially important early in the development process when a variety of viewpoints can help anticipate and solve problems before they become barriers to success. Development speed can also be important in highly competitive markets (such as disposable diapers) when being first to market affords a competitive advantage. Once Kimberly-Clark had refined the Pull-Ups product through use tests, it skipped its usual test marketing to gain a first-mover advantage over arch-rival Procter & Gamble. Using a geographically designed national rollout of Pull-Ups, the company was able to achieve a full five-year lead over P&G.

When a product is not the first in a market, yet is attractive, being second puts a different set of parameters on the development process. Such was the case for Glaxo in the second story considered in this chapter. To be second in a pharmaceutical market, even when it is growing, usually means a market share under 10 percent. Therefore, any investment must be balanced against the degree of true product superiority. An expeditious, yet effective, product refinement process is necessary because products must satisfy demanding regulators (such as the Food and Drug Administration in the United States), not to mention physicians and their patients.

Glaxo decided to compete against SmithKline's new Tagamet anti-ulcer drug, which was a major success. The Glaxo science team found a new ingredient for their "H_2 blocker" anti-ulcer treatment that enabled them to conceptualize a new product. However, the process of refining such a drug normally took about 10 years. The time/benefit tradeoff clearly made this process an unacceptable investment. A five-year cycle time was deemed to be advantageous, but risky. Nevertheless, an innovative drug design process with parallel testing to meet regulatory and drug efficacy requirements was implemented. By focusing the design process on Tagamet's vulnerabilities, Glaxo molded Zantac into a product with superior characteristics, a necessary condition to crack the tough market of gastrointestinal physicians.

Development speed is not always an ideal goal, especially when quality or market readiness is at issue. The success of Gillette's Sensor shaving system, the third story in this chapter, is a case in point. Gillette took about 13 years to realize its new shaving system. The idea for it emerged in 1977, but the product was not officially launched until January 1990. Gillette, known for its expertise in developing shaving products, conducted exhaustive use testing for the new system. This effort included the use of a panel of some 200 company employees and more than 5,000 consumers.

Gillette may appear to have been managing its product life cycle, that is, delaying launch to minimize cannibalization of its current technology and its strong market position. However, Gillette's business was under pressure from the increasing popularity of disposable razors, which were cheaper and much less profitable than shaving systems. Gillette realized it needed to move the market back to shaving systems, but to do so required a proven superior product. Use testing was crucial to ensure that the new shaving system would be measurably better than other devices.

Taken together, the three success stories provide a well-rounded view of the importance of product refinement, albeit with different twists. Kimberly-Clark wanted a first-mover advantage over its major competitor; Glaxo was second to market, but needed a superior product to succeed; and Gillette wanted to maintain its leadership position by bringing the market back to a quality-based positioning from a price-based one. How these companies achieved product refinement under varied conditions provides interesting insights into success.

Kimberly-Clark Corporation: Huggies Pull-Ups

Susan L. Aiken and Amy S. Nichols

Accidents are bound to happen, and no doubt the child will be more than a little upset by the fact that he has soiled or wet his new pants—but you should not be. Resist the tendency to scold or punish. Do not even disapprove; after all, it is an accident.

Your Growing Child, *Time Life Books, 1987*

Kimberly-Clark Corporation, maker of Huggies brand disposable diapers and Kleenex brand tissues, introduced disposable training pants to the U.S. market in 1989.[1] The product, Huggies Pull-Ups, provides a transition from diapers to underwear for children in the toilet training process. With revenues of more than $400 million by 1992, Pull-Ups was a significant market success, with greater annual dollar sales than all baby shampoos, oils and lotions, and powders combined. Pull-Ups became an integral part of the way many children are toilet trained.

THE DISPOSABLE DIAPER MARKET PRIOR TO PULL-UPS

Prior to the launch of Pull-Ups in 1989, the distinction between the diaper and training pants markets was clear. Within the diaper category, consumers could choose between cloth and disposable diapers. Disposable diapers were first launched in 1961 by Procter & Gamble (P&G) under the Pampers brand, and demand for the product grew rapidly. Because consumers wanted convenience, disposable diapers eventually dominated the market. The $3.5 billion disposable diaper market was driven by strong competitive and environmental forces. Dominated by Kimberly-Clark (with Huggies) and its arch-rival P&G (with Pampers and value-priced Luvs brands), the disposable diaper market was a battleground in the quest for the thinnest, driest, most comfortable, and most environmentally safe product.

The two leading companies conducted their product development in secrecy. They frequently filed lawsuits against each other for alleged patent violations. Products were developed with code names and at unusual development sites. For example, at one point in the development of Pull-Ups, the project was known as Omega and was located in a former Ford dealer's garage in Neenah, Wisconsin.

Although the major producers held the greatest market share nationwide, the entry of regional grocery and drugstore chains into the disposable diaper business with their own private-label brand names created additional competition and a stronger emphasis on price. Consumers began to see disposable diapers as a commodity rather than a special product. Competing with a low cost strategy, regional chains easily entered the market with "me-too" products that met basic needs.

These private-label and regional brands captured significant sales, but generally lacked the research and development resources to generate continuous product improvements or undertake product breakthroughs. Consequently, Kimberly-Clark and P&G began to compete on the basis of continuous innovations in disposable diapers. They also searched for new opportunities, such as the "toilet-training" market.

THE MARKET OPPORTUNITY

As a child grows and reaches the age to begin toilet training (usually between 15 and 30 months), parents put the child in "training pants" as an interim measure between diapers and underwear. Traditionally made of cloth and resembling heavily padded underwear, training pants provide absorbency should a child have an accident. They look much like regular underpants, which gives them "big kid" connotation. Suppliers of cloth training pants include several children's food and apparel companies such as Gerber, Carter Company, Dundee Mills, Spencer, and Louisiana Knits.[2]

The disadvantages of cloth training pants are that they have no plastic covering to prevent leaks and they require washing. For most parents who had grown accustomed to the convenience of throwing away soiled diapers, washing training pants became a new and unpleasant activity. Parents and children were likely to be upset when accidents occurred in cloth training pants because of the work involved in washing them.

Using large diapers is an option for many parents with children in training. However, large diapers encourage children to act like babies rather than rise to the challenge of becoming a "big kid" in training pants. Further, as children grow larger, they become unwieldy on a changing table. A disposable training product would certainly have advantages for both children and parents. Kimberly-Clark estimated the annual size of the disposable training pants market to be some 300 to 600 million units and $150 million to $300 million in sales. The unusual aspect of the market was that although about four million children on average entered toilet training each year, they left the market about a year later once training was completed. The market size depended on birth rates, but the opportunity was deemed attractive enough to pursue.

THE DEVELOPMENT OF PULL-UPS

The evolution of Pull-Ups can be viewed in terms of a four-stage new product development process: idea, concept generation, prototyping, and product/marketing program.

Idea Generation

The new product idea came from consumers with problems. As increasing numbers of parents began to rely on disposable diapers, Kimberly-Clark became aware of the difficulties parents faced in switching to cloth training pants. After receiving numerous requests directly from parents to develop a disposable training pant and investigating the market opportunity, Kimberly-Clark's managers became convinced that such a product was worth pursuing.

Concept Generation

The concept behind Pull-Ups training pants was to satisfy the needs of a child in training and to provide convenience for parents. Kimberly-Clark set out to develop a product that would both encourage training and prevent leakage should an accident occur. Previously, parents had to choose among products that met one of those criteria, but not both. Cloth pants reinforced training by implying that the child was growing up, but they leaked. Plastic pants did not leak, but did not encourage training. Disposable diapers afforded protection, but lacked the psychological benefit of implying a more grown-up stage and did not encourage use of the toilet.

The basic concept of disposable training pants developed quickly as a result of Kimberly-Clark's expertise in disposable diapers. The company would adapt its diaper technology to the next stage of child development. It determined that Pull-Ups should seem as much like cloth training pants as possible in terms of thinness, comfort, and ability to be pulled up and down by a child, yet be disposable. The core concept was clear: absorbent, easy-to-use, and comfortably fitting disposable training pants that protect the child and facilitate the toilet training process. Although the product was easy to conceptualize and define, development of a working prototype proved to be difficult.

Prototypes

The prototype stage posed the biggest obstacle to Kimberly-Clark. The company's R&D costs exceeded $12 million and the development of a working Pull-Ups prototype spanned a five-year period. Despite their expertise in the absorbency material needed for the pants, company engineers had difficulty identifying a suitable material for the waistband. The project nearly failed in the prototype process. Product testing repeatedly showed that the materials chosen could not withstand being pulled up and down.

Rather than abandon the project, Wayne Sanders, the recently promoted president of Kimberly-Clark's Infant Care Sector (and subsequently the CEO of the firm), was convinced the idea was a good one and looked within the company for help. After consultation with several people, he soon found a stretchy nonwoven synthetic material that the company was developing for another purpose. A successful prototype was finally developed.

The training pants were constructed with a highly absorbent material and included a liner with elastic legs and waist that help provide protection. The pants also had soft, stretchable side panels made from Kimberly-Clark patented material. They fit like pants and were strong enough to be pulled on and off like underwear. A spun bonded fiber was woven to provide an outer cover. The pants had a clothlike feel, yet were coated to prevent leakage. In case of an accident, the bonded side seams of the pants could be torn away for easy removal of any mess. Patterns could be printed on the outer cover. With the working prototype, Sanders moved ahead to the next phase of development.

Product and Marketing Program

After overcoming the obstacle of developing a suitable prototype, Sanders prepared for a full commercial launch. To get the product on the market quickly without alerting competitors, he decided to eliminate the customary practice of test marketing and proceeded directly to a phased national launch plan. The marketing program addressed the product's features, promotion, pricing, and distribution.

The final product had been designed to look very much like training pants. Initially, the pants were white and came in three sizes for children from roughly 20 to 50 pounds. To reflect the concept of Pull-Ups as the next step in child development, the advertising concentrated on the "Big Kid" theme. A colorful "Big Kid" handbook was included with each package to explain to parents how the product could be helpful in toilet training.

The television advertising campaign was designed to reach some 95 percent of mothers about 13 times each. In addition, print ads appeared in family and women's magazines such as *Parents, Better Homes and Gardens,* and *Woman's Day.* Kimberly-Clark also distributed a large number of coupons at launch to stimulate trial and repeat purchase. The price of Pull-Ups was about twice that of disposable diapers (about 50 cents apiece retail). The company distributed the new product intensively through its Huggies channels.

Product Launch

Launched first in Denver and Phoenix in May 1989, Pull-Ups quickly achieved a 3.3 percent share of the diaper market. This initial success confirmed the company's opinion and led to continued rollout across the country. Although such a rollout precludes formal testing of critical marketing decision variables (such as alternative advertising themes), it does facilitate a refinement of the basic launch program in an adaptive mode. Consumer problems, trade problems, production problems, and other issues that emerge during the initial rollout can be identified and resolved.

To implement the rollout, the United States was divided into 13 regions and Pull-Ups was launched systematically over a two-year period according to the following schedule:

Ship Date	Region
5/15/89	Denver/Phoenix
7/17/89	Remaining Northwest
8/1/89	Southern Pacific
9/18/89	Southwest
4/16/90	Southern
4/16/90	Southeast
5/01/90	Carolinas
6/18/90	North Central
2/11/91	East Central
2/11/91	Atlantic less Carolinas
3/18/91	Pittsburgh/Buffalo
5/15/91	Balance of Northeast
5/15/91	Metro East
By May 1991	Total United States

LAUNCH RESULTS

The Pull-Ups product achieved considerable success after its rollout. Its acceptance indicated that parents believed in the concept of disposable pants that fit and resemble underwear and can be used in toilet training. In 1991, the product's first full year of nearly national levels of distribution, sales revenue reached $253 million. By the end of 1992, sales had grown to $423 million and Pull-Ups had a 10.6 percent share of the overall disposable diaper market!

Pull-Ups provided a truly new way for parents to toilet train their children and created a profitable new category for Kimberly-Clark. Because an estimated four million children begin toilet training each year and another one million children are bed-wetters, Kimberly-Clark believes there is room to grow in the market, which it estimates to be two billion training pants a year in the United States. Remarkably, Pull-Ups successfully entered the disposable diaper market with virtually no cannibalization of Huggies' other diaper products, which also grew in volume throughout the Pull-Ups success.

Kimberly-Clark's research has shown that mothers prefer Pull-Ups four to one over other toilet training products across all three sizes of training pants. In the same market research study, consumers were asked to rate Pull-Ups on several key attributes on a 10-point scale. Pull-Ups scored 9.0 or better on ease of fit, absorbency, overall fit, and containment of urine. The product clearly fulfilled its core benefit promise.

REASONS FOR PULL-UPS' SUCCESS

Huggies Pull-Ups succeeded for a variety of reasons, including an effective new product champion supported by top managers, a solid base of technical experience with disposable diapers, strong marketing skills, and retailer cooperation and acceptance of the new product. Three other important factors that drove the success of Pull-Ups were a tenaciously pursued product design that works, compelling consumer problems awaiting a solution, and a first-mover advantage in establishing a new market segment.

Persistence in Product Design

The need for an absorbent, easy-to-use, and comfortable disposable toilet-training product for growing children was voiced by parents and heard loud and clear by Kimberly-Clark (and probably its major competitors). However, designing and delivering a new product to meet that need was not easy. The company spent several years and $12 million in R&D to pursue the market opportunity. Clearly, the determination of Wayne Sanders in searching for additional technologies and the right materials to solve the design problems ultimately paid off.

Kimberly-Clark's experience in designing Pull-Ups shows the importance of assembling a multifunctional team of experts early in the development process. The technology for Pull-Ups' success was available within the organization, but not in the garage where the product was being developed for part of the time. Even a multifunctional team, however, cannot guarantee solutions to major problems. Persistence and determination are necessary when a new product opportunity seems achievable but development is stymied by a difficult problem.

Fortunately, the Pull-Ups technical problem was resolved and a product was designed that fulfilled every major quantifiable consumer need from absorbency to pantlike fit. The product received high ratings in consumer tests and was even preferred four to one over other approaches to toilet training. Kimberly-Clark was rewarded for its persistence with significant sales response and high repeat purchase rates among users (about 80 percent), which indicated considerable satisfaction.

A Clear and Present Consumer Need

From the time a child is born to the time he or she is toilet trained, parents are engaged in what is commonly known as the "maintenance stage" of child rearing. Maintenance consists of feeding, dressing, washing, combing hair, and changing diapers. As a child grows and matures, less maintenance is required. Changing diapers is the duty parents say they would most like to relinquish. Toilet training therefore implies growing up for children (becoming a "big kid") and liberation for parents.

Toilet training is one of a child's first lessons in responsibility. For some, learning to use the toilet is a simple rite of passage; for others, toilet training can be a very emotional and trying experience. In either case, parents invest a lot of emotion and energy in training their children. For example, in Time Life Books' *Your Growing Child*, parents find explicit directions about how to choose the right time for toilet training, how to prepare for toilet training, how to select the child's first potty, how to introduce the child to the potty, how to train the child, and how to react when accidents occur. The book states that each step is crucial to a successful training process.

Toilet training is therefore a multistep endeavor that, if taken seriously, leads to anxiety. Parents do not want to alienate their children or cause undue stress that may come about through accidents. Because parents are under pressure *not* to get upset over accidents, their choice of training products is important. If cloth training pants are soiled, parents must wash them, which may cause undue apprehension and resentment. Pull-Ups helps parents reduce the accident anxiety because the soiled pants can be tossed in the trash.

Cultural and demographic changes in the United States have influenced parents' toilet training needs and in part explain the success of Pull-Ups. For example, with the increase in dual-income families and single-parent households, parents have less time to spend with their children. This decrease in time translates directly into a search for more convenient products. Many parents simply do not want to take the time to wash reusable cloth training pants. Moreover, working parents do not want to waste their brief daily parenting time wrestling their children onto a changing table or consoling them over accidents. All of these factors combine to form a segment of parents who are willing to pay a premium for the convenience of disposable pull-up training pants.

Consumer need therefore was based in both the physical and emotional aspects of toilet training for children and their parents. The physical benefits of Pull-Ups include disposability, absorbency, use, look, and comfort. The pants go on and off like underwear, look like underwear, feel like underwear, and have a pantlike fit. The emotional benefits derive from the product's convenience, which mitigates the stress of toilet training.

First-Mover Advantage

Once the product was perfected, Wayne Sanders' decision to bypass the usual test marketing practices and accelerate the launch of Pull-Ups gave Kimberly-Clark a substantial first-mover advantage. The Pull-Ups launch caught its major competitors off guard, both strategically and technologically. P&G took five years to respond with a comparable product. A five-year lead in a fast-moving market enables the market leader to solve all operational problems and establish a strong presence in the market.

Unfortunately, the market turnover of users is high; that is, consumers enter the market during the time the child needs the training pants (at about the age of two years) and leave about a year later after toilet training is achieved. Hence, Kimberly-Clark must work hard to defend and maintain its early lead, a reasonable task given the company's accumulated experience in R&D, production, and marketing.

CONCLUSIONS: BUILDING ON THE SUCCESS

After the launch, Kimberly-Clark continued to refine and build on Pull-Ups' initial success. The company extended the product line from three to six in early 1992 by creating three sizes for boys and three sizes for girls. Even though competitors had yet to enter the market, technical and marketing improvements would further strengthen the product's first-mover advantage. The two new lines were 20 percent thinner, provided better absorbency, and offered more patterns and prints on the outside of the pants. These new size and design elements addressed the tendency of children to begin to notice gender differentiation in their toilet training years.

Kimberly-Clark launched Pull-Ups Good Nites in 1994. These disposable underpants provided help for parents whose older children have a bed-wetting problem. The aggressive launch campaign reflected Kimberly-Clark's desire to cover every segment of the market (estimated at about $100 million in this case). Rather surprisingly, in 1994 Kimberly-Clark also began supplying Wal-Mart Stores with a private-label brand of training pants called "Atta Boy" and "Atta Girl," which sell for about 20 percent less than Pull-Ups. Clearly, Kimberly-Clark anticipates a tough battle with P&G and other competitors in all key segments.

The emergence of competition from P&G and regional retail brands continues to challenge the future growth of Pull-Ups. Kimberly-Clark will pursue expansion into global markets and persist in evolutionary improvements on Pull-Ups to defend its position and early lead. Competing with P&G and local companies in Europe, Japan, and other parts of the world will tax Kimberly-Clark's resources because the company is not as well positioned there as the others. Nevertheless, Kimberly-Clark has laid the groundwork for Pull-Ups to maintain its success in the United States, if not globally.

Glaxo Holdings PLC: Zantac

Andrew P. Corsig, Thomas P. Soloway, and Richard M. Stanaro

The stomach is the teacher of the arts and the dispenser of invention.

Persius (A.D. 34–62), Satires

Glaxo Holdings PLC of Great Britain is one of the world's largest pharmaceutical firms.[3] It has not always had success in new products, and going into the 1970s had a reputation as a somewhat conservative, if not stodgy, organization. However, its anti-ulcer drug Zantac, a "me-too" new drug product that became the market leader, made Glaxo a global contender in the highly competitive pharmaceutical industry. In 1983 at the launch of Zantac, Glaxo was sixteenth in the world pharmaceutical industry; by 1992, it was number two! During that period of time, the market value of Glaxo rose from $4 billion to $36 billion.

Glaxo's introduction of Zantac challenged the then-dominant SmithKline Beecham PLC (SmithKline) and its very successful breakthrough drug, Tagamet. To compete with SmithKline in a rapidly growing market for peptic ulcer drugs, Glaxo pursued aggressive innovations in product development and marketing and overtook Tagamet. The story of how Zantac became the best-selling prescription drug in the world in a relatively short period of time begins with an understanding of the human problem it addressed.

ULCER DISEASE

Peptic ulcer disease is a serious disorder of the digestive system that creates an unhealed hole or open sore in the tissue lining the gastrointestinal (GI)

242

tract. The condition causes discomfort, pain, disability, and in rare cases death. Although knowledge of peptic ulcer disease predates Hippocrates, the exact cause of peptic ulcers was a mystery and a topic of intense research in 1973. The only effective methods of treating ulcers then were painful and risky surgery or the use of over-the-counter (OTC) antacid products such as Rolaids, Tums, Maalox, or Mylanta to treat symptoms.

The overall incidence of peptic ulcer disease is high; between 10 and 12 percent of the world's population is affected. The disease is prevalent in all economic and social classes and, despite stereotypes, is found in people with all types of personalities. In addition, although ulcer disease occurs in all age groups, it is most common in women over the age of 65. The growth of the drug opportunity for this market was estimated to be some 20 to 30 percent a year.

In the early 1970s, David Jack, head of Glaxo's research laboratory, had completed work on asthma drugs and was searching for a new project. Glaxo's drug Ventolin was very successful at treating asthma. However because it was not marketed aggressively (especially in the United States), it was not a financial success. Consequently, Jack was sensitive to the market potential for new drugs. Because ulcers were a common problem and represented a large and growing global market opportunity, he began research on a safe and effective ulcer treatment.

As part of the research process, Jack attended a lecture by James Black, a distinguished researcher and Nobel Prize recipient. Black worked for SmithKline and was researching ulcer disease. At the lecture, Jack learned of a new theory for the treatment of ulcer disease. The lecture focused on acid secretion, which was thought to aggravate ulcers and prevent healing. Black theorized that histamine, a naturally occurring agent in the human body, was the key to controlling acid secretion. The theory was simple. Histamine binds to a gastrointestinal cell at a location known as an H_2 receptor site. After attaching, the histamine instructs the cell to secrete hydrochloric acid. At the time, Black was experimenting with compounds called "H_2 blockers," which could block the action of histamine. Because H_2 blocker compounds are similar in chemical structure to histamine, they compete for the H_2 receptor sites on gastrointestinal cells. When H_2 blocker compounds bind, they inhibit the cells from secreting acid.

The lecture spurred Jack into action. He immediately began searching for his own H_2 blocker compound. However, after three years of experimenting with different compounds, Jack and his research team were unable to find a safe drug. At the same time, SmithKline had made great strides in its research. By 1977, with the help of James Black, the company had discovered and launched Tagamet, the first H_2 blocker drug.

Tagamet immediately revolutionized ulcer treatment and appeared to the medical community to be a wonder drug. It gave physicians an extremely safe and effective way to treat ulcer patients. Tagamet healed approximately 90 percent of ulcers within three months and had no known contraindications. In addition, most of its side effects were mild, transient, and reversible.

THE DEVELOPMENT OF ZANTAC

The emergence of Tagamet thoroughly discouraged David Jack and his team. They realized that the opportunity to be the first to capture the ulcer market had quickly disappeared. Still, they decided to take one last stab at the problem, modifying the molecular structure of a compound called "ranitidine" (Tagamet was based on cimetidine). Incredibly, the compound passed all tests and proved to be the breakthrough that the team had been seeking. Unfortunately, the breakthrough seemed to come too late.

Traditionally, "me-too" drugs have not fared well in the pharmaceutical market. Each successful innovation is usually followed by a host of such drugs, which in total rarely capture more than a 10 percent market share. Jack was determined that Zantac would be different; however, he faced two major challenges:

- Tagamet was becoming wildly successful. By 1982, five years after introduction, Tagamet had worldwide sales of $620 million and was the best-selling prescription drug in the world. If Zantac was not developed quickly, it would never catch Tagamet.
- Additional competitors were threatening market entry. Both Merck and Eli Lilly were known to be working hard to develop their own H_2 blocker agents. How close these competitors were to launching their products was not clear, but Glaxo would definitely be an also-ran if it could not be second in the H_2 blocker market.

Jack realized that to get Zantac to the market quickly, he would need to dramatically reduce the typical 10-year development time for new drugs. That much time was necessary because drug regulatory agencies (such as the U.S. Food and Drug Administration) required extensive test data to

ensure that the drug would be safe for human use. To meet that requirement and shorten development time, Jack conceived the first "parallel"
development process in the pharmaceutical industry. Instead of following
the traditional lengthy sequential process of testing first with rats, then
with monkeys, and so on, Jack decided to perform all testing simultaneously. For example, researchers performed long-term toxicity tests before the results of short-term tests were known.

The decision was fraught with risk. If critical tests were not passed, iso-
lating the problem areas would be difficult until all data were in. The par-
allel process doubled the work and consequently the expense of testing.
Research expense rose from £17 million in 1976 to £40 million in 1981.
This dramatic increase in research costs put considerable pressure on
Glaxo's profitability during the new drug's development.

Fortunately, Paul Girolami, Glaxo's influential finance director, was
able to accept the risky development project and championed the product
throughout the organization. Zantac made it through testing without major problems, despite the fact that nine of 10 new drugs fail testing. Furthermore, the parallel process reduced development time significantly.
Zantac was ready for launch in 1982, after only five years of development
and testing. It thus gave Glaxo a major advantage over Merck and Eli Lilly,
which were testing their own products at that time.

PREPARING FOR THE U.S. ULCER MARKET

In 1982, Glaxo decided to launch Zantac into the $362 million U.S. market
for anti-ulcer preparations. That market represented 3.5 percent of all
prescription sales and just over 1 percent of the total prescriptions written. However, the average prescription price of anti-ulcer drugs was
$18.10, far surpassing the $14.46 average for anti-arthritic drugs, the second most widely prescribed drug category. SmithKline's Tagamet was
the top-selling anti-ulcer drug, but other competitors were beginning to
appear. For example, in 1982, Marion Laboratories had captured 2 percent of the ulcer market with its non-H_2-blocker drug, Carafate.

In launching Zantac in the United States, Glaxo carefully considered
buyer behavior. Because of the societal mechanisms established to deliver
health care, the purchase behavior for ethical pharmaceuticals is unusual.
Patients generally have little knowledge of medicine and must rely on
physicians to obtain prescription drugs. The doctor's prescription is
therefore the means by which patients gain access to drugs in a pharmacy.

This system has interesting implications for new product development. Glaxo's product had to satisfy the needs of not only end users, but also physicians, who are the real decision makers in the buying process.

An important aspect of a market of physicians is the process by which information is diffused into the medical community. Influential specialists (gastroenterologists in this case) want the most recent information available about a particular problem. If those specialists adopt a new product, the more numerous general practitioners typically follow their lead. Consequently, it is essential in the launch of a new pharmaceutical to get the drug into the hands of the specialists as quickly as possible.

Doctors judge drugs on the basis of three major criteria: effectiveness, safety, and degree of side effects. Patients also consider those factors, but often have deeper needs on a more personal level. For example, for many people, taking medicine is a sign of weakness, aging, and/or a general decline in health. Any physical deterioration threatens a person's quality of life and often raises great fears. However, if a medicine ameliorates symptoms or resolves a problem, patients are very pleased. Therefore, how patients are treated and reassured (or not) by their physicians, and the ease and convenience with which the drug can be taken, can affect their use and acceptance of a new drug. Finally, another area of difference between doctor and patient needs is that physicians do not pay for the medication they prescribe; patients or their health insurance companies do.

THE LAUNCH OF ZANTAC

Paul Girolami assumed responsibility for developing the launch marketing plan for Zantac. He began with a focus on the needs of physicians. He knew that the overall goals of physicians were to relieve symptoms, promote complete healing, and prevent complications and recurrence. In addition, he knew that an anti-ulcer product's ability to relieve the patient's pain and its ability to heal the ulcer (healing rate) were the two prime characteristics that influence physicians' selection of anti-ulcer therapy.

Girolami's challenge was to position a "me-too" product as superior to Tagamet, which had been described in literature as a "wonder drug." Like many drugs, Tagamet had numerous side effects, none of which were significant in the patient's overall treatment. The drug had proven safe in trials and over time in use. Nevertheless, these side effects proved to be Zantac's window of opportunity and Tagamet's "Achilles' heel."

Girolami and his marketing team decided to alleviate selected side effects through product refinement and then attack Tagamet on those effects. Tagamet could not deny them, because pharmaceutical companies are required to publish a list of side effects for every drug. To implement this competitive marketing strategy, Girolami planned an aggressive launch marketing program that covered product improvements, premium pricing, strategic alliances for distribution, and assertive advertising.

Achieving Product Superiority for Zantac

Girolami wanted to launch Zantac with features superior to those of Tagamet, even though both drugs addressed the same problem. He therefore focused on the issues of dosage and side effects. Like Tagamet, Zantac was originally formulated for twice-a-day use over a six-week period. Girolami wanted a once-a-day dosage, knowing that people hate taking medicine. Taking one pill a day would be easier for patients and would bolster compliance.

Girolami also wanted the drug to be suitable for life-long use without undue side effects. Tagamet and the original Zantac formula had been designed for use only until the ulcer was healed. Girolami sent the product back to the research laboratory. Ultimately, through careful research, certain Zantac side effects were eliminated or reduced in relation to Tagamet's. For example, researchers were able to eliminate the anti-androgenic (testosterone-inhibiting) effects of Zantac that were common to Tagamet. In addition, some patients, particularly the elderly, experienced central nervous system (CNS) effects such as confusion, agitation, disorientation, or hallucinations while taking Tagamet. Glaxo researchers were able to formulate Zantac to alleviate CNS effects among users, a positive feature for physicians whose patients were complaining about such symptoms. Thus, although Zantac was a "me-too" product behind the leader, it brought additional value to the market.

Pricing

Girolami opted for a premium pricing strategy in the launch of Zantac. This decision surprised the board of directors because it defied conventional wisdom. Girolami argued that Zantac would be positioned as an overall superior product with added value, and therefore should be priced accordingly. Further, Glaxo needed to recover its R&D costs, not to mention the cost of the aggressive marketing program needed to catch up to

Tagamet. Despite some intense opposition, Girolami and the premium price decision prevailed.

Distribution

Girolami was determined to launch Zantac globally in all major markets. He was also determined to use Zantac to establish Glaxo in the United States. Building distribution from scratch would take too long, so Girolami decided to pursue a strategic alliance with an established U.S. firm through a licensing arrangement. At first he chose Merck to take the license, but changed his mind at the last minute. He believed that once Zantac was launched as a "Merck" product, it would always be that.

Consequently, Girolami decided to use Hoffman-LaRoche, which had excess capacity and a relatively low profile in the United States. Girolami was confident that LaRoche would do a good job with distribution and sales without jeopardizing Zantac's name. Further, the arrangement was implemented on a temporary basis, thereby giving Glaxo some flexibility to change distribution arrangements in the future.

Advertising

Advertising carried the important positioning message to differentiate Zantac from Tagamet in the minds of the key segment of gastrointestinal physicians. A carefully designed long-term advertising campaign showed Zantac's superiority on side effects as "the first advance" over Tagamet. Further, the campaign would stress different side effects from year to year. This repetitiveness would reinforce the logic of Zantac's superior effectiveness. The launch campaign announced: "Introducing the first advance in H_2-antagonist therapy." Glaxo emphasized the following advantages in ads placed in key trade journals read by gastroenterologists:

- No reported mental confusion
- No significant interference with hepatic drug metabolism
- No detectable anti-androgenic effect
- More convenient administration
- Single dose action for up to 12 hours

Glaxo also actively supported research among gastrointestinal physicians. With a continual flow of new product forms and reduced side effects,

Glaxo created the impression that its product was much more progressive than SmithKline's Tagamet, and was the *de facto* leader in the anti-ulcer drug category. The market responded accordingly.

LAUNCH RESULTS

Zantac's launch had an immediate impact on the ulcer-treatment market and threatened Tagamet's position as the best-selling drug in the world. Within the first week of availability, Zantac claimed 7,000 new prescriptions. In the second week, the number climbed to a staggering 19,000. Five months after the introduction, the number was 40,000 and climbing. At the time, Zantac represented 24 percent of new prescriptions and 17 percent of total prescriptions written. Tagamet's share of the market plummeted from 94 percent to 76 percent. By the end of the year, Zantac had stolen some 100,000 new patients a month from the former market leader.

By 1985, Zantac sales at the pharmacy level totaled $29 million. By the beginning of 1986, prescriptions had risen 41 percent and sales were up by almost 65 percent. In 1987, the dizzying sales rate began to slow; prescriptions increased only 34 percent to 11.3 million and retail sales increased only 44 percent. However, Zantac had finally surpassed Tagamet in U.S. sales. Growing 29.4 percent, Zantac reached $542 million in sales.

By 1987, most of Glaxo's success came at the expense of Tagamet, which for the first time in its history had a decline in both prescriptions and sales. Zantac had finally assumed its position as the sales leader in the anti-ulcer ethical pharmaceutical market. Far behind in third and fourth places were Marion's Carafate and Merck's Pepcid. Glaxo's ultimate success was achieved in 1991 when Zantac became the first drug ever to reach $1 billion in U.S. sales. Continual improvements and research on the drug showed it was also effective in treating severe heartburn. By June 1993, global sales had reached $3.5 billion, or about 70 percent of the world market for the H_2 blockers! In the United States during 1993, Zantac sales reached some $2 billion in comparison to $678 million for Tagamet.

FACTORS CONTRIBUTING TO ZANTAC'S SUCCESS

In a conservative organization, strong leadership from product champions like David Jack and Paul Girolami is necessary to bring change. Subsequently both were knighted, and Sir Paul Girolami became chairman of the company. The two leaders were largely responsible for engineering the Zantac success. Without their wisdom, risk taking, and decision making, Zantac would not have been created. They drove Zantac's success through four major actions: pursuing a growing market, refining the product to beat the competitors, accelerating new product development for faster entry, and hammering a vulnerable leader with a targeted positioning.

A Large and Growing Market

Stomach ulcers and related gastrointestinal problems are common to people all over the world. The market for anti-ulcer products is not only large, but also rapidly growing. This growth is partly due to innovation. SmithKline's drug Tagamet enabled doctors to treat and possibly heal ulcers without surgery. Doctors with patients who suffered from ulcers were quick to prescribe the new medication.

The emergence of a competitor (Glaxo) with an improved product further spurred market growth because more information was disseminated to doctors and patients. Also, Zantac offered reduced side effects, a feature physicians could cite as a benefit to their patients. A large and growing market is not necessary for a new product's success, but can speed the acceptance of one that meets consumers' needs better than current products.

Refining and Differentiating the Product

A product that is not the first entrant into a market must be superior to previous entrants to succeed. Product superiority was critical for Glaxo for two reasons. First, the company needed a financial success from the attractive market opportunity, but a strictly "me-too" product might never recoup investments, especially if it realized only the typical 10 percent market share of an also-ran. Second, the company could differentiate itself from competitors only with a truly superior product. Creating such a product would be difficult, as Tagamet had received approval from regulators and was shown to be effective in practice.

Tagamet had side effects (though not debilitating ones), which became the basis for Glaxo's differentiation of its new product. By continually refining, improving, and offering new forms of Zantac over the years, Glaxo was able to differentiate its product quickly and effectively from SmithKline's Tagamet and achieve a position of market leadership.

Accelerated Product Development

By using parallel processing in its new product development, Glaxo was able to cut its usual development time in half. The company was able to beat competitors to market and secure a loyal customer base. As history has shown, the timing of Zantac's market entry was critical to its success. Glaxo's accomplishments would not have been possible if Merck or Eli Lilly had established a presence in anti-ulcer medications prior to Zantac's appearance. However, the acceleration of new product development was not without risk. Had the simultaneous drug-testing procedures failed, the entire project may have been scuttled.

Aggressive Positioning against a Vulnerable Competitor

Glaxo's positioning strategy attacked SmithKline where it was most vulnerable, on Tagamet's side effects. Glaxo turned Tagamet's weaknesses into Zantac's strengths and used aggressive advertising to give information-hungry gastrointestinal physicians the evidence they needed to prescribe Zantac. SmithKline had difficulty responding to the attack because Tagamet's side effects were listed irrefutably in the information brochures about the drug as required by regulators.

Despite Glaxo's aggressive competition, however, Tagamet dollar sales continued to increase by 6 percent. The market for anti-ulcer drugs was growing more than 20 percent a year during the 1980s. Such market growth can lull an incumbent leader, whose sales continue to grow, into believing that the new competition is good for business, not bad. The leader may delay competitive response and allow the new entrant to continue to make inroads. It is difficult to say how serious a threat SmithKline believed Glaxo to be (especially while sales were increasing), but Tagamet was in a difficult and vulnerable market position, of which Glaxo took full advantage.

POSTSCRIPT

Science marches on. In 1994, the medical community began to accept the conclusion that the bacterium *H. pylori* causes peptic ulcers. Experts recommended two weeks of antibiotic therapy to cure the ulcers. For all practical purposes, this therapy replaces one of the uses of Zantac and

Tagamet. Antibiotics are seen as cheaper and better than H_2 blockers. The H_2 blockers speed ulcer healing, but if the patient stops the course of treatment, the chance of ulcer recurrence is high. The patient may have to take the drug for years. The antibacterial treatment completely eliminates the *H. pylori* that causes the ulcer in two weeks.

The new therapy was a major threat to Zantac, which in 1993 represented about half of Glaxo's $8 billion in sales. However, Glaxo had repositioned the drug over the years, shifting its therapeutic emphasis from ulcers to severe heartburn, an even more common ailment. Glaxo therefore had less than 30 percent of its Zantac business at risk to the new antibiotic therapy.

Patent expirations posed another threat to Zantac's position. Zantac patents expire in 1995 and 2002 and Tagamet's patent expired in 1994. By mid-1994, some 10 drug manufacturers had released generic versions of Tagamet, which sold at a much lower price than Tagamet and Zantac. Tagamet launched a generic version targeted to health maintenance organizations at a significantly lower price. In response, Zantac began exploring strategic alliances with health maintenance organizations and developed an over-the-counter version of Zantac. Meanwhile, the entire U.S. health care system entered a period of political and social turbulence. Such challenges will continue for Zantac, but they are the natural consequence of the extraordinary new product success that put Glaxo on the world map as a leading pharmaceutical firm.

The Gillette Company: Sensor

Webster K. Fletcher and Katherine D. LaVelle

Of a thousand shavers, two do not shave so much alike as not to be distinguished.

Samuel Johnson, quoted by James Boswell in
Life of Dr. Johnson, *1791*

Babies haven't any hair.
Old men's heads are just as bare;
Between the cradle and the grave
Lies a haircut and a shave.

Samuel Hoffenstein, Songs of Faith in the Year After Next

The Gillette Sensor shaving system represents one of The Gillette Company's most successful new product launches.[4] The new men's razor captured 8.8 percent of the $2.2 billion wet shaving market in 1991, with sales exceeding $150 million. The Gillette Company sold more than 27 million razors and 300 million cartridges. The Sensor was the best-selling razor in every market in which it was introduced. Overall, sales exceeded forecast by 30 percent in its first year. The new product eventually served as a platform for an entire line of men's grooming products.

Gillette is no stranger to new product success. The Gillette Company began in 1901 and two years later King C. Gillette introduced the world's first safety razor with disposable blades, an event that changed the future of shaving around the world. During the first year of production, Gillette sold 51 razors and 168 blades. One year later, sales rose to 90,884 razors and

123,648 blades. This trend continued over the years and, despite ups and downs, Gillette dominated the shaving business. It also developed and introduced complementary product lines and diversified into unrelated product areas.

The Gillette Company competes in several "core category" areas, including men's and women's grooming products, writing instruments and correction products, oral care products, and high quality small household appliances. Major brand names include Gillette, Right Guard, Dry Idea, White Rain, Soft & Dri, Paper Mate, Parker, Liquid Paper, Waterman, Oral-B, and Braun. Although based in the United States, Gillette scans the world for market opportunities.

With 1992 revenues at $5 billion, a 64 percent market share in the United States, a 70 percent share in Europe, and an 80 percent share in Latin America, Gillette was clearly a leader in global markets. In 1992, blades and razors generated about one third of Gillette's worldwide revenues, but nearly two thirds of the company's profits. Although Gillette has several business lines, its success with razors has given the company a reputation as the world's leading maker of shaving products.

Among men over the age of 40, the Gillette name conveys a sense of family tradition and represents a passing on of values from father to son. The Gillette name taps warm memories of rites of passage from boyhood to manhood. Through market research, the company discovered that older men relate the Gillette name to baseball and the Friday-night fights, televised programming sponsored by Gillette in the 1950s. The Gillette name has strong brand recognition and tremendous value; therefore any new products the company develops must maintain and enhance that value.

THE BUSINESS ENVIRONMENT PRIOR
TO SENSOR'S ENTRY

Before the introduction of the safety razor, men had shaved for centuries with the less comfortable, less safe straight razor. The safety razor breakthrough changed shaving from a barbershop procedure to one that could be done at home with sturdy metal implements, or shaving systems. Traditionally, a man valued his razor as an important personal tool.

Gillette, which has introduced most of the major shaving product advances in the market since the turn of the century, has long been known for its innovative culture. In 1946, it introduced the first blade dispenser for the Gillette Blue Blades to eliminate the need to unwrap blades. In 1960, it introduced silicone-coated blade edges to improve the quality, safety, and comfort of the shave. In 1971, it introduced the Trac II, the first razor with twin-blade cartridges. Users no longer needed to touch the razor blade.

A classic marketing strategy known as the "blades and razor" strategy emerged from the Gillette view of products as "systems." The razor is developed and sold at a relatively low price to encourage adoption of the shaving "system," then blades are sold on a repeat-purchase basis for profitability. However, in 1974, the French firm Societe Bic SA launched the first disposable razor in Greece. The Bic disposable gave a poorer shave, but consumers responded positively, giving Bic a 10 percent market share in Greece in a very short time. As Bic began to roll out its launch through Europe, Gillette, after considerable internal discussion, launched disposables in the United States before Bic: Daisy for women in 1975, followed by Good News! for men in 1976. The "shaving systems" business would never be the same.

The Disposable Razor Market

After their introduction in the mid-1970s, disposable razors became enormously successful. By 1988, disposable sales represented 52 percent of the overall wet shaving market. An entire generation of first-time shavers would choose a disposable razor for their first shave, a trend that would have important strategic ramifications for the shaving systems market. Predictably, the disposables' success came at the expense of the traditional shaving system, a particularly disturbing fact because Gillette's profit is typically 25 to 30 cents per cartridge refill and only 8 to 10 cents per disposable razor.

By the mid-1980s, Gillette executives had begun to worry that consumers' increasing use of disposable razors was threatening its market position and corporate image. Although a leader in the disposable market with its Good News! razors, Gillette realized that growth of the disposable segment was forcing the entire market to focus on price, creating a rash of discount price promotions. The company believed that this trend was impeding its ability to meet its long-term business objectives.

Gillette engaged in extensive market research to determine consumer perceptions of its company name and product lines, and feelings about shaving in general. Throughout the 1970s and 1980s, this research showed the strength of the Gillette brand and its universal association with quality men's shaving products. The Gillette Company's dominance and positioning in the 1950s and 1960s had caused men to have an almost nostalgic view of Gillette, relating the company closely with the rituals of male grooming and, more broadly, passage into manhood. Among respondents, shaving had a particularly strong association with fatherhood, grooming, sports, growing up, and manhood in general. As the company progressed through the 1980s, however, users of the Good News! disposable razor, particularly younger men, increasingly related Gillette and shaving to convenience, plastic, and low price.

Gillette managers realized that this trend would continue to diminish the significant role that shaving and Gillette played in men's psyche. With the prevalence of disposable razors, buying decisions were increasingly based on price, not on quality or other less tangible factors that historically had been Gillette's strength in the market. Gillette research showed that buyers of disposable razors tended to be less loyal to specific brands than system users. Clearly, the trend toward price-motivated buying decisions and the emerging commodity status of its core product troubled Gillette.

To address these concerns, Gillette created a new vision for its branded products during the late 1980s. The purpose was to consolidate Gillette as "the premier male grooming brand" and to bring quality and value back to shaving products. The trend toward inexpensive disposable razors did little to help the company maintain a reputation as an upscale, high quality producer. It needed to return to its roots in product innovation.

Financial Pressures

Adding to Gillette's concerns about the disposable razor market were two fierce takeover attempts in the mid 1980s. In 1986 the company averted a $4.1 billion unsolicited purchase offer from Revlon Inc., and shortly thereafter fought another proxy battle with the buyout firm Coniston Partners. Gillette survived these takeover attempts, but a consequence of the raiders' attacks was an added sense of urgency to reinvigorate Gillette's innovative culture.

Concerned that stockholders would lose faith in the company's ability to retain its position as market leader, Gillette needed to develop a new product that would impress stockholders and industry analysts. By offering the promise of its next new technology (Sensor), the company was able to convince shareholders that keeping Gillette together would be worth more than breaking it up. In effect, facing a growing but less profitable disposables market that was cannibalizing the more profitable shaving systems products, and the threat of financial takeovers, managers felt pressure to move ahead with the Sensor project.

SENSOR DEVELOPMENT

Development of the Gillette Sensor took place over 13 years and involved a total outlay of some $310 million: $75 million in R&D, $125 million in capital investment, and a $110 million launch-year advertising budget. A combination of market research, product refinement, manufacturing development, and crisis management led to the most successful product launch in Gillette history.

The Gillette Company had long prided itself on its new product development efforts, not hesitating to introduce products that were certain to cannibalize successful current lines. All new product development focused on consumer needs and problems related to shaving. The Gillette Blue Blade, the Trac II razor, the Atra, and the Daisy and Good News! disposable razors were all created to improve shaving.

The Idea for Sensor

The idea for Sensor emerged after the launch of the Gillette Atra razor in 1977. John Francis, a design engineer in Gillette's Reading, England, R&D facility, thought to attach two very thin shaving blades (of his earlier design) to some sort of springs for flexibility. The idea was that the springs (or their equivalent) would allow the blades to "float" and contour to the face for a closer shave. He built a crude prototype, thereby creating the first suspension system for razorblades.

Francis' initial design was a system of fluid-filled compressible tubes that allowed the blades to move independently. This device would have been too complex and expensive to manufacture on a large scale. Further, other aspects of the product design did not conform well to the tube concept. For example, a skin guard that stretched the skin before the blades cut the beard would not work well with the tubes. Consequently, Gillette set out to develop a product design that would meet all constraints, especially those of mass production.

Product Design and Manufacturing

By tapping the company's manufacturing and design expertise, Sensor engineers were able to design a product that was truly a breakthrough. To reduce the costs associated with the original suspension design, engineers developed a system of cantilevered springs integrated into the cartridge. Continued testing, however, revealed that the styrene used on most other razors lost its resilience over time. After experimenting with different resins, the engineers selected Noryl, a resin that proved more durable and better suited to this unique application.

By 1983 they had a working prototype that was use tested by 500 men. The results were favorable, with preference for the prototype being substantially greater than that for Atra or Trac II. Gillette considers itself highly expert on shaving facial hair and uses a variety of product use-testing approaches. For example, in addition to testing by actual consumers, test shaving is done each day by selected employees who come to work unshaven. Every aspect of the shaver and the shaving process was analyzed in detail.

With a satisfactory prototype, Gillette was able to turn to manufacturing issues. The product design had to be suitable for mass production so that scale effects would lead to reduced costs. However, the complexity of the floating blades and the overall design created major production problems. For example, the cartridge design required that steel supports be joined to the blades. These supports had to be secured to the blade bodies with total reliability, without damaging the fragile blade edges and at a rate sufficient to keep pace with the other high speed assembly operations. To solve this problem, engineers developed a laser welding system that provided the accuracy necessary for the tiny and complex cartridge components.

With the new system, the 15 needed welds could be done without damage to the surrounding structure. Once welded, the blades moved down the production line at the rate of five every two seconds and were inspected by high resolution cameras that compared each weld's image with computer-stored perfect welds. Some 100 electrical or mechanical inspections were made on each final blade cartridge assembly.

Managing and Refining Sensor's Development

By 1981, the design was far enough along in terms of market research, R&D, and manufacturing that Sensor development was moved from the Reading, England, R&D facility to Gillette's South Boston manufacturing center, although the British office continued to contribute to Sensor development.

As in many important new product development projects, various controversies over technical issues arose among the design engineers and required considerable discussion and testing. This form of *creative conflict* is often the best way to refine the design of a complex new product. In these cases a chief technical officer is required to resolve such strategic differences.

However, as design and marketing plans developed, another type of controversy emerged over the strategic direction of the new razor. Boston planners were developing both a disposable and a cartridge-system version of Sensor in an effort to serve both of those major markets. Reading managers, including head of European operations John W. Symons, argued that Gillette was relying too heavily on disposables and pushed for a cartridge-only Sensor. In a shakeup that would determine the future course of Sensor development, Gillette CEO Colman M. Mockler put Symons in charge as executive vice president of the shaving group. This move provided clear direction to the project: the emphasis would be on the shaving system over the disposable.

Symons then replaced much of the Boston razor management team with his own European staff. He assembled a nine-person Sensor team who would begin an intensive 15-month effort to meet the January 1990 production deadline. The cross-functional "crisis" team of product designers, engineers, and R&D people used ongoing product testing to continuously improve the new razor. The Sensor was tested by more than 5,000 men, who compared it to Atra Plus, considered to be the best product then on the market. Results of this testing showed that Sensor provided significantly better performance on every designated shaving attribute.

PRODUCT LAUNCH

Sensor helped Gillette return to the shaving systems concept with a vengeance. The final product reflected the efforts of the Gillette design team to give Sensor a masculine look and feel. The handle casing was made of stainless steel, with black plastic trim and grips. The device was reminiscent of past high quality shaving systems, and very different from the light plastic disposable razors. Ergonomics was used to shape the handle to the fit and weight that would be comfortable in a man's hand.

A plastic shaving "organizer" was designed to hold the new Sensor razor and a packet of five blade cartridges. It not only provided a handy travel kit and facilitated retail display, but also consolidated the image of the Sensor as a return to the shaving system, bringing quality and value back to shaving.

The retail launch price for the initial package was set at $3.75, less than the prices of Atra and Trac II, to encourage trial and adoption of the new system. However, blades would be priced at $3.79 for five cartridges, about 25 percent more than other Gillette blades, which would yield an estimated eight cents more gross profit per cartridge! This pricing represented a convincing return to the classic "blades and razor" strategy.

Gillette was determined that Sensor would not fail through lack of awareness. The Sensor global launch program was budgeted at about $110 million, whereas the advertising budget for all Gillette products during 1987 was $284 million. Prior to the official Sensor launch, Gillette had developed the tag line: "Gillette: The Best a Man Can Get." This theme emphasized both the quality of the shaving experience that Gillette products provide and the overall brand image of Gillette quality within the broader men's grooming segment.

Promotion for the Sensor launch began in September 1989 with sales and press briefings that were held simultaneously in 19 countries around the world. This effort generated initial excitement that resulted in a barrage of public relations and free media coverage. With the decision to launch during the Super Bowl in late January, Gillette began "teaser" ads during television sporting events at the beginning of that month, using the line: "Gillette is about to change the way men shave forever." Finally, Sensor was officially launched on January 28, 1990, with three spots during the Super Bowl, all continuing with the theme "The Best a Man Can Get."

The Super Bowl ads were immediately followed by additional TV spots and a print campaign in general media such as *USA Today, Time,* and *Newsweek.* A strong television campaign in March during major sporting events (especially basketball) and on prime time was designed to continue the momentum. To energize the trade, which would provide distribution for the Sensor, Gillette used trade magazines and selective television advertising.

To get the new razor into users' hands as quickly as possible during the launch year, Gillette mailed five million coupons for two dollars or three dollars off and placed 50 million free-standing inserts (FSIs) of equal value in a variety of media. At that price, Gillette was essentially providing the razor free, certain that most of the trials would result in long-term use. Its most aggressive promotion involved mailed kits containing a razor, three replacement cartridges, and a one-dollar-off coupon to 400,000 men who were confirmed users of competing products.

SUCCESS!

The Gillette Company's launch of Sensor was nothing short of an overwhelming success. Sensor first-year sales of more than $150 million surpassed optimistic forecasts by 30 percent. Internationally, Sensor became the best selling razor in every one of the 15 markets in which it was introduced. By the end of 1991, the product had similar sales results in more than 59 countries, with sales topping $300 million.

Perhaps more important to Gillette was the growth of the overall shaving systems market in relation to the disposables market. The dollar-value market share of disposable razors declined from 49 percent in 1989 to 41 percent by 1993, largely because of the introduction of the Sensor shaving system. In addition, the average sales ratio of blades to razors was more than 12 to one in the first year, indicating substantial repurchase rates by men trying Sensor for the first time. Finally, about 36 percent of new Sensor sales were taken away from competing products.

The new Sensor product and launch marketing program were so successful that demand for the product exceeded Gillette's ability to manufacture the new razor and its cartridges. Sales were appreciably ahead of forecasts and the sophisticated manufacturing process was difficult to accelerate on short notice. Such high demand was a tribute to both the product and the promotional efforts, but created problems with distributors, retailers, and some customers. In some countries, the Sensor launch had to be postponed until supplies could be produced in sufficient quantity. With some scaling back of promotion, sensible market allocations, and acceleration of production to the extent possible, Sensor's pace of growth continued after the first six months of growing pains. Nevertheless, profitability was delayed.

The success was recognized by stockholders (stock price rose from the mid-$20 range in 1989 to about $60 in 1992), but Gillette did not rest on its laurels. It began to leverage the Sensor success with extensions of the brand. In 1993, Gillette launched a new line of men's toiletries and grooming products. It also began laying the groundwork for its next-generation Sensor, to be launched in the mid-1990s.

In September 1992, Gillette introduced Sensor for Women, the world's first razor designed to address all of the shaving needs of women. Its slogan was: "Finally, a Razor Worth Holding Onto." The women's Sensor featured a specially designed wide handle that made the razor easier to hold in the shower or bath than the traditional man's razor. It had a feminine appearance, cool colors, and the original Sensor blade technology. It was introduced at $3.99 and 7.6 million units were sold in its first six months on the market. Dollar sales of some $40 million, including blade cartridges, far exceeded the forecast!

The success of the Sensor products drew competitors. Warner-Lambert's Schick brand was number two in the U.S. market with a 13 percent share. The company introduced its Tracer line in 1990, aimed at slowing Sensor's domination of the system segment. Although Tracer lacked the breakthrough technology and product design embodied in Sensor, it was capable of attracting at least some of Sensor's customers. Wilkinson Sword, Gillette's major European competitor, introduced a new system razor that became a significant threat in key European markets. However, Gillette began acquiring parts of Wilkinson's business (country by country).

KEYS TO SENSOR'S SUCCESS

Numerous factors undoubtedly contributed to Sensor's overwhelming success. Fundamental to that success was Gillette's ability to meet consumers' needs. Recognizing that a man wants to look and feel his best, Gillette used its design and manufacturing strengths to establish the product's core benefit: delivering a better shave through high technology. Dedication and commitment to product design and refinement led to significant improvements over currently available products. Other key success factors were a commitment to superior manufacturing processes, strong marketing support, managers' willingness to take a risk, and leadership.

Product Refinement with Alpha and Beta Testing

Gillette's Sensor success shows that a new product entering a competitive market must do more than just meet the needs of consumers. The new product must be superior in every respect. Its design must be refined to the point that even if consumers cannot explain just why the product is better, they know that it is and are moved to action. To achieve this kind of refinement, the company must study the product and its user in depth.

Gillette undertakes what is perhaps the most comprehensive ongoing study of facial hair in the world. Every day, roughly 200 volunteer employees from throughout the company participate in alpha testing. They begin their work day at the South Boston R&D facility with a shave. They shave in small booths complete with sinks and mirrors, using a variety of razors, shaving creams, and aftershave lotions. Women make up 29 percent of the razor market, so female employees participate by shaving their legs. Afterward, the volunteers answer numerous questions from researchers who are measuring the performance of each product.

In addition to obtaining user feedback, Gillette takes a more scientific approach. Researchers use a boroscope, a tiny fiber-optic video camera, attached to a razor to record the dynamics of the actual shaving process. They measure such things as the angle of cut whiskers, the balance of the razor, and the motion of the skin guard. The company has found, for example, that there are 30,000 whiskers on the average male face, and that they grow by about 15/1,000th of an inch a day.

Subsequently, Gillette conducts beta testing of the products with actual users to gain further insights. When the Sensor for Women was developed, focus group participants were given the new razors to take home for use. They later returned to the focus groups to discuss their experiences. By thorough product testing to understand the fundamental function of its products, Gillette is able to develop innovative concepts and prototypes that are continuously improved. Gillette has up to 20 different prototypes in testing at any one time. Its dedication to continuous product development and perfection led to the development of the finely tuned Sensor.

Superior Design and Manufacturing to Preempt Competition

By investing resources in a complex and meticulously designed product, the company achieved short-term success while creating a long-term competitive advantage. The product design and manufacturing processes led to a "floating blade" technology with 22 patents, a feat not easily duplicated by competitors. Because of Gillette's first-mover advantage and aggressive placement of razors in the hands of shavers, competitors would be forced to make a huge investment in research and development to surpass the Sensor. Simply learning how to manufacture the product (or a close facsimile) would be a formidable task.

Financial and Marketing Strength

The Gillette Company backed Sensor's introduction with strong financial and marketing support. As a profitable global enterprise and industry leader, Gillette could afford to launch the product with an impressive campaign, spending more than $110 million on advertising and promotion in Sensor's first year. This effort created the product excitement and consumer demand that were needed to generate a return on Gillette's sizable investment. Numerous new products fail simply for lack of sufficient resources to create an impact on the market and overcome consumer and trade resistance.

Taking the Risk

Because of Sensor's huge success, the magnitude of The Gillette Company's gamble with the new product may not be apparent in retrospect. The company was very profitable without Sensor. It did not need to take the chance of trying to switch consumers from disposables to a new shaving system. Even though market research and product testing indicated that the product was a winner, there was a possibility (as shown by textbook statistics) that the new product would fail. Gillette therefore undertook an aggressive advertising ($110 million) and public relations campaign. With $200 million at risk in development, the company was not going to be lax in informing the market about the new product.

Clearly, Sensor could have failed. Disposable razors had been widely accepted. Moreover, consumers may not have perceived enough difference between the new Sensor and its predecessors, Trac II and Atra, to change their behavior. Nevertheless, Gillette managers believed in their new product enough to invest a significant amount of money and time to support it. They were willing to take the risk.

Leadership

After eight years of development work, strategic differences arose between the American and British management groups over whether the product should be a disposable razor or a shaving system. This decision could have stalled the project interminably. The arguments on both sides were convincing. The issue was finally resolved by the CEO's decision to back one option over the other. This situation exemplifies the crucial role of leadership in new product development. The product was on the market 15 months after the decision. Otherwise, its launch may have been delayed by years of discussion. Decisive leadership came at the right time and from the right person for the Gillette Sensor.

CONCLUSION

As The Gillette Company looks to the future, the company continues the effective implementation of a long-term competitive strategy. Its product and brand positioning has bolstered its strength in the men's grooming market and provides a platform for future growth. The success of the Sensor has enhanced the Gillette name and image and provided a brand identity that can be leveraged for growth into new markets. The recent successful launch of Sensor for Women is a direct result of the strength of the brand and the renewed perception of Gillette as a technology leader.

By sticking to its key competitive guidelines, learned through a humbling loss of market share during the mid-1960s, Gillette has been able to rebuild and expand its brand franchise. Gillette has learned valuable lessons from Sensor and must continue its aggressive new product development. The next-generation razor and blades are undoubtedly on the drawing boards or being tested by company executives.

9

Tracking the
New Product

New product development is a continual process that does not end on the day of the launch. The new product, its marketing program, and their performance must be monitored and tracked very closely after launch. For most new products, launch provides the first opportunity to understand how the product performs under actual use conditions. The information generated is much more telling than the information gathered during planning and development.

The market's response to the launch marketing program also must be tracked. Conditions in the business environment at launch could be much different from those during planning and development and could lead to unexpected results. For example, advertising may not be as effective as anticipated because of competitive reactions, or distributors may doubt that the new product will attract consumers and may postpone their cooperation.

To prepare for any number of contingencies, a company must carefully plan the implementation of a new product launch, anticipating responses to changing business conditions. However, even if a company is prepared for contingencies, it must establish a monitoring and tracking capability to know what to change and when.

A tracking capability requires data collection on selected measures to identify and diagnose problems quickly and efficiently. The process of diagnosis is particularly important because it determines the type and timing of changes needed to pursue success. For example, in the first story in this chapter, Fuji Photo Film Company launched its QuickSnap single-use camera in Japan and had almost immediate success. However, the product was launched in the United States along with Kodak's Fling version of the single-use camera, and both products had very slow market acceptance.

Trying to understand why the acceptance rate was so low for a product that should have been popular was central to determining what changes were needed. For example, both companies had to overcome ecological concerns about disposability (Kodak changed its product's name from Fling to FunSaver) and establish the credibility of the concept. In effect, consumers wanted proof about the product's performance. Also, American consumers were not as involved in photography as Japanese consumers, and therefore were much slower to adopt the new idea of disposability. The use of promotion helped overcome some of the market resistance.

Once the needed changes are identified, they must be implemented. This process is exemplified in the second story, which recounts the actions of MTV after its launch. Even on launch day, the MTV team knew that much remained to be done if they wanted to succeed. Most important, they had to persuade record company executives that providing free video clips for MTV's new 24-hour music television format would enable the companies to increase their record sales. Without free film clips, the newly launched MTV channel could fold.

The MTV team also had to persuade advertisers (the main source of their revenue) that the new cable channel could help them reach the attractive target market of people 24 to 34 years of age. However, they first had to persuade cable television distributors to buy into the new program to get the breadth of coverage necessary to deliver a large audience to advertisers. How MTV used market research, creative advertising, product development, distribution, pricing, and segmentation to achieve its far-reaching success after launching the new cable channel exemplifies the implementation of postlaunch changes.

The third story in this chapter shows how Snapple, a small entrepreneurial firm, beat the odds and achieved success against giant competitors. This David and Goliath story illustrates the importance of strategically focusing on a growing segment of the market and continually improving the new product and its performance. Being the leader in the rapidly growing New Age beverage segment gave Snapple an early advantage against industry giants Coke, Pepsi, and Lipton, but sustaining the advantage took special effort.

Relentless implementation of advertising and distribution proved to be critical to Snapple's continued competitive success after launch. Further, the founders of Snapple actively engaged in *learning* their business well and adhered to key principles to sustain their advantage. Their actions show the importance of maintaining a clear strategic focus for a new product while modifying the product and program as necessary to ensure continuing success.

Fuji Photo Film Company, Ltd.: QuickSnap

Wendy E. Hyer and Katherine A. Stocker

A picture shows me at a glance what it takes dozens of pages of a book to expound.

Ivan Turgenev, Fathers and Sons, 1862

The Fuji single-use camera reached Japanese retail shelves in 1986, and was an instant success.[1] In its simplest form it is basically a roll of film encased in a cardboard box with an inexpensive plastic 35mm lens. The camera is purchased at a convenient location, the pictures are taken, and the entire camera is sent in for processing. Ironically, Fuji and Kodak launched single-use cameras in the U.S. market in 1987, and both were initially unsuccessful. Consumers doubted the reliability and quality of single-use cameras and environmentalists denounced the cameras as generating waste.

However, by 1992, some 22 million single-use cameras had been sold in the United States, and the category as a whole had become a $200 million market. Surprisingly, the product actually expanded the entire photography market. It enabled the consumer to take pictures anywhere at any time. The story of how this new product concept was developed and launched provides insight on the Japanese new product development processes and shows the difficulty of achieving success in a competitor's home market.

THE PHOTO FILM BUSINESS

Photography has broad appeal. From children, to parents, to swinging singles, to grandparents, *everyone* has a reason to take pictures. In fact, amateur photographers spend more than $10 billion annually. Nearly 46 percent of point-and-shoot camera owners consider themselves beginners, and people are becoming camera users at a younger age. In fact, in one study, 80 percent of teenage boys said they own cameras.

Why is photography so popular? For the picture taker, a photo is an inexpensive and permanent record of a memory, usually a happy memory. The cost of a photo is very low in relation to its lifetime value. Despite economic downturns, people continue to marry, have babies, and make memories. Photography enables young couples, new parents, and grandparents to capture moments in time and share them with friends. Single people use photography to record events with friends. Sports enthusiasts photograph action events to share with other sports enthusiasts.

People also use photography to capture their youth, so that memories live on as they age. Pictures create a feeling of nostalgia, helping people to relive past events. Because the opportunity to capture memories is fleeting, picture-taking is impulsive and the majority of pictures taken are unplanned and unanticipated.

In the early 1980s, however, growth in the camera market was stagnant. Consumers were weary of the increasing sophistication of 35mm cameras, and longed for simplicity and convenience. The transitory nature of picture-taking opportunities represented a real concern for consumers as they struggled to master the latest technology.

Fuji's Background

Fuji Photo Film Company, Ltd., based in Tokyo, Japan, started in the 1930s as a maker of motion picture film. Initially the company had difficulty gaining consumer acceptance as a quality producer of film, but teaming up with a German emulsions specialist enabled it to overcome its product deficiencies. By the early 1960s, Fuji had expanded operations into Brazil, the United States, and Europe. In addition, it had expanded its product line.

Total sales in 1990 were $8.6 billion, including sales of magnetic tape (audiotape, videotape), commercial products (color scanners, copiers, motion picture film), and consumer photographic products (cameras, electronic imaging equipment, photographic paper). Fuji has participated in joint ventures with Rank Xerox in the United Kingdom (1962), B&F Microdisks (1989), and DuPont (1989). By 1994, Fuji was Japan's leading manufacturer of photographic film and paper, holding a 73 percent share of the market for color film and an 85 percent share of the single-use camera market in Japan.

Fuji launched an effective attack strategy against Kodak in the United States, eroding Kodak's overall market share from 90 percent to 65 percent. Not complacent, Kodak began to make inroads into Fuji's territory in Japan through a strategic counterattack. The two photographic giants will continue to clash around the world wherever an opportunity arises.

The Fuji Culture

Fuji strives to give employees broad experience throughout the company. Organized in functional divisions and subsidiaries, Fuji follows a practice of promoting from within, thereby guaranteeing well-rounded executives who are knowledgeable about all aspects of the business. In sharp contrast to the usual Japanese business practice, Fuji's R&D division promotes on the basis of merit, not seniority or age.

Fuji executives control hierarchy by minimizing separation of the functional business segments. This practice fosters continual innovation through the synergy of cross-functional relationships. Also, unlike many Japanese firms, the company encourages innovation by actively soliciting suggestions from employees, customers, family members, and vendors. The three principles or "action guidelines" for Fuji operations are: (1) be thoroughly customer oriented, (2) think and act globally, and (3) strive to create innovation.

Fuji's Strengths

Fuji's core competitive strengths are its competence in measuring and addressing consumer needs and its ability to develop and introduce new products faster than its competitors. The company created the first magnetic tape product in 1960 and produced the world's fastest color negative film in 1976. It was the first company to develop the plastic 35mm lens, and was able to draw on its experience in mass producing video cartridges to speed development of the inner plastic casings for the single-use camera. In addition, Fuji created "drop-in" film loading after listening to customer concerns about the difficulty of loading film.

Fuji tends to increase R&D expenditures during critical phases of product development, and has sought to strengthen relationships with its service and distribution channels. These efforts contribute to successful product launches. Fuji is determined to innovate as technology evolves, and to use innovation to gain competitive advantage.

THE DEVELOPMENT OF QUICKSNAP

Fuji's new product development process begins with ideas or concepts that arrive *directly* from consumers' comments and distributors. Although research and development functions are centralized in Tokyo, Fuji often tests ideas and concepts with its distributors all over the world to screen them and get feedback before creating a prototype. Distributors take suggestions and complaints from consumers and send them to Fuji in Tokyo, which then conducts focus groups and concept tests. Once a market opportunity is identified, Fuji creates a prototype.

The idea for a single-use camera came from focus group research on cameras conducted in the United States, the United Kingdom, and Japan throughout 1982 and 1983. Consumers were concerned about taking their cameras into high risk environments. They wanted an inexpensive camera that would take good pictures, but if lost or dropped would not be a great financial loss. To address these needs, Fuji's defined the objective of developing 35mm quality in a low cost shell.

Ironically, the idea for such a product (called *"utsurun-desu"* in Japanese, or "film with a lens attached") had originated in Fujifilm more than 20 years before, perhaps as a response to the Japanese consumer's obsession with single-use items. Fuji had tried to make the product, but was unsuccessful. Finally in 1986, spurred on by consumer requests from the 1982 focus groups, Fuji succeeded in perfecting the product technology.

The core product concept represented six major attributes: low risk, pocketable, portable, under $10, able to deliver quality, and care free. By delivering all these attributes at a reasonable price, Fuji could give consumers added value. People could take quality pictures anywhere without worrying about an expensive 35mm camera—at the beach or on a mountaintop. Fuji delivered a product that addressed unmet needs. The single-use camera reintroduced impulsiveness in picture-taking activities, and in fact expanded the opportunities to take impulsive shots.

LAUNCH MARKETING STRATEGY

Consistent with its history, Fuji first introduced the new camera in the domestic market to gain an understanding of consumer response, product problems, and any production difficulties. Once satisfied with the product's market performance in Japan, Fuji would roll it out to other markets.

The Launch in Japan

Fuji believed the Japanese consumer would stringently test its product's merits. Traditionally, the Japanese have been much more involved in photography than people in most other countries. They are considered shrewd and critical consumers of photographic products. If they liked the new camera, it would be adopted quickly.

The first single-use camera (110 film format size) was launched in Japan in July 1986. The product was called "*Utsurun-desu.*" The simplicity of its design appealed to the Japanese sense of aesthetics, and its disposability was admired by a society that views many things as impermanent. Advertising was limited during its introduction. Instead, Fuji relied on word of mouth among a society of consumers to whom photography was important and any innovation was a news event.

Fuji also capitalized on the parent/child relationship in Japan. Japanese parents tend to involve their children in photography much earlier than parents in other cultures. Consequently, Fuji positioned the *Utsurun-desu* as an inexpensive and easy way for parents to encourage and develop their children's photographic skills. The camera also became increasingly popular with teenagers and older people. For the consumer, the ease of use merely underscored the camera's advertising tag line: "Don't miss the shutter chance!"

Soon after the product was launched in Japan, Fuji pursued an intensive distribution strategy that was piggybacked on its distribution strengths for regular film. No vacation resort or tourist area would be far from convenience stores and vending machines that would carry the *Utsurun-desu*. The single-use camera would be available in every possible sales outlet, from large camera shops to railroad station kiosks.

The new product's success in Japan was quick and sizable. In 1989, Fuji had a commanding 90 percent share of the Japanese single-use camera market. By 1992, it controlled 70 percent of the Japanese market for film and the single-use camera represented 20 percent of its film sales.

The Launch in the United States

Encouraged by its initial success with the single-use camera in Japan, Fuji entered the U.S. market in 1987. Americans shoot more than 16 billion pictures a year (28,000 a minute). Fuji therefore believed that the United States represented an attractive opportunity for its new product. The U.S. market presented major challenges, however. First, the U.S. market was much larger and more diverse than the Japanese market. Second, the United States had more environmentalists who would be concerned about the disposability aspect of the camera. Third, American consumers were familiar with and had an overwhelming preference for Kodak products. Fourth, and perhaps most important, Kodak had entered the market in 1987 with its own 110 format size version of the single-use camera.

Apparently Fuji's 1986 launch in Japan gave Kodak the lead time necessary to develop its own single-use camera. Using a crash program and a cross-functional new product development team, Kodak was able to achieve the fastest product development in company history. The end result was a low cost product with high quality and few problems during manufacturing. When Kodak launched its version of the 110 format size camera, Fuji launched its 135 format single-use version of QuickSnap into both the Japanese and U.S. markets. However, all of this activity had little impact in the U.S. market because of slow acceptance of single-use cameras by American consumers.

Part of the reason for this slow start was American consumers' skepticism toward new photographic products. In addition, the photographic industry was under pressure because of environmental concerns about its operations. Environmentalists condemned the single-use camera for adding to the waste stream. Kodak responded by changing the name of its single-use camera from "Fling" to the less-wasteful-sounding "FunSaver." In addition, Kodak began a recycling program to alleviate worries about the environmental impact of the camera. For example, photo finishers are encouraged to return the entire camera to the manufacturer for reuse and recycling. The industry also made a concerted effort to stop referring to the cameras as disposable, using the terms "one-time-use" and "single-use" instead. By responding to environmental concerns, both Fuji and Kodak were able to reduce a major barrier to sales growth.

Over time, Kodak and its marketing campaign began to increase acceptance of the single-use camera and expand its market in the United States. Kodak's strong brand recognition, built over 100 years, helped to alleviate early consumer skepticism and, in effect, enlarged the market.

Thus, Fuji was able to benefit from Kodak's actions, which legitimized the product. Both companies also gave many cameras away in promotions to prove that the print quality was equal to that of regular point-and-shoot cameras.

Although Fuji is the second largest (to Kodak) film manufacturer in the world, its advertising budget was limited. Its advertising funds were used to encourage sales of standard film rather than single-use cameras. In fact, only one TV advertisement for the QuickSnap was produced. Initially, Fuji relied on sales promotional techniques to gain trial and adoption. For example, in addition to using promotional giveaways, Fuji gained exposure by customizing the single-use camera for companies to use as gifts or promotions, otherwise known as premiums.

As market acceptance increased, the advertising budgets of both Kodak and Fuji steadily grew to fuel demand. Advertisements were generally limited to tourists and the mass market to build consumer recognition. Kodak's advertisements had the tag line: "This picture was taken by someone who didn't bring their camera." Fuji's showed expensive cameras being accidentally damaged and used the message: "You should have had a QuickSnap."

Fuji's distribution channel in the United States initially centered on supermarkets and camera shops. Soon after the launch, however, it blanketed the market to include discount, convenience, mass merchandise, and drug stores where regular film is sold. Drug and discount stores have increasingly become primary sales outlets for photographic products. In addition, because many single-use camera purchases are made on impulse, supermarket register display racks are popular. Camera stores are less important for distribution because they typically concentrate on more sophisticated cameras that use high margin accessories.

The price of the basic Fuji QuickSnap model, which took general outdoor shots, was $6.95. Subsequently, an $11.95 flash model was introduced for indoor and dimly lit outdoor settings. A panoramic QuickSnap at $11.95 provided a wide-angle lens to capture scenery and large groups. Fuji also introduced a $12.95 all-weather camera that could take underwater shots.

WHERE IS THE SUCCESS?

The success of the single-use camera was uneven for Fuji. With an estimated 90 percent share of the very demanding Japanese photography market, Fuji achieved a significant success with the 1986 launch of the *Utsurun-desu* in Japan. However, its subsequent U.S. launch of the Quick-Snap was relatively less successful. By 1992, Fuji held about 20 percent of the U.S. market and Kodak held 80 percent.

Acceptance of Fuji's single-use camera concept in the United States was very slow, but eventually gained momentum. Overall sales of single-use cameras grew an average of 50 percent each year between 1988 and 1992. Sales grew from 2.8 million in 1988 to 22.0 million in 1992. By then the market was attractive enough to lure additional competitive entrants (Konica, 3M, and others).

A more telling measure of the camera's success is the fact that the sales generated by the single-use camera were incremental and did not appreciably cannibalize regular film sales. Industry experts estimate that 50 percent of the pictures taken with single-use cameras would not have been taken without them. Because the cameras are preloaded, recyclable, and inexpensive, consumers are willing to use them in places where they would not take an expensive camera, such as at the beach or on the ski slopes.

EXPLAINING THE PATTERNS OF SUCCESS

Fuji's initial success with the single-use camera in Japan is explained largely by the company's approach to new product development. First, Fuji is highly customer-driven, not in the sense of using traditional marketing research, but in the sense of listening carefully to customers and retrieving information from them in as direct a format as possible. The idea for QuickSnap emerged directly from consumer problems and concerns about using expensive 35mm cameras in difficult situations. Second, Fuji's organizational culture fosters innovation. In particular, the use of cross-functional teams composed of people from manufacturing, design, and marketing produces synergy through continual communication and interaction. This synergy in turn increases the speed, flexibility, and quality of new product development.

The success of the single-use camera in the United States is indirectly attributable to Fuji's performance in Japan, although Fuji did not benefit from it as much as Kodak. When Kodak observed Fuji's Japanese success in 1986, it knew it would be only a matter of time before Fuji launched in the United States. Kodak was compelled to develop its own single-use camera. Using new product development methods similar to those Fuji had used (cross-functional teams, and so on), Kodak was able to launch the Fling single-use during 1987. However, its market response was nothing like Fuji's in Japan.

American consumers were not as intensely interested in photography as Japanese consumers. Word of mouth about the new product took longer to circulate from early users to later adopters than it did in Japan, where the word spread quickly. Further, U.S. environmentalists had concerns about the disposability of the product. Kodak's use of the Fling name implied "fling it away when you're done with it." After Kodak changed the name and increased its promotional efforts, many of the initial barriers to consumer adoption were overcome and success followed.

Even if Fuji had entered the U.S. market in 1986, a year before Kodak, it is not likely to have achieved any greater success. The market simply took time to develop. Perhaps only Kodak would have been able to develop the U.S. market. Kodak's tremendous credibility on the subject of photography among American consumers gave it the edge in overcoming the market barriers to success. In retrospect, the fact that Fuji was able to garner a 20 percent share of the U.S. market can be considered a success.

Cultural familiarity and loyalty to a brand explain the significant difference in market share between Fuji and Kodak in Japan and the United States. Each new product performed exceedingly well in its home market, where consumers were comfortable with the brand names, and poorly in its competitor's market. Despite differences in brand preference, the product itself satisfied a need that is apparently global among consumers—the need for inexpensive and convenient way to capture memories.

A VIEW TO THE FUTURE

Because the single-use camera has proven to be so convenient and easy to use, it has spurred 35mm film sales. Single-use cameras are the only bright spot in the otherwise dormant film industry and now account for 5 percent of the U.S. film market.

As long as prices stay in a reasonable range, new uses for and new models of single-use cameras are likely to continue the market growth. For example, cameras for specific sporting events provide growth opportunities. Special wide-angle cameras sell briskly at professional football games. Cameras with special lenses can be developed for a variety of specific sports enthusiasts, such as cyclists, swimmers, and rock climbers. Also feasible are lenses that produce wavy or distorted photos (like funhouse mirrors).

Fuji has shown that consumers may not always want the fanciest and most complex camera, but instead may prefer the simplest and most functional! By listening to its customers and meeting the needs of various market segments, Fuji will be able to produce a continual stream of new products built on the single-use principle. The brand extension possibilities include a variety of film speeds, lenses, accessories, and packaging.

Many opportunities for expansion are available outside the United States, Japan, and Europe. With the opening of Eastern Europe and other less-developed areas of the world, a huge untapped market awaits. The single-use camera may be a perfect vehicle for introducing the joys of photography to consumers who are not able to make a large initial camera investment. The convenience, ease of use, high quality, and recyclability of the single-use camera, coupled with Fuji's innovative capabilities, should enable the company to seize the worldwide opportunities and maintain a position as one of the world's major producers of these cameras.

MTV Networks: MTV

David J. Benjack and J. Michael MacKeen

Ladies and gentlemen! Rock and roll!
John Lack, introducing MTV, August 1, 1981

The launch of MTV, Music Television, on August 1, 1981, started a new age in television.[2] MTV, the product, served as a new promotional tool for recording artists, a new advertising vehicle for manufacturers, a unique program format for cable operators, and an exciting new entertainment channel for a young, music-loving audience.

With a reported initial investment of $20 million, MTV grew from just another cable television concept to an emerging global television network. By 1992, MTV was in 57 million homes in the United States, 40 million homes in Europe, and 24 million homes in Latin America. Furthermore, MTV launched new channels in Asia and Australia, expanding its 1991 in-home subscriptions. Globally, MTV broadcasted into 215 million homes in 75 countries!

THE SITUATION PRIOR TO MTV'S SUCCESS

In 1979, the recording industry went into a recession largely attributed to disco music, which was expected to be a long-term success but turned into a short-lived fad. The direction of rock music was not clear, especially among consumers 12 to 34 years of age. These young consumers in the so-called "baby-boom" generation represented an attractive target to national advertisers. They were a large and important spending group because of their trend-setting tendencies, but were difficult to reach.

The rapid rise and fall of disco made radio stations jittery about the kind of music to play, so they returned to the tried-and-true successful stars of the 1960s and 1970s in their programming. They were reluctant to play recordings by new artists. As a consequence, young listeners became bored with the lack of new music. Music plays a fundamental role in the social fabric of young consumers. They associate music with memories of school, dating, friendships, and special occasions. Certainly, they would be receptive to innovations in music that would become part of their experience of youth.

Meanwhile, in the late 1970s, the market for cable television was emerging. Few creative programs were offered in the early days. Cable channels such as ESPN (round-the-clock sports), CNN (round-the-clock news), HBO (round-the-clock movies), and others offered programming that reflected specific types of network television programs (news, sports, movies, sitcom reruns, documentaries, and so on). Consumers, especially the young ones who were attractive to advertisers, were not impressed by these offerings. Cable companies faced sluggish sales and clearly recognized the need for alternative programming.

Young consumers needed new music, record companies needed to recover from the postdisco sales slump, and cable companies needed to revitalize their programming. These unmet needs created the opportunity for MTV to use musical video clips as an entertaining way of introducing and promoting artists and records through cable television.

THE DEVELOPMENT OF MTV

In January 1979, John A. Lack was appointed executive vice president of programming and marketing for Warner Cable Corporation (WCC). Because cable television at the time was still fairly new, his primary responsibility was development of new programming for Warner's various cable operations, including the Nickelodeon Channel, which had about one million subscribers and was targeted to children and teenagers. In an effort to develop new programming (and profitability) for Nickelodeon, Lack asked Mike Nesmith to put together a series of video clips of rock music for a program idea called *Pop Clips*.

Nesmith, formerly of The Monkees rock group and TV sitcom, was a pioneer in the area of video clips. He envisioned the promotional as well as the entertainment value of such clips and had previously formed his own production company, Pacific Arts Corporation. Reportedly, some 50 half-hour shows for the *Pop Clips* program were produced for Nickelodeon. They became the forerunner idea for a 24-hour music video channel, an idea that many people in the industry probably had at the time (including recording artist Todd Rundgren). However, Lack was in the enviable position of making it a reality through Warner Cable.

Lack's working concept was a 24-hour music channel that added value by enabling (1) more new music and artists to be seen and heard than could be introduced on radio, (2) advertisers to reach the elusive 12-to-34 age group, and (3) innovation and creativity to stimulate a staid cable television environment. To achieve the concept, which he dubbed "MTV" for "music television," Lack assembled a team. It included young, successful individuals in radio programming (Robert Pittman) and promotion (John L. Sykes). They all knew the importance of numbers in the business, so they commissioned a market research study to test the feasibility of the concept among consumers in the 12-to-34 age group. The results were very positive.

When the MTV concept (along with the data) was presented to the directors involved in the various Warner companies, it received approval in the form of a $20 million investment to continue. From that point on, implementation was an operational problem. Robert Pittman, who was most instrumental in operationalizing the concept, set to work on the key problem of persuading record company executives to provide *free* video clips of their artists. He also had to persuade cable operators to pick up the MTV program signal and convince advertisers that MTV could deliver the 12-to-34 target audience.

On March 4, 1981, the arm of Warner designated to manage cable programming (Warner-Amex Satellite Entertainment Company, or WASEC) formally announced that a 24-hour music video channel would be launched on August 1, 1981. This announcement was evidence of serious commitment on the part of WASEC and energized the MTV team. However, to transform MTV from concept to reality, the team had to surmount major hurdles related to the product, sales, and distribution.

Creating the Product

MTV was somewhat unusual because the development of its product depended almost entirely on people outside the firm. The videos were to be supplied by record companies free of charge. This inexpensive source of programming would make MTV a profitable venture more quickly than other forms of programming. However, record companies did not see the value of investing to create music videos that would give their artists exposure on a new, unproven cable channel. Because of declining sales in the late 1970s and into the 1980s, many record companies were short of capital and several were downsizing. In this uncertain environment, record executives were reluctant to champion a new, risky idea. Furthermore, most record companies did not have a large library of promotional videos for their artists and were not interested in raising their expenses by producing videos to be used by MTV.

The shortage of videos threatened MTV's viability. Because it was committed to launch, MTV would have to go on the air with a limited stock of video clips. Lack and his team realized they needed more convincing evidence to persuade record executives that MTV would actually increase the sale of records, and that therefore the channel should receive videos free of charge. Consequently, they planned a market research study immediately after launch to provide actual data.

Sales

Once the physical product was in place, although limited in quantity, Lack and Pittman needed advertisers that would support the network. They defined the potential advertisers as firms needing to reach consumers from 18 to 34 years of age. The actual audience turned out to be younger, with viewers ranging in age from 12 to 26 years. Initial response from advertisers was weak. Spots were priced at $1,200 a minute, but the salesforce was reportedly selling them for as little as $350 a minute. Advertising agencies were still uncertain about cable television at the time because of the difficulty of measuring the effectiveness of small channels not monitored by the Nielsen rating service.

Almost in desperation, the MTV team devised a risky strategy for attracting advertisers. They offered to produce advertisements for any company that advertised on the channel. Because MTV would be usurping the function of the client's ad agency, this offer alienated the very ad agencies that MTV would depend upon for future ad dollars. MTV put its long-term revenue stream at risk to get support in the short term. The strategy was mildly successful, with only about 30 percent of the commercial time reportedly sold to 13 national advertisers at the launch of the channel.

Distribution

To create a successful channel, Lack and Pittman needed to establish a large viewer audience that could be profitably sold to advertisers. The distribution channel that would bring MTV to the potential audience was the nation's network of local cable operators. The team had to convince cable operators to carry MTV. They had an advantage because of their affiliation with Warner Amex Cable Corporation (WACC), one of the nation's largest cable operators. The internal sell was easier than convincing an unaffiliated operator, but several of WACC's cable franchises were still wiring cities and had not begun to broadcast.

Many independent cable operators had reservations about adopting MTV. Most operators used 12-channel transmitters and were broadcasting on all available channels. The operators were hesitant to discontinue a channel and replace it with MTV. Some operators encountered resistance to MTV from local PTA and religious groups, which regarded MTV as morally deficient, exposing young people to sex and violence. There was also a generation gap to overcome. Many cable operators had grown up before rock and roll became popular and did not see the attraction of a music network dedicated to it.

To entice cable operators, MTV was positioned as a vehicle for increasing the number of households subscribing to their systems. Lack told operators that MTV would create demand for cable service among teenagers and young adults who were currently not cable users. These people would install cable so they could get MTV. He also showed how the stereo broadcast capability, which MTV required of its operators, could be sold as an additional purchase option for $1.50 per household per month, thereby increasing revenues. This appeal worked for some, but not many, cable operators.

At launch, MTV's initial distribution was so thin that industry executives were surprised when the channel called itself a network. The channel was represented in some midwestern and southern cities, but not in the key New York and Los Angeles markets. MTV executives had to travel to New Jersey to watch the network premier. Lack of distribution in these major markets made the channel difficult to sell to advertisers.

TRACKING THE LAUNCH

Just after midnight on August 1, 1981, MTV was formally launched. The first video clip aired, appropriately or not, was "Video Killed the Radio Star" by The Buggles. Everyone at MTV was delighted, but they knew their work had only begun. They were still a long way from success. They needed to prove to the recording industry that MTV could boost artists' record sales and to advertisers that MTV attracted a desirable target market.

The team used market research to track record sales and radio play of artists represented on MTV. By mid-1982, data indicated that artists exposed on MTV were selling records in markets where they did not have any radio exposure. These results were important because they demonstrated that MTV did influence record sales and was launching artists that radio had ignored. Later in 1982, *Billboard* obtained similar results from its own survey, reinforcing MTV's original conclusion that exposure on MTV would increase record sales.

The market research results gave MTV new power to settle the issue of paying record companies for video clips. Pittman told record companies that paying for videos would bankrupt MTV. Given the firm's shaky financial status, this assertion was not far from the truth. Because MTV was increasing record sales, Pittman argued, it was in the best interest of the record firms to keep the channel on the air and supply it with music videos.

When MTV executives watched the network premier, they saw that the product they had created did not match the product they had envisioned. The programming needed refinement. Pittman felt the show was too much like regular television and lacked the enthusiasm and irreverence associated with rock and roll. In the first few weeks of operation, he reportedly changed the look of the studio from a typical talk show setup to a simulation of someone's basement or garage and added unusual items and rock and roll trappings.

The role of the hosts or "veejays" was also changed. The five original veejays had no idea how they were supposed to act. No one had decided whether they should simply announce the music or attempt to become personalities themselves. Most of the original five had no television experience and had to learn to interact with the camera. As late as 1986, the MTV team was still debating exactly who the veejays should be and what role they should perform. Eventually, the veejays became extremely popular by personifying the music that was played during their air time and developed followings of their own. Ratings began to rise and the channel began to build audience.

Meanwhile, the team challenged its advertising agency to create a campaign that would better promote MTV to cable operators. The agency came up with the unusual strategy of using a pull rather than a push campaign. The phrase "I Want My MTV" became the slogan of choice and the agency designed an advertising program around it to influence consumer demand. The advertisements featured well-known singers telling people to call their local cable operator and demand MTV. The campaign succeeded. In January 1983, Group W, a major cable operator in Los Angeles and upper Manhattan, added the channel.

Although advertising revenues grew steadily through the first two years, it was not until after MTV persuaded major cable operators to sign on that significant advertiser support was attracted. With proof to record industry executives that MTV could generate sales, increasing availability of the channel, and a steadily improving programming format on the air, MTV's growth on all key measures became exponential.

WHAT MADE MTV SUCCESSFUL?

Although proof of performance was necessary, the original MTV concept provided an opportunity for all potential stakeholders. Record companies gained a promotional vehicle, advertisers gained access to an audience that other media could not reach, teenagers and young adults found a new source of entertainment, and cable operators got attractive programming that could be used to market a basic cable subscription. The fundamental "win-win" nature of the concept is the most important reason for MTV's success.

In addition, the original concept was successful because it was not a threat to any established products. MTV had no significant direct competitors. The only potential losers in the success of MTV were FM radio stations that were competing for listener attention and for advertising revenues from blue jeans and soft drink marketers. The influence of these stations may have waned as music video grew, but many have since become adroit niche marketers.

Another key reason for MTV's success was its ability to evolve as the environment changed. From the moment of launch, it was a work in progress. It had to prove its benefits through market research and persuasion. Further, throughout its first decade, MTV survived challenges and difficulties by adapting both its format and its business practices to the current situation. The two most important adaptations were the decision to broaden the format beyond traditional album-oriented rock and roll and the decision to pay record companies for exclusive rights to new videos.

MTV faced a controversy in February 1983 over its rock and roll programming format, which excluded most black artists performing urban contemporary music. MTV was publicly charged with racism because it refused to air videos by black artists. For example, industry professionals charged that MTV was not airing Michael Jackson's "Beat It" video even though the song had become number one on both the pop and urban contemporary charts. This controversy posed a threat to the channel's advertising revenues and to its supply of videos from record companies that had popular black artists under contract. Pittman wisely decided to adjust the format to include a wider range of music, and MTV arranged the world premier of Michael Jackson's "Thriller" video.

Another significant policy shift enabled MTV to build a major barrier to competition. Originally, the channel obtained all of its videos free of charge from record firms that produced them as promotional material. This policy helped MTV get started. However, by 1983 the video music environment had changed. Hollywood film directors were making videos that cost hundreds of thousands of dollars to produce. Record firms were unhappy that MTV did not share this expense.

Several potential competitors had been announced to challenge MTV. Ted Turner's Black Entertainment Television as well as the developers of the Financial News Network (FNN) decided to start music video organizations. Pittman met these challenges in one swift move. He offered to pay record companies for the short-term exclusive rights to their videos. With protected access to most new releases, MTV effectively locked other video channels out of the market while still avoiding huge production fees.

Pittman also created competitive barriers by segmenting the market with product extensions. For example, in late 1984 he acquired the remains of Ted Turner's failed music video network and turned it into VH-1, a rock video channel aimed at the "thirty-something" viewer. This strategy of segmenting the market created some cannibalization of the MTV channel, but broadened the company's overall market and discouraged potential competitors.

MTV segmented its own channel by adding theme programs featuring a specific type of music or original programming. *Club MTV* and *Yo! MTV Raps* appealed to dance and rap music fans and *MTV: Unplugged* featured popular rock singers performing acoustic versions of their songs. The channel added a game show called *Remote Control*. Even news shows were added to the program schedule, originally five- to 10-minute clips and later 15- to 20-minute shows hosted by Kurt Loder, former columnist for *Rolling Stone*.

In 1992, MTV competed with major networks for election coverage with a "Choose or Lose" campaign, designed to promote voting among its 18 to

24 year old viewers. An off-taste cartoon show, *Beavis and Butt-Head*, further demonstrated MTV's flexibility in maintaining viewers and capturing new ones. Continual monitoring of the market and aggressive evolution to accommodate a variety of music tastes reportedly helped MTV to reach more than $400 million in revenue by 1992 with double-digit annual growth.

CONCLUSION: LESSONS LEARNED

The MTV story demonstrates that truly new product concepts are difficult to bring to life. The MTV team had adequate funding and other advantages because of corporate support. The various Warner companies operated cable franchises and record companies. Yet the operation took three years to show a profit and another two to pass the total-project breakeven point. The MTV story teaches that even with a great concept, patient tracking and refinement of the new product are essential to its success.

A second lesson from the MTV story is that competing with the firm's current products and risking some cannibalization can be a successful strategy. Pittman's technique of segmentation was particularly successful because the cable industry was in the early stages of its life cycle and many firms were evaluating market entry. Pittman's moves precluded their entry and ensured a strong position for his firm.

The MTV story exemplifies the value of dedicated product champions who take emotional ownership of a project. MTV exists today because Lack believed in his concept enough to hang his career on it, and because Pittman personally convinced key stakeholders to take the chance on the idea. Aspiring product developers need to realize the difference between creating or planning a product and taking personal responsibility for its success or failure.

The final lesson from MTV's success is the value of a fresh perspective obtained from synergy among concepts and technologies. MTV created an entire new industry because people whose viewpoint had developed in the radio business were hired to run a television business. Cable and commercial television had operated for decades before MTV was launched, but network television people did not envision such a channel because they had established ideas about how TV should operate. The synergy principle can be applied in other organizations by finding employees and project team members who have gained skills and experience in other industries.

MTV is clearly much more than a new product. What started as a commercial venture to reach a targeted age group of consumers has become a major breakthrough in music broadcasting and, more interestingly, a part of the global culture. It has evolved in such a way that it is difficult to discern whether MTV leads or follows the youth culture, or whether it has in fact become one with the culture. MTV is an object of praise, criticism, and even academic study because of its influence on society. The MTV innovation has forever changed television, the music industry, and the world in which we live.

Snapple Beverage Corporation: Snapple Iced Tea

Christopher Melly and Michele A. Munn

"Take some more tea," the March Hare said to Alice, very earnestly.
Lewis Carroll, Alice's Adventures in Wonderland, 1865

Snapple was established in 1972 as Unadulterated Food Products, Inc.[3] The founders were three Brooklyn natives, Hyman Golden, Leonard Marsh, and Arnold Greenberg. Golden and Marsh are brothers-in-law and Greenberg and Marsh have been best friends since high school. All three had extensive entrepreneurial experience, acquired as a result of operating their own businesses from a very early age. In fact, Golden and Marsh were operating a window-washing service and Greenberg was running a health foods store until Snapple finally demanded their full attention.

A BRIEF DESCRIPTION OF SNAPPLE'S LONG ENTREPRENEURIAL HISTORY

Snapple emerged in 1972 from the simple idea of selling all-natural fruit drinks to health food stores in New York City. The founders' formula was clear: deliver a true health drink at a premium price to health-concerned consumers at stores they visit often. At a price almost twice that of traditional canned sodas, Snapple delivered 10 ounces of natural fruit-juice beverage in 11 flavors. All ingredients were natural. Because the product

290

was not unique, the founders were patient in slowly developing a base in New York City, determining how consumers responded, and later expanding regionally.

Being true entrepreneurs, Snapple's founders initially leveraged their time and resources in bringing Snapple products to market. For example, rather than establishing their own production facilities, they chose to subcontract production to independent organizations. They also signed agreements with health store distributors to place the product in selected outlets.

The next several years constituted a period of slow growth for Snapple. Each of the founders maintained a role within his own business and operated Snapple on the side. However, Snapple's business gradually grew to the point that, in 1979, the founders decided to hire their first full-time salesperson. In the early 1980s, Snapple's business continued to expand with sales increasing by approximately $1 million a year. This growth came about because consumers liked the product, and also because Snapple expanded its product line and distribution. By 1983, Snapple had 18 flavors in fruit juices, fruit juice drinks, and regular and diet sodas and seltzers. It also extended its products' availability to delicatessens and supermarkets. Subsequently, it began to expand into major regional markets, such as Boston and Washington, DC.

By 1987, the founders could no longer ignore the mounting evidence of success. They became active in the business and generated new product ideas. Snapple's business took off, with sales jumping from $13 million in 1987 to $205 million by 1992. In March 1992, the T.H. Lee Company acquired Snapple for $140 million and sold back 30 percent of it to the three founders (10 percent each), who remained active in the company's management. Snapple went public on December 15, 1992, and the stock immediately closed 45 percent above its offering price of $20. A major factor in this explosive growth was Snapple's innovative process for "hot-fill" bottling of freshly brewed tea. This new iced tea product launched in 1988 propelled Snapple's success.

SNAPPLE'S ICED TEA DEVELOPMENT

During its entrepreneurial years, Snapple introduced at least one new product each year. Typically, new products were simply different flavors that extended the brand name. One of the founders would have an idea for a flavor and then delegated the responsibility for developing the physical product to a variety of independent flavor houses. The idea for Snapple's very successful tea originated from Golden, although he did not necessarily visualize tea as the product. His idea was simply that Snapple's product line needed a "cool summertime drink." Golden then directed a flavor house to develop such a drink that would be of very high quality with natural ingredients, consistent with Snapple's health tradition.

The flavor house brought back a product that was essentially the now well-known real-brewed iced tea. Iced tea was selected because it was a widely accepted, almost universal summertime thirst quencher that could be produced with all natural ingredients. The product was created without any substantial aid from market research studies, focus groups, or test markets. Golden was simply sticking to the principle of basing new products on wholesome ingredients and good taste. The new drink followed logically from the company's strategic focus on the health market and Snapple's earned image as "healthy."

However, implementing the product idea was not as easy as coming up with it. Snapple's innovation was to fill the bottles directly with hot tea, then seal them without any preservatives. This process is very similar to the home canning process used to preserve fruits and other foods. The result was a "real-brewed" tea with a true tea taste and no preservatives, a product that would enable Snapple to maintain its health image and offer a tasty drink.

Snapple uses independent copackers to prepare, bottle, and warehouse its products. To ensure quality and consistency, it purchases the raw materials and supplies them directly to the copackers. The company's copackers are chosen carefully and subjected to intense quality control testing. Each copacker is monitored, and quality control representatives from the company test and taste samples from each production run. The product is bottled in sturdy 16-ounce glass bottles with a single distinctive label. The glass bottle contributes to the quality of the overall product. At the time of launch, most ready-to-drink iced teas were packaged in cans and many were made from concentrates.

The market responded enthusiastically to the new product. In 1991 the new brewed tea comprised 55 percent of Snapple's sales, captured 15 percent of the entire iced tea market, and became the leader of the real-brewed iced tea market. In New York, Snapple's most penetrated market, Snapple's tea had a 94 percent increase in sales in 1991. Performance was equally astounding in some of Snapple's newer markets. For example, in San Francisco, Snapple's share of the market for iced tea went from 3.1 percent to 48 percent from 1991 to 1992. In the same time period, Snapple's share of the Los Angeles market grew from 0.7 percent to 21.3 percent.

Snapple popularized real-brewed ready-to-drink iced tea and quickly became the industry standard. Competitors attempted to duplicate Snapple's efforts and made advertising claims of being as good as or better than Snapple, thereby conceding Snapple's quality. Snapple's tea also led to several new flavors and brand extensions. It is largely responsible for Snapple's growth in product offerings to 52 products in five market segments (real-brewed tea, fruit drinks, fruit juices, natural sodas and seltzers, and sports drinks).

SNAPPLE'S MARKETING

Launching the new Snapple real-brewed iced tea depended largely on distribution and promotion. A premium price was necessary, not only for image reasons, but also because the company's all-natural ingredient costs were higher than those of most beverages.

Building Distribution

Originally, Snapple products were marketed only through health food distributors, with subsequent expansion on a regional basis into delicatessens and supermarkets. However, the company's growing success, along with the potential of the new brewed iced tea, began to attract larger, established distributors. Snapple was also able to secure franchised distributors that exclusively distribute Snapple products. This form of distribution is very effective because it increases the company's influence on the merchandising and display of its products.

Snapple continued to penetrate the supermarket chains, including Shoprite, Pathmark, Jewel, Kroger, Lucky, Vons, Winn Dixie, Safeway, and Publix. By the second quarter of 1992, Snapple was available in 51 supermarket chains, in contrast to only 18 chains in 1991. The additional distribution into supermarkets was very beneficial. It gave Snapple "billboard" shelf space because of the large number of Snapple products (52). To further promote the billboard display concept, Snapple implemented a program with its distributors to share the cost of purchasing coolers. The coolers were placed in retail outlets in exchange for primary product display within them.

Promotional Program

In 1988, the total advertising budget was $1 million; by 1992, it was $15 million. Snapple markets all of its beverages under the Snapple name to concentrate its marketing efforts behind a single brand. Ironically, the Snapple brand name was derived from a failed carbonated apple juice drink!

Snapple's most dominant advertising theme, "Made from the Best Stuff on Earth," reinforces its concept of all-natural, high quality health drinks. With a relatively low initial advertising budget, Snapple had to use creative approaches to generate awareness and trial. Its initial offbeat approach involved radio advertising using the controversial personalities Howard Stern and Rush Limbaugh. The company defends the use of these two men by claiming that a lot of people listen to both. It also readily admits that once people try the product, word of mouth contributes significantly to awareness, resulting in rapid sales growth in newly entered markets.

SNAPPLE'S SUCCESS FACTORS

The success of Snapple's real-brewed ice tea was astonishing for this relatively small beverage company with humble entrepreneurial beginnings. It is all the more surprising in an industry made up of giants that are true marketing superpowers. Snapple's success is therefore due not so much to what the company did prior to launch, but how it managed to thrive after launch.

A Concentrated Beverage Industry

The beverage industry encompasses all nonalcoholic carbonated and non-carbonated drinks, including sodas and colas, iced tea, lemonade, fruit-ades, bottled pasteurized water, and carbonated mineral water. In 1994 the overall size of the market was about $62 billion, and the dominant players, Coke and Pepsi, held 72 percent of the entire market. The eight largest companies in the industry controlled 97 percent of the market, leaving only 3 percent to be fought over by regional and specialty companies like Snapple.

With so much concentration of sales among so few companies, Snapple might have been ignored by the industry giants. Companies like it have come and gone for years. For example, bottled water products with a dash of fruit juice flavor started quickly, but then declined. Consequently, the Pepsi–Lipton Tea partnership took four years to respond to Snapple's real-brewed ice tea with Lipton Original bottled tea.

As expected, Lipton Original struck very hard, even hurling charges against Snapple's claims about its brewing process. With Pepsi's efficient distribution system, Lipton Original was able to launch nationally in a relatively short period of time and achieve significant share. Snapple's sales also grew substantially during this time, indicating the benefits of being first with a good product. Part of Snapple's growth was due to the fact that many former Lipton distributors switched to Snapple once Lipton aligned with Pepsi. Nevertheless, Snapple doubled its advertising budget to an estimated $30 million in 1993 (from $15 million in 1992).

Riding the New Age Beverage Wave

Underlying the success of Snapple (and other niche beverages, some of which have not survived) was the drastic change of buyer behavior brought about by health concerns since the mid-1970s. The industry responded initially by removing, one by one, all ingredients that consumers perceived as bad. The most important characteristics became "diet" and "caffeine free." Eventually, consumers' desire for healthy ingredients led to a variety of new drinks known as "New Age" beverages.

New Age beverages are not traditional carbonated drinks (such as colas), nor bland bottled waters, but a combination of healthy, easy-to-drink, and tasty ingredients. They are natural products, containing no additives, artificial ingredients, preservatives, or artificial flavors. They are characterized as being lighter, healthier, and more "gulpable" than other drinks and usually are sold in wide-mouth glass bottles (for gulping) that convey an impression of wholesomeness. Such products include natural sodas, sparkling juice drinks, flavored sparkling waters, and sports drinks. Since its inception in 1972, Snapple's basic marketing strategy has placed it at the forefront of the New Age drink market.

Although Snapple's efforts may not have created the New Age beverage market opportunity, its success is certainly due to its persistent focus on meeting the needs of the niche market segment that generated the New Age market trend. Snapple's founders did not veer from their strategic business definition and were rewarded with a market that grew consistently over time. Even giant Coke entered the New Age market in 1994 with its line of Fruitopia beverages.

Persistent Postlaunch Marketing Efforts

Snapple did not wilt in the face of stiff competition. The company's continued aggressive marketing efforts have succeeded in winning loyal and experienced distributors. Further, Snapple recruited top industry employees to improve and intensify its distribution, a key to success in the beverage market. Snapple's consumer advertising has been innovative and exciting, attracting consumer awareness and trial. When necessary, the company has increased its advertising expenditures to match those of its toughest competitors. By maintaining a premium price and expensive packaging in distinctive 16-ounce wide-mouth glass bottles, it has reinforced its carefully developed image of all-natural healthiness and quality.

The strong and growing "health" positioning associated with the Snapple name may give the company a competitive advantage over industry leaders such as Coke, Pepsi, and Lipton, which do not have (nor necessarily want) such a narrow positioning. Coke, for example, launched an entirely new brand name (Fruitopia) to compete effectively in the New Age market.

As Snapple continues to fulfill the needs of health-conscious consumers, its taste benefits may appeal to people who simply enjoy a refreshing drink. Iced tea is a very popular thirst quencher for everyone, and iced tea as a foundation enables Snapple to attract consumers outside the health-conscious segment. The all-natural, high quality image of Snapple is consistent with the historically wholesome and homey image of iced tea. Iced tea is perceived as very American and natural, enabling Snapple to capitalize on a positive perception. Iced tea also provides a good-tasting base to which flavors can be added, such as lemon, peach, and raspberry.

CONCLUSIONS

Snapple's future will be challenging, as Coke, Pepsi, Lipton, Nestlé, and other beverage companies will undoubtedly threaten its position. However, the fact that many consumers have already accepted Snapple as the standard helps Snapple defend its position. Snapple's financial strength enables it to compete effectively and sustain a strong position in the ready-to-drink iced tea market. For example, in 1994 Snapple built a bottling plant, which improves its cost position, and acquired stakes in several distributors.

Snapple's competitiveness will depend on continued new product development, most notably products beyond iced teas. Whether the founders can still generate a new idea each year or should employ more systematic new product development processes to generate the next success is an open question. Another is whether new product development should continue to be implemented by outside firms or be internalized for better control.

Finally, Snapple's launch of its beverage lines in Europe during 1994 guarantees future opportunities for the upstart company from Brooklyn. With an advertising budget of some $65 million in 1994 (up from $30 million in 1992), Snapple hopes to become a global brand name. No doubt it will do battle with Coke, Pepsi, Lipton, and other major competitors around the world. In many cultures, tea has a different meaning as a beverage than it does in the United States. Whether tea in bottled form will be well received is uncertain. Global expansion will challenge Snapple's creativity in developing appealing new products and its capability to market and distribute them.

10

Lessons from the New Product Success Stories

The secret of success is constancy to purpose.

Benjamin Disraeli, 1872

It should be apparent after reading 24 success stories that new product development is highly situational. What works in one situation may not work in another. For example, recall that Fuji found success with single-use cameras, but Gillette found success by moving the market away from single-use shavers and back to high tech shaving systems. Developing a list of rules for success would not be useful because the rules would not apply in every situation.

However, some valuable lessons can be learned from the new product success stories. Drawing insights from success stories in the form of lessons might be helpful in constructing useful decision guidelines for specific situations and purposes. For example, if getting a product on the market as soon as possible is important, certain conditions might be identified that would indicate bypassing a test market in favor of a quick launch. Such insights do not eliminate decision risk, but provide guidance in addressing the many difficult decision problems inherent in new product development.

SOME LESSONS FOR NEW PRODUCT DEVELOPMENT

Anyone involved in new product development who has read the 24 success stories can develop his or her own insights, lessons, and guidelines from them. This chapter briefly lists some of the kinds of lessons that might be learned from the stories. Each new product success story contains useful information, but its interpretation will vary according to the experiences and purposes of the reader.

The selected lessons briefly reviewed here (and summarized in Figure 10.1) are merely illustrative of the kinds of guidelines that might be developed to enhance the intellectual processes involved in new product development. There is no implied order to the list, nor are the lessons independent of each other. A combination of some or all may bring success, as well as any single one. The lessons are presented simply to stimulate and improve thinking and decision making in a complex and risk-laden endeavor.

Understand Consumer Needs

All of the new product successes met a consumer need better than other products on the market. Some products filled unmet consumers needs. The Baby Jogger stroller enabled parents to run and pursue an active lifestyle with their children, without the guilt of leaving them at home. The *Carmen Sandiego* educational/fun software for children gave teachers and administrators an important rationale for their classroom computer purchases, thereby satisfying needs instrumental to their occupational roles.

Often the psychological aspect of consumer needs must be probed in designing a product. The managers at Ault Foods were surprised to learn from their research that consumers found it difficult to believe an ice cream product could taste good with absolutely no fat; consequently, they marketed a product with 1 percent fat, a more credible claim. The success of Huggies Pull-Ups depended on understanding the psychology of parent and child in the highly sensitive process of toilet training. Recognizing psychological needs early in the new product development process facilitates refinement of the new product during testing and launch.

Follow Market Trends

Favorable market trends can not only inspire new product ideas, but also contribute to new product success. Baby Jogger, Ault's Sealtest Parlour 1% ice cream, Snapple, The Body Shop, and Slim-Fast all were developed in recognition of the growing trend for health-related concerns among consumers. Calyx & Corolla's successful flower delivery service was based on a careful analysis of trends in the ways consumers were using

☐ Understand consumer needs
☐ Follow market trends
☐ Employ market segmentation
☐ Leverage a product's global opportunities
☐ Align strategic partners and build relationships to manage difficult business environments
☐ Participate in the new product's regulatory environment
☐ Select a new product development philosophy best suited to the organization's culture
☐ Treasure good leadership and support product champions with adequate resources
☐ Build cross-functional terms
☐ Leverage and manage creative resources
☐ Empower employees who interact with customers
☐ Carefully assess the role of market research
☐ Run the numbers
☐ Define a clear core product concept
☐ Develop a superior product
☐ Pursue total quality management for new products
☐ Strive for innovative design based on design principles
☐ Consult lead users for new product ideas—with caution
☐ Increase the use of information technology in product design
☐ Select a positioning consistent with the core product concept
☐ Invest in and protect the brand name
☐ Prepare appropriate new product launch communication programs
☐ Achieve adequate distribution availability by launch date
☐ Provide sufficient value in introductory pricing
☐ Implement an integrated and resonating launch marketing program
☐ Assess market entry timing: First-mover *dis*advantage?
☐ Persevere for effective execution: Testing, retesting, and training
☐ Anticipate the competition that a successful new product almost always attracts
☐ Do not give up easily on a good new product idea: The entrepreneurial instinct
☐ Plan to be patient—accelerate product development when possible, but success takes time
☐ Adhere to strong business principles
☐ Foster a bias toward *process* over *project* success

Figure 10.1 Checklist of selected lessons from new product success.

flowers. Indirectly these trends were related to health concerns, or giving flowers instead of candy as gifts.

Interestingly, the success of Philips' compact disc depended on demographic and social trends, but was enhanced by the success of MTV beginning in the 1980s. Recording firms clearly benefited from their artists' exposure on MTV. Of course, not all successful new products are based on a growing market opportunity or favorable trends. Some products, such as the Lever 2000 bar soap and Starbucks coffee, succeeded in very mature markets with little or no growth. However, small but growing trends within those markets led to segmentation opportunities.

Employ Market Segmentation

At some level, consumer needs become heterogeneous across a population. The process of segmentation helps discover groups of consumers whose needs are similar within groups and different between groups. Through market research, Lever Brothers found a segment of consumers who wanted the combined benefits of moisturizing, deodorizing, and antibacterial efficacy in a bar soap. Courtyard by Marriott relied heavily on market segmentation to find opportunities for growth without cannibalizing other Marriott hotels.

Other new products, such as Starbucks, The Body Shop, and Snapple, built their initial success on market segments that grew over time, revealing that segmentation is a highly dynamic process. Although some products do not appear to employ segmentation, such as *USA Today* and MCI Friends and Family, certain kinds of consumers with similar needs *self-select* in response to the product. *USA Today* appeals to the segment of consumers who are highly mobile, and Friends and Family appeals to those who may be more gregarious than others among their circle of friends. Thus, market segmentation is at work, even if not formally implemented.

Leverage a Product's Global Opportunities

Many of the new product successes are global in terms of market opportunity. Philips' CDs, The Body Shop, *USA Today*, Gillette's Sensor, the Laser sailboat, and MTV are a few of the products that have a global presence. Their global success implies a certain universal level of human need. Young people around the world respond similarly to rock and roll (MTV). However, cross-cultural opportunities must always be examined for differences in needs (in addition to regulatory, political, legal, and other institutional characteristics and differences).

The rapid success of Fuji's single-use camera in Japan but slow acceptance in the United States shows some of the nuances of cross-cultural differences. Japanese consumers tended to be more responsive to camera innovations than American consumers. Similarly, paragliders were very successful in Europe and other parts of the world, but not at all in the United States (possibly because of differences in geographic terrain, laws, and attitude toward freedom). New products must be examined carefully for their global potential. In a world of increasing communication, the emergence of global consumption patterns provides substantial opportunity.

Align Strategic Partners and Build Relationships to Manage Difficult Business Environments

Alignment with key stakeholders can help a company to capitalize on market opportunities in difficult business environments. For example, Philips, strong in technology, benefited from a partnering relationship with Sony, strong in marketing and brand name, in successfully launching the compact disc. Both Calyx & Corolla and Starbucks had to align key partners to achieve success. The alliance between paraglider manufacturers and schools that taught paragliding was important in getting the business off the ground.

Aligning partners and building relationships may take considerable effort. MTV had to take the risk of launching its network before it had adequate video clips or advertiser support. Not until the company had post-launch market research results could it prove to record company executives that providing free video clips would be profitable, and persuade advertisers that MTV could very efficiently and effectively reach a highly attractive target market.

Participate in the New Product's Regulatory Environment

Not surprisingly, several of the success stories involve regulators, either as facilitators of or barriers to success. Cellular One was made possible by the processes of the Federal Communications Commission. Paragliders are somewhat limited in the United States by lack of FAA recognition. The original version of Slim-Fast failed in the market in 1977 after the Food and Drug Administration (FDA) publicized its concern about dietary products. MCI was aided by legal and regulatory decisions. Drug firms, such as Glaxo, must satisfy a barrage of FDA test requirements. By participating in the regulatory aspects of a new product during its development, a company can take advantage of regulatory benefits and anticipate and overcome barriers as they arise.

Select a New Product Development Philosophy Best Suited to the Organization's Culture

The success stories exemplify at least three general philosophies that might drive an organization's new product development processes: *proactive, reactive,* and *interactive.* The Body Shop, Ault's Parlour 1%, *USA Today,* MCI Friends and Family, Huggies Pull-Ups, Courtyard by Marriott, Gillette Sensor, and Lever 2000 are all examples of proactively developed new products. That is, the companies purposefully decided to develop new products as part of their strategic direction and pursued development accordingly.

In contrast, Slim-Fast, Ford's Taurus, and Zantac were developed reactively in response to market conditions. Slim-Fast proceeded very cautiously, perhaps because of its previous experience with a regulatory agency. Ford was clearly reacting to the success of the Japanese auto manufacturers, and Zantac was reacting to Tagamet's success. Notably, all of the products were major successes, so a reactive philosophy should not necessarily be viewed negatively. Sometimes it is the only way an organization can move ahead.

Perhaps a more progressive philosophy of new product development involves the establishment of close and ongoing interaction with customers and other stakeholders. Starbucks views each retail store as an opportunity for dialogue with its customers about coffee. Thus, the company simultaneously educates the customer and retrieves useful information for new product ideas and general operations. Calyx & Corolla performs a similarly interactive dialogue with customers who call in for orders and information. Fuji pursues an aggressive program of listening to the direct and personal concerns of customers, who were the source of the Quick-Snap idea.

MTV has pursued a continual change of its programming over the years by interacting closely with its primary audience. It interacts through a variety of means, including parading by the target audience a variety of video clips and personalities that are in effect created by members of the target audience. By pushing many different emotions to the limit with the audience, it eventually reaches a happy medium and becomes synchronized with them. The combination of television and rock and roll fuses the viewer and the MTV organization into a potent emotional and commercial interaction that is mutually reinforcing.

Clearly, the culture of the organization largely determines which of the three philosophies would best guide its new product development. In a highly competitive and rapidly changing market environment, proactive and reactive approaches may be too slow to ensure competitive advantage. Interacting with potential buyers in an ongoing dialogue about their needs may prove to be the ideal approach, albeit the most challenging one.

Treasure Good Leadership and Support Product Champions with Adequate Resources

Organizational leadership in new product development comes from two sources, the formal structure of authority and skills and expertise in championing a new product effort. Formal approval and support of a new product development effort is almost a necessary condition for new product success. Ford could not have proceeded with the Taurus project without approval and support of top managers. Leadership and support were essential at Unilever to continue the search for a product and technology that would deliver the desired consumer benefits in Lever 2000. The Gillette Sensor was nearly stalled by intraorganizational differences of opinion about the form of the final product until top managers clearly set the direction. Good leadership is often difficult to find and should be valued when it is found.

The other kind of leadership involves the efforts of product champions to focus an organization's actions and resources on "their" new product project. A sense of ownership and pride infuses the product champions, as well as respect for the challenges and risks ahead. The champions must be resourceful in putting together a development process that fits the organization's culture. Then top managers must support the champions' efforts with adequate resources.

Almost every one of the new product successes considered in this book had a known champion who led the cause. Sometimes it was an entrepreneurial organization's founder (Anita Roddick for The Body Shop, Howard Schultz for Starbucks, Ruth M. Owades for Calyx & Corolla, C. Daniel Abraham for Slim-Fast), an organization's visionary (Alan Neuharth for *USA Today*, Wayne Schelle for Cellular One, Doug Carlston for Broderbund Software), an inspirational designer (Bruce Kirby for the Laser, Phil Baechler for the Baby Jogger, Laurent de Kalbermatten for paragliders), or the new product manager (Hiroshi Tanaka for the Canon PC copier, Lewis Veraldi for the Ford Taurus, Gérard Théry for Minitel, Wayne Sanders for Huggies Pull-Ups). In every case, someone rose to the occasion to build and maintain the project's momentum.

Build Cross-Functional Teams

One of the first tasks of a new product champion is to build a team that will have responsibility for carrying out the many activities necessary to coordinate development. Almost every success story provides evidence of the value of using cross-functional teams. Product champion Alan Neuharth hand-picked a team to go off site and create a national newspaper, whereas Canon used an extensive system of parallel teams to produce a high quality breakthrough copier in record time. Cross-functional teams were instrumental to the success of nearly every product.

Kimberly-Clark's experience with Huggies Pull-Ups illustrates why such teams are valuable early in the development process. Several years of work was almost abandoned until the search for a suitable waistband material was extended throughout the organization. Perhaps early inclusion of a variety of organizational members with different and cross-functional capabilities would have been helpful to Kimberly-Clark. The synergy of ideas from different perspectives can often expedite the solution of problems, thereby shortening the development process.

Leverage and Manage Creative Resources

A good practice in new product development is to generate as many new product ideas as possible and carefully screen them. Therefore, creativity must be fostered within an organization, a task that is very difficult to accomplish in practice. Creative people sometimes tend to be temperamental, preoccupied with the technical details to the neglect of practical business issues, and may fit poorly in traditional organizational structures. Nevertheless, creativity and creative people are essential for most organizations intent on serving markets with new products and services.

The design of the Laser sailboat involved several key designers, but they were able to work together because they established agreed-upon design principles at the outset. Further, they took pride in creating a truly innovative class of sailboat. The entrepreneurial creativity and persistence shown by Phil Baechler in developing the Baby Jogger illustrates the role of creativity throughout the development process. Whenever development problems arise, creativity can contribute to their solution.

Perhaps the best example of managing creativity in organizations is found in the Broderbund Software story. The company's creative teams were empowered to create the product, the only limitation being to stay within the framework of practical business requirements. The software field is rife with projects that are over budget, underfunded, or simply lacking in creativity of design and implementation.

Empower Employees Who Interact with Customers

Two firms that rely on their employees to deliver their concept paid special attention to empowering their employees. At the store level, Starbucks trains its front-line employees, gives them equity in the company, and gives them the authority to deliver the quality of service necessary to complete the consumption experience. The Body Shop is highly selective of its franchisees, who must pass a rigorous evaluation process. The retail salesforce is also rigorously screened and trained extensively in informational rather than persuasive selling. They are able to provide substantive information to consumers about The Body Shop's naturally-based personal care products.

By using telecommunication services (800 numbers) and other creative approaches, any organization can make it easy for its customers to call the organization for help and information. However, as in the case of MCI's Friends and Family product, the customer service employees must be thoroughly trained and empowered to provide customer satisfaction.

Carefully Assess the Role of Market Research

The fact that several of the new products achieved success with little or no formal market research may be surprising. For example, the Laser sailboat, the Baby Jogger, and Snapple were developed with virtually no formal market research. Perhaps the developers of the products either had blind faith in their success, had keen sensitivity to the needs of their markets, were willing to take the risk of failing, or could not afford or did not value market research.

In contrast, the development of Courtyard by Marriott, Minitel (with its extensive test markets), and Sensor (with thousands of consumers involved in use tests) was accompanied by considerable market research. Marriott, for example, needed market research not only to design a better hotel, but also to overcome expected organizational resistance to the Courtyard concept. Similarly, MTV needed market research to accelerate its development and acceptance among key stakeholders after launch. In some sense, the use of market research may be part of the organization's philosophy about new product development (reactive, proactive, or interactive).

Run the Numbers

Throughout new product development, a variety of measures should be taken regularly. Chief among them are the size of the market opportunity, a sales forecast, and estimates of profitability (based on estimates of cost). In almost all of the stories, these factors are of concern. Ruth Owades would not go into business with Calyx & Corolla until she was satisfied that the market size and profitability numbers were adequate.

The Courtyard by Marriott story exemplifies the use of sophisticated market-based new product forecasts and analyses. However, even the best new product forecasting can be off, as was the case of Gillette in underestimating the demand for the new Sensor razor. Accuracy is not the objective in new product forecasting; rather, the process of continually doing the forecasting provides some control of the project and a sense of reality to balance the ever-present bias of optimism.

Define a Clear Core Product Concept

In almost every new product success considered, from Starbucks to Snapple, a clear definition of the core product concept linked to a fundamental consumer need was instrumental to success. Starbucks was not selling coffee, but rather a total consumption experience based on romance, theatrics, and community. Snapple was not selling beverages, but rather health and good taste. Broderbund was not selling software, but rather fun, mystery, and fantasy for children.

Besides linking the product to a consumer need, which in turn is linked to an organization's business strategy, a clearly stated product concept can be communicated to and understood by various members of the organization. New product development processes work best when everyone involved has a clear understanding of the desired outcome. However, formulating new core product concepts is not an easy task, nor is the task of maintaining their integrity throughout the development process. For success, both tasks require a clear understanding of consumer needs.

Develop a Superior Product

Whether through persistent improvement of technology, strategic alignment of key stakeholders in the value chain, or other means, successful companies strive to create the *best* product in a category. Ford Taurus achieved success in building a high quality car by studying the "best-in-class" product features of the top-selling cars in the world. By aligning flower growers and delivery services, Calyx & Corolla was able to transport flowers from the grower to the consumer faster than anyone else, thereby giving the flowers greater longevity than even local florists could provide. Gillette spent 13 years and hundreds of millions of dollars to develop superior shaving quality through its state-of-the-art Sensor shaving system. Starbucks Coffee Company insists on a superior product through "fanatical quality control."

Pursue Total Quality Management for New Products

Developing a superior product requires attention to the quality with which it is made. Total quality management is desirable, but it is a costly process for many organizations. Changing the operations of a company that is not accustomed to the pursuit of quality may take years. However, total quality management can be emphasized in the new product development process.

In today's highly competitive business environment, new products that are not built on quality principles will be at risk. Quality products not only work better for consumers and reduce the chance of recalls, but also have shorter development time and lower cost in the long run. Japanese companies such as Canon and Fuji are consistent in their pursuit of quality, and reap benefits accordingly. Canon's total quality management effort resulted in a breakthrough low cost, high quality copier for small office and home office use. American companies have picked up the quality challenge as exemplified by successes of Ford's Taurus and Gillette's Sensor. Quality assurance is critical even for Calyx & Corolla's flower delivery service.

Strive for Innovative Design Based on Design Principles

Even for a product that works well, having wonderful style and an aesthetically pleasing design is a great advantage. The success of Ford's Taurus was due largely to its innovative design, a design that was copied by numerous competitors (the ultimate compliment). When France Telecom developed the Minitel display terminal, the ergonomics of product design was crucial to its eventual use in homes. Consider other examples: the aesthetics of Starbucks' coffeehouses contributed to the consumption experience, the shape and feel of the Lever 2000 bar of soap contributed to its "human touch" and "body parts" themes, and the simple yet elegant design of the Laser sailboat gave it a classic appeal.

The design of the *USA Today* newspaper racks to look like television sets helped its target consumers (raised on TV) to identify with the newspaper. The design of Snapple's bottle with a wide mouth for "gulping" effectively differentiates it from soda bottles and cans. The package design for the Sensor makes the razor easy for consumers to use while traveling and for retailers to display on shelves. The design details of a product determine its look and feel and influence the entire consumption experience. Good design requires clear and agreed upon principles that guide development and help settle disagreements within the organization. For example, the design principles specified for the Laser sailboat deserve much credit for the boat's success.

Consult Lead Users for New Product Ideas—with Caution

A common practice in new product development is to consult lead users for direction on new product ideas, design issues, and product improvements. In the case of the Laser sailboat, interaction with the small group of lead users defining the sailboat racing community was important to obtain their reactions to the new product. However, the need for caution in designing products for lead users is illustrated in the paraglider story. When hang gliders were designed for lead users, the products became so complex, expensive, and difficult to operate that the larger and more profitable segment of less-skilled users abandoned the sport. In the Fuji QuickSnap case, many Japanese and later American consumers, adopted the disposable 35mm camera for its simplicity of use in comparison to their increasingly complex 35mm versions. Consulting lead users can be helpful, but their suggestions should be assessed very carefully.

Increase the Use of Information Technology in Product Design

Several of the new product successes relied on information technology to deliver their benefits. MCI invested in and depended on information technology to implement its Friends and Family service. The national newspaper *USA Today* began to make progress toward profitability when information technology made regional editions possible that could cater to regional advertisers. France Telecom's Minitel is an elementary prototype of the information superhighway. Finally, like Calyx & Corolla, every company should maintain a database of its customers, not only to enhance marketing, but also to identify new product development opportunities by speaking with customers directly.

Select a Positioning Consistent with the Core Product Concept

A new product's positioning in the minds of target consumers should be based on the core concept. The entire marketing program helps define the positioning, but the product's name (and related symbolism) is often the primary avenue to the consumer's mind. Many new products' names are highly descriptive of their major benefits: Huggies Pull-Ups, Gillette's Sensor, Slim-Fast, QuickSnap (and even Kodak's FunSaver), and Baby Jogger. All relate directly to the benefits consumers are seeking or the problems they want to solve. Using such names helps implant the promotional message about the new product in the consumer's mind.

However, a name related to consumer benefits is not absolutely necessary for positioning success. For example, to clarify its natural benefits to consumers, The Body Shop positioned itself directly opposite traditional cosmetics industry firms. Consider also Glaxo's Zantac for stomach ulcers and heartburn. What if it had been named Stomach-Ease instead? The product is prescribed by physicians, and perhaps the mystery, lore, and life-giving expertise of the profession (and its potions) are enhanced by such exotic names as Tagamet, Mevacor, Vasotec, or Premarin. Thus, successful positioning can be based on symbolic imagery. When product names or symbols do not describe a benefit or create a favorable association, additional promotion may be necessary to give them meaning. To compete effectively, Glaxo heavily promoted Zantac through considerable advertising and personal selling to create meaning and awareness for its name.

Invest in and Protect the Brand Name

For a new organization, the corporate image or name becomes whatever is made of it. The Starbucks, Calyx & Corolla, The Body Shop, and MTV names would reflect their eventual successes. However, long-established organizations may have years of effort and considerable resources invested in shaping and protecting a brand name. New product development can become risky for them. When Marriott introduced the lower priced Courtyard by Marriott hotel, it was very concerned about the effect on the company's upscale reputation. When Ault Foods developed its new low-fat ice cream, it was very cautious in testing the product to make sure it would be credible to Canadian consumers before using the well-known Sealtest Parlour name.

Leveraging the equity in a brand name is a popular strategy, especially for introducing new products. However, care must be taken to avoid jeopardizing the brand. For example, Broderbund Software licensed a variety of products under the Carmen Sandiego name before realizing the importance of protecting the name's integrity. A name that appears on unrelated products and services may begin to lose its prestige among consumers.

Prepare Appropriate New Product Launch Communication Programs

All new product launch programs require some form of communication with consumers, retailers, and other key stakeholders. However, the type of communication depends on the spread of the target audience, the nature of the product and the consumer's buying process, the effectiveness of various media in reaching consumers, and the budget available.

For example, Starbucks, paragliders, The Body Shop, and the Baby Jogger relied heavily on word of mouth. The innovative and memorable aspects of those products became the basis for interpersonal communication. Calyx & Corolla relied on an effective catalog displaying its flowers, with an equally effective database of mailing addresses. Other companies relied on effective advertising in mass media, primarily because their audiences were large and geographically diffuse. Slim-Fast, Lever 2000, Canon's PC copier, Gillette's Sensor, Cellular One, Zantac, MCI, and Snapple all needed substantial and creative advertising to build initial awareness, trial, and credibility.

Achieve Adequate Distribution Availability by Launch Date

If the product is not on the shelves or available to buy, success will not be possible. Although Snapple's growth was in part attributable to growth of its target segment, the company's efforts to expand distribution after its brewed iced tea launch were essential to its success. Advertising would have been useless without availability. Distribution was also central to other successes, including Fuji's QuickSnap, MTV, *USA Today*, and Cellular One. Retail companies (Starbucks and The Body Shop) can grow by expanding outlets, and once in place, the stores become a platform for new products and creative merchandising.

Provide Sufficient Value in Introductory Pricing

New products are risky for potential buyers. Therefore, the value proposition for a new product should be inherently clear at the launch to reduce barriers to adoption for people who are interested in the new product. For example, France Telecom used pricing to overcome consumers' reluctance to give up their telephone books. With government support, it provided the Minitel terminals free! To build a catalog of service providers, the company offered consulting help along with low introductory advertising prices.

Ford gave Taurus an innovative and stylish design (resembling that of higher priced European cars), high quality, and a very competitive price to deliver high value to the potential buyer. Lever Brothers used heavy couponing, in effect a price discount, to encourage trial and repeat purchase of its new bar soap. MTV offered advertising time at huge discounts to attract an initial base of advertisers at the launch of the new channel.

For some products, price is a primary symbol of quality and value, especially when quality is determined by subjective factors. Snapple retains a premium pricing strategy in part to communicate the high quality of its natural ingredients and reinforce its health positioning. Starbucks charges a premium price for a cup of its unusual tasting coffee as a symbol that the coffee and the experience are significantly more prestigious than a simple cup of coffee bought at a convenience store.

Implement an Integrated and Resonating Launch Marketing Program

In highly competitive business environments, making an impact with a new product marketing program is difficult. Consumers are bombarded with several hundred commercial messages a day, and retailers are overloaded with requests for space on their shelves. A highly integrated marketing program that resonates in the market after launch is necessary to create a strong impression. Resonance is an *echoing* effect that reinforces the core product concept in the market.

Integrated marketing programs were used for several of the new products, and the Lever 2000 program is an excellent example. The family target market, the high tech/high touch positioning, the product name implying a new century (the year 2000) contrasted against a creative and playful advertising campaign emphasizing 2,000 body parts, the soap's design in a soft, curvilinear, easy-to-hold shape, the strikingly modern package, and promotion with coupons and free samples to encourage trial and repeat purchase—all combined to create a highly resonating and successful launch program.

Assess Market Entry Timing: First-Mover *Dis*advantage?

Contrary to the proverb, the early bird does not always get the worm. Sometimes a company can learn from the market leader and bring a superior new product to the market as a follower. Such was the case with Glaxo's Zantac. Not being first to market, Glaxo knew it had to develop a product that took advantage of Tagamet's vulnerabilities. In the long run, Zantac's market share surpassed Tagamet's. Established market leaders are often vulnerable to new products. AT&T had difficulty responding to MCI's new Friends and Family service without jeopardizing its own profitability. Also, Slim-Fast was a very cautious entrant after the initial success of the Cambridge Diet, but went on to be the market share leader.

Further, if the market is not ready to buy, being first to market may not matter. Entering the U.S. market before Kodak would not have helped Fuji because American consumers were reluctant to buy either company's single-use camera and had to be persuaded about its efficacy. Kodak was in a better position than Fuji to do the persuading because of its high credibility in the United States at the time. Fuji actually benefited by riding on Kodak's coattails.

Generally, a first-mover advantage makes sense when competitors can offer a comparable or better product and when early customers are profitable and influential ones. Lever 2000, Huggies Pull-Ups, and Snapple are products that are relatively easy to imitate. However, because of their market lead combined with their experience and aggressive marketing, they may be able to retain their strong positions. Cellular One benefited by being first to market with its cellular service because it captured the influential early adopters of the product. Also, once frequent travelers stayed at the Courtyard by Marriott, their interpersonal influence and loyalty (based on a product carefully designed to meet their needs) were to Marriott's long-run advantage.

Persevere for Effective Execution: Testing, Retesting, and Training

All of the new product successes depended on effective execution of numerous tasks and activities. Flowers sold by Calyx & Corolla had to arrive in excellent condition or the business would fail. The Gillette Sensor had to be manufactured with exceptional precision to deliver a smoother shave. Further, Gillette conducted thousands of use tests among consumers to ensure that the product worked well. MCI's Friends and Family service involved sensitive communication between its hundreds of telemarketers and the millions of people nominated to the Friends and Family circles. Further, the telephone bills had to be executed with precision in figuring the correct discounts to lend credibility to the overall service. Extensive training of the telephone sales and service representatives was therefore essential.

Anticipate the Competition That a Successful New Product Almost Always Attracts

In almost every new product story, competition was present before the new product was introduced, and it usually increased after the new product became successful. Contrary to the popular assumption, success does not ensure a monopoly position for a new product, especially a technology-based product. Cellular One competes with numerous other telephone services, both cellular based and not. Even though France Telecom is a state-owned monopoly, its Minitel constantly competes with other information technology systems that are not state subsidized. MTV may not have a direct competitor, but it certainly must vie for the attention of its target age group with other programming and leisure time activities.

Truly new products have a chance to defend their position, but must do so aggressively. MTV secured its position by acquiring exclusive rights to major video clips produced by record companies. Racing Strollers, Inc. took out several patents for its Baby Jogger stroller. In addition to patents, Gillette's Sensor is protected by a complicated product design and manufacturing process that is difficult for competitors to duplicate effectively.

New products that can be imitated must be very aggressive in defending their positions. Lever Brothers must innovate continually to defend its Lever 2000 bar soap against a multitude of competitors. Similarly, Slim-Fast, Huggies Pull-Ups, Starbucks, The Body Shop, Zantac, and Snapple all used aggressive marketing to defend their positions after launch.

Do Not Give Up Easily on a Good New Product Idea: The Entrepreneurial Instinct

Several of the stories illustrate the value of persistence in new product development, especially if market research or trends support it. When the Laser sailboat was first proposed as a design, it was rejected; however, the designers believed in it enough to risk building their own business on it. Kimberly-Clark almost gave up on Huggies Pull-Ups, but persisted in the belief that the product could eventually be made. This entrepreneurial instinct is present in both startup and established organizations, and can be a driving force in new product development. However, the product champion's bias for optimism must be balanced by careful attention to the financial aspects of the product and the market opportunity.

Plan To Be Patient—Accelerate Product Development When Possible, But Success Takes Time

Few of the new products had short development cycles or were overnight successes. Starbucks began in 1971, Snapple in 1972; neither achieved substantial success until the 1990s. Gillette took 13 years to develop the Sensor. *USA Today* took more than 10 years to make a profit and MTV took more than three years. Courtyard by Marriott required five years of development time, in part for market research to create the best design, but also to persuade the organization that the product would be a success without jeopardizing the Marriott name. MCI's Friends and Family was launched just six weeks after the idea was proposed, and was taking major market share from AT&T a year later. However, its seemingly rapid success was preceded by several years and several millions of dollars of investment in computers and information technology.

Speed is often crucial in new product development, and every effort within reason should be made to reduce development time and costs. For example, Glaxo's effort to reduce development time from 10 to five years was clearly to its advantage. However, the developer of a new product must recognize that it takes time for organizations to make new products and services, for markets to accept the new offerings, and for other stakeholders to approve and otherwise adopt them. The lesson is: Hurry, but be patient!

Adhere to Strong Business Principles

Several of the successful organizations expressed strong business principles. Anita Roddick listed eight principles defining a "credo" for The Body Shop. Canon espoused a "three J's" corporate philosophy built on respect for the individual (self-motivation, self-awareness, self-reliance), and credits it for many of the company's new product successes. Similarly, Fuji follows three principles credited for much of the company's innovativeness: be thoroughly customer oriented, think and act globally, and strive to create innovation. An organization that shares a common set of principles is prepared to act as a community in uncertain situations. To be effective, such principles must be clear and communicable to all members of the organization.

Foster a Bias toward *Process* over *Project* Success

All 24 success stories show that a new product development *project* can be successful. Ford succeeded with the Taurus, and subsequently with the Mustang. However, these were *project* successes and not organizational *process* successes. The Mustang *project* was kept alive by a "skunk works" group in Ford who were ardent Mustang fans; it was not the outcome of an organizationwide innovation process learned from the Taurus. Ford failed to adopt a view of new product development as an ongoing process of innovation.

The benefit of an ongoing process of development is the speed with which the organization can respond to environmental changes. Further, a continual mode of development fosters learning among individual members of the organization and thereby leads to personal and organizational growth. Fuji's philosophy, which includes striving for innovation, illustrates this approach.

CONCLUSIONS

As is evident from the sheer number of lessons that can be learned from the success stories, new product development is a complex activity. By necessity it involves almost all aspects of the organization, and when it is a *new* activity for the organization it puts tremendous stress on everyone involved. The strain of an intense new product development effort is often responsible for breakdowns in the process. That is why it is so important to incorporate new product development as an *ongoing* activity within the organization.

As markets change, the need for new products will be continuous, whether incremental innovations or major breakthroughs. Change brings complexity and with it a need for rapid generation of knowledge and understanding on a regular basis throughout the organization. As a consequence, new product development is a highly intellectual process. The 24 case studies and the lessons to be learned from them are intended to aid that intellectual process.

Notes

Chapter 1: Learning from New Product Success

1. The Acuvue example is based on a Georgetown MBA marketing class project by Henry E. Chon, Johanna Eigen, Matthew S. Myers, Chet B. Steiner, and Anna M. Wagner completed in December 1993.

2. This brief illustrative case study is based on John R. Wilke, "Beech's Sleekly Styled Starship Fails to Take Off With Corporate Customers," *The Wall Street Journal*, October 29, 1993, pp. B1+.

3. See Abbie Griffin and Albert L. Page, "An Interim Report on Measuring Product Development Success and Failure," *Journal of Product Innovation Management*, 10 (September 1993), pp. 291–308.

4. For additional discussion of the numerous factors involved in new product development, see Robert J. Thomas, *New Product Development: Managing and Forecasting for Strategic Success* (New York: John Wiley & Sons, 1993).

5. Albert L. Page, "Assessing New Product Development Practices and Performance: Establishing Crucial Norms," *Journal of Product Innovation Management*, 10 (September 1993), pp. 271–290.

6. The Black & Decker example is based on a Georgetown MBA marketing class project by Hideo Fukuoka, Paul F. Pelosi, Jr., H. Sean Ross, Carrie C. Sauer, and Sarah S. Saunders completed in December 1993.

7. The discussion of this example is based on Zachary Schiller, "At Rubbermaid, Little Things Mean a Lot," *Business Week*, November 11, 1991.

8. The discussion of this example is based on the following articles: Jim Carlton, "Sales of Apple's Hand-Held Computer Have Weakened Since Its Introduction," *The Wall Street Journal*, December 13, 1993, p. B1; Jim Carlton, "Apple's Sales Data Suggest to Analysts that New MessagePad Is Floundering," *The Wall Street Journal*, January 25, 1994, p. B3; G. Christian Hill, "First Hand-Held Data Communicators Are Losers, but Makers Won't Give Up," *The Wall Street Journal*, February 3, 1994, pp. B1+; Bradley Johnson, "Nuts about Newton? Nah!", *Advertising Age*, pp. 3+; Walter S. Mossberg, "In Newton, Apple Has the Germ of an Idea with Weighty Potential," *The Wall Street Journal*, August 5, 1993, p. B1; Kyle Pope, "Compaq to Delay Hand-Held Computer after Bad Reviews of Pen-Based Rival," *The Wall Street Journal*, January 25, 1994, p. B3; Ken Yamada, "Imminent Debut of Newton MessagePad Has Apple Crowing and

Critics Carping," *The Wall Street Journal,* July 30, 1993, pp. B1+; Steven K. Yoder, "Apple's Newton Moves Briskly in Early Sales," *The Wall Street Journal,* August 19, 1993, p. B2; Bart Ziegler, "What Apple Learned from the Newton," *Business Week,* November 22, 1993, p. 110.

9. The discussion of this example is based on G. Pascal Zachary, "Agony and Ecstasy for 200 Code Writers Beget Windows NT," *The Wall Street Journal,* May 26, 1993, pp. 1+.

10. Page, op. cit.

11. The discussion of this example is based on Jeff D. Felberg and David A. DeMarco, "New Idea Enhancement at Amoco Chemical: An Early Report from a New System," *Journal of Product Innovation Management,* 9 (December 1992), pp. 278–286.

12. The Teva Sandals example is based on a Georgetown MBA marketing class project by Yenii Chen, Faik Erdenir, Karin Lesica, Stephanie Scherr, and Ichio Shinohara completed in December 1993.

13. The discussion of this example is based on Albert L. Page and Harold F. Rosenbaum, "Developing an Effective Concept Testing Program for Consumer Durables," *Journal of Product Innovation Management,* 9 (December 1992), pp. 267–277.

14. The discussion of this example is based on Joseph Weber, "The Nicotine Patch Looks a Bit Ragged," *Business Week,* April 5, 1993, p. 28.

15. The discussion of this example is based on the following articles: Raymond Serafin, "The Saturn Story," *Advertising Age,* November 16, 1992, pp. 1+; Raymond Serafin, "Saturn Recall a Plus—for Saturn!", *Advertising Age,* August 16, 1993, p. 4; James B. Treece, "Here Comes GM's Saturn," *Business Week,* April 9, 1990, pp. 56+; Joseph B. White, "Saturn Recalls 30% of Its Cars in New Setback," *The Wall Street Journal,* February 14, 1991, pp. B1+; Joseph B. White, "GM Struggles to Get Saturn Car on Track after Rough Launch," *The Wall Street Journal,* May 23, 1991, pp. 1+.

Chapter 2: Aligning Strategic Opportunities

1. Julia Flynn Siler and Dori Jones Yang, "Fewer Cups But a Much Richer Brew," *Business Week,* November 18, 1991, p. 80.

2. Alice Z. Cuneo, "Starbucks' Word-of-Mouth Wonder," *Advertising Age,* March 7, 1994, p. 12.

3. Starbucks Coffee Company prospectus, April 1992.

4. Howard Schultz, President, Starbucks Coffee Company, telephone interview, October 22, 1992.

5. Siler and Yang, op. cit., p. 80.

6. The Specialty Coffee Association of America, report, 1992.

7. Walker McCoy, "Know Your Beans," *Food and Wine,* August 1992, p. 34.

8. Starbucks Coffee Company prospectus, April 1992.

9. H. Gupta, "Prospectus Shows Sales Have Boomed at Starbucks," *The Seattle Times,* May 22, 1992.

10. J. Stark, "Starbucks: At the Helm of Seattle's Espresso Adulation," *Tea and Coffee Trade Journal*, April 1991, p. 11.

11. Schultz, op. cit.

12. Ibid.

13. Starbucks Coffee Company promotional material, Corporate Profile 1992.

14. "The Story of Good Coffee From the Northwest," Starbucks Coffee Company promotional material, 1992.

15. See Ken Know, "Coffee Matters," Starbucks Coffee Company customer newsletter, November/December 1992.

16. Ibid.

17. Kathleen Deveny, "For Coffee's Big Three, a Gourmet-Brew Boom Proves Embarrassing Bust," *The Wall Street Journal*, November 4, 1993, pp. B1+.

18. Barbara P. Nobel, "Benefits? For Part Timers?", *The New York Times*, August 16, 1992, Section 3, p. 1.

19. Starbucks Coffee Company prospectus, April 1992.

20. Charles McCoy, "Entrepreneur Smells Aroma of Success in Coffee Bars," *The Wall Street Journal*, January 8, 1993, p. B2.

21. Starbucks Coffee Company prospectus, April 1992.

22. Siler and Yang, op. cit.

23. Schultz, op. cit.

24. Patrick M. Reilly, "Competitive Floral-Delivery Networks Claim a Rose Isn't a Rose Isn't a Rose," *The Wall Street Journal*, February 14, 1994, pp. B1+.

25. Carolyn Lochhead, "A Fight with Foreign Petal Pushers," *Insight*, April 10, 1989, p. 42.

26. Ellie Winningham, "Growing a New Market Niche," *Working Woman*, February 1991, p. 42.

27. Patti Hagan, "Hearts and Flowers: The Nosegay Express," *The Wall Street Journal*, February 14, 1991, p. A10.

28. "A Career by Mail," *Martha Stewart Living*, February/March 1992, p. 36.

29. 1-800-Flowers press release, August 18, 1992, p. 1.

30. Rebecca Piirto, "The Romantic Sell," *American Demographics*, August 1989, pp. 38–41.

31. Robert Levy, "Flower Power in the Supermarket," *Business Month*, March 1987, p. 62.

32. Kate Foster, "The Perfect Gift," *SAF–Business News for the Floral Industry*, November 1990, p. 30.

33. Ibid.

34. "Ruth Owades—A Budding Entrepreneur," *Sales and Marketing Management*, June 1992, p. 32.

35. Lochhead, op. cit., p. 43.

36. Foster, op. cit.

37. Phil McCombs, "The Women's Catalyst," *The Washington Post*, November 13, 1992, p. C1.

38. Rick Cahill, Marketing Director, Sun Petal Growers of Miami, Inc., interview, December 1, 1992.

39. Cahill, op. cit.

40. Winningham, op. cit.

41. "A Career by Mail," op. cit., p. 38.

42. Stephanie Stron, "In the Mailbox, Roses and Profits," *The New York Times*, February 14, 1992, p. D5.

43. Ibid.

44. Ruth Owades, President of Calyx & Corolla, personal interview, November 18, 1992.

45. "Business is Blooming," *Catalog Age*, January 1991, p. 1.

46. Cahill, op. cit.

47. Linda Luttrop, Marketing Manager, Federal Express, Inc., personal interview, December 2, 1992.

48. "Business is Blooming," op. cit.

49. Reilly, op. cit.

50. Mark Poirier, "Small Expectations," *Catalog Age*, February 1992, p. 1 and Leah Rickard, "Blossoming Opportunities," *Advertising Age*, July 18, 1994, p. 24.

51. Reilly, op. cit.

52. Owades, op. cit.

53. Paul Miller, "Pay More, Get Less," *Catalog Age*, April 1992, p. 1.

54. This success story is based on the following sources: "Ten Years of the Compact Disc," Press Office, Philips Consumer Electronics, The Netherlands, 1992; "Philips Goes Japanese," *The Economist*, July 10, 1982, p. 80; Thane Peterson and Larry Armstrong, "Philips Assails a Japanese Stronghold in the U.S.," *Business Week*, April 22, 1985, p. 52; Udayan Gupta, "Compact Discs Picking Up Speed," *Advertising Age*, June 7, 1983, pp. 35+; "Digital Audio Builds Towards a Sales Crescendo," *Business Week*, January 30, 1984, pp. 62–63; "We Have Heard the Future and It Works," *The Economist*, May 15, 1982, p. 92; "Sony's One and Only," *Broadcasting*, March 28, 1983, p. 95; "Laser Music: Sony Launches Digital Audio Discs," *Time*, March 21, 1983, p. 8; Kinya Murata, "Much Hope Is Laid on Compact Discs," *The Nihon Keizai Shimbun Japan Economic Journal*, August 23, 1983, pp. 30+; Patrick Oster, "Philips: Playing by Its Own Rules at the World Cup," *Business Week*, June 20, 1994, p. 80; and Jeffrey A. Trachtenberg, "Sony, Philips Forge Alliance to Create Digital Disk Player for 2 Hours of Video," *The Wall Street Journal*, May 20, 1994, p. B2.

Chapter 3: Capitalizing on the Business Environment

1. *Cellular One Employee Handbook*, "Cellular History," Chapter 3, p. 8.

2. Ibid., "General History," Chapter 2, p. 2.

3. Cellular Telecommunications Industry Association, "How Cellular Works."

4. For additional information on this process and the results of demand forecasts for this new technology, see Robert J. Thomas, "Problems in Demand Estimation for a New Technology," *Journal of Product Innovation Management*, 3 (September 1985), pp. 145–157.

5. Emily Nelms, American Personal Communication, Washington, DC, personal interview, December 4, 1992.

6. For a discussion of this analysis, see Robert J. Thomas and Wayne N. Schelle, "To Settle or To Fight: Deciding Which Is Worth More," *Telocator*, June 1984, pp. 47+.

7. Frank Kuznik, "The Road Warriors," *Regardie's*, July 1985, pp. 64–69.

8. Ibid.

9. Ibid.

10. Cellular Telecommunications Industry Association, *State of the Cellular Industry*, 1992, pp. 28–29.

11. "Surge in Semi-Conductors," *Barron's*, October 14, 1991, p. 25.

12. McCaw Communications Annual Report, 1991.

13. Ault Foods Limited, *A New Kind of Dairy Company*, brochure, undated.

14. Ibid., p. 3.

15. Scott McMurray, "Fat Substitute Market Grows Crowded as Hercules Launches a Pectin Product," *The Wall Street Journal*, September 24, 1991, p. B4.

16. Cheryl Pellerin, "Lowering Cholesterol: An Oat-Based Fat Substitute ConAgra Is Speeding to Market," *Technology Transfer Business*, Fall 1992, p. 25.

17. "Unilever Unit Serves Up Fat Substitutes," *The Wall Street Journal*, January 8, 1992, p. B1.

18. For discussion of Nutrasweet's experience with Simplesse, see "Maker of Simplesse Discovers Its Fake Fat Elicits Thin Demand," *The Wall Street Journal*, July 31, 1991, pp. A1+.

19. Ault Foods Limited, "Unique Canadian Technology Produces First 100 Per Cent Milk-Based Fat Replacement," press release, undated.

20. The preparation of this story would not have been possible without the kind and generous help of Jamie Fagan, Intern, Refrigerated Division; Keith Gillespie, Brand Manager, Parlour; Massoud Poustchi, Marketing Director, Refrigerated Products; and Moni Eino, Corporate Vice President, Operations; all of Ault Foods Limited.

21. This discussion is based on Richard L. Celsi, Randall L. Rose, and Thomas W. Leigh, "An Exploration of High-Risk Leisure Consumption through Skydiving," *Journal of Consumer Research*, 20 (June 1993), pp. 1–23. See also A. Brannigan and A. A. McDougall, "Peril and Pleasure in the Maintenance of High Risk Sport: A Study of Hang-Gliding," *Journal of Sport Behavior*, 6 (March 1983), pp. 37–51.

22. Parachute canopies are porous and allow about 30 percent of the air pressure to escape through the membrane. Paraglider canopies are not porous at all.

23. Glide ratio is the ratio of the distance a glider travels horizontally to the distance it drops vertically. Glide ratio is one or two for square parachutes, seven for paragliders, 12 for hang gliders, and 21 for fixed-wing glider planes.

24. Jerry Adler et al., "Been There, Done That," *Newsweek*, July 19, 1993, p. 42.

25. Michael W. Miller, "At the Ski Jump, Philosophy in Motion," *The Wall Street Journal*, February 24, 1994, p. A14.

Chapter 4: Pursuing Market Acceptance

1. Phyllis Berman with Amy Feldman, "An Extraordinary Peddler," *Forbes*, December 9, 1991, pp. 136+.

2. "Ultra Diet Quick Meal Replacement Drink," *Lookout–Foods Edition*, August 27, 1991, p. 141.

3. "Ultra Slim-Fast Frozen Desserts and Novelties," *Lookout–Foods Edition*, June 25, 1991, p. 104.

4. "Slim-Fast Lines Make Debut," *Chain Drug Review*, June 17, 1991, p. 120.

5. "A Company That's Getting Fat Because America Wants To Be Thin," *Business Week*, November 19, 1984, p. 70.

6. "The Protein Fad," *Newsweek*, December 19, 1977, p. 71.

7. Ibid.

8. "New Warnings About Those 'Easy Diets'," *U.S. News & World Report*, July 10, 1978, p. 61.

9. Thompson Medical Annual Report, 1983.

10. "When Dieting Goes Wild," *U.S. News & World Report*, October 8, 1984, p. 58.

11. "A Company That's Getting Fat Because America Wants To Be Thin," op. cit.

12. Berman, op. cit.

13. Ibid.

14. Ron Stern, President of Slim-Fast Foods Company, personal interview, December 10, 1992.

15. "The Protein Fad," op. cit.

16. Stern, op. cit.

17. Ibid.

18. "The Protein Fad," op. cit.

19. Stern, op. cit.

20. "Slim-Fast Foods Company Backgrounder," Slim-Fast Foods Company, 1991.

21. "A Company That's Getting Fat Because America Wants To Be Thin," op. cit.

22. Ibid.

23. "Ultra Diet Quick Meal Replacement Drink," op. cit.

24. Ibid.

25. The authors thank the following individuals for their time and help through personal interviews: Ronald Stern, president of Slim-Fast Foods Company,

Patricia Sagawa, Slim-Fast user, and Paul Korody, vice-president of government affairs, ConAgra.

26. Information Audit Department, The Body Shop International, West Sussex, England, fax communication, September 1994.

27. Ibid.

28. Bo Burlingham, "This Woman Has Changed Business Forever," *INC.*, June 1990, p. 34.

29. "What Is Natural," The Body Shop, company brochure.

30. Dennis Chase, "P&G Gets Top Marks in AA Survey," *Advertising Age*, January 29, 1991, pp. 8–10.

31. Burlingham, op. cit., p. 36.

32. Jean Sherman Chatzky, "Changing the World," *Forbes*, March 2, 1992, p. 83.

33. "What Is Natural," op. cit.

34. "Against Animal Testing," The Body Shop, company brochure.

35. "Reuse, Refill, Recycle," The Body Shop, company brochure.

36. "Trade Not Aid," The Body Shop, company brochure.

37. Rahul Jacob, "What Selling Will Be Like in the 90's," *Fortune,* January 13, 1992, p. 63.

38. Laurie Freeman, "Personal Care Products Fill Specialty Niche," *Stores*, May 1991, p. 60.

39. Connie Wallace, "Lessons in Marketing—From a Maverick," *Working Woman*, October 1990, p. 81.

40. Burlingham, op. cit., p. 42.

41. Burlingham, op. cit., p. 37.

42. Burlingham, op. cit., p. 37.

43. Burlingham, op. cit., p. 37.

44. Wallace, op. cit., p. 82.

45. Burlingham, op. cit., pp. 37–38, and Patrick M. Reilly, "Shoppers Buy Up a Bounty of Natural Beauty Products," *The Wall Street Journal*, June 8, 1994, pp. B1+.

46. France Telecom, "La Lettre de Teletel," April 1992, No. 8, Les Chiffres, 1991.

47. Wallys W. Conhaim, "Maturing French Videotex Becomes Key International Business Tool," *Information Today*, January 1992.

48. The following discussion about the development of Minitel is based largely on Marie Marchand, *The Minitel Saga*, translated by Mark Murphy (Paris: Larousse, 1988). This book describes the entire project in detail. Other useful references are: Wallys Conhaim, "French Videotex: Reaching Out for New Markets," *Information Today*, January 1991, pp. 28+; Wallys W. Conhaim, "France Telecom Joins Forces with U.S. West to Develop Videotex Gateways in the U.S.," *Information Today*, November 1991, pp. 37+; Blayne Cutler, "The Fifth Medium," *American Demographics*, June 1990, pp. 25+; Shlomo Maital, "Why the French Do It Better," *Across the Board*, November 1991, pp. 7–10; Carol Wilson, "The Myths and Magic of Minitel," *Telephony*, December 2,

1991, p. 52; *Information and Communications Technologies in Europe*, Commission of the European Communities Directorate-General XIII Telecommunications, Information Industries and Innovation, 1991.

49. Marchand, op. cit., p. 40.

50. James Pressley, "French, German Phone Concerns Form Venture on Business Communications," *The Wall Street Journal*, December 8, 1993, p. B8.

51. The authors thank Cece Drummond and Stefan Gayraud, both of France Telecom, for their help on the project.

Chapter 5: Motivating the Organization

1. Dean Foust, "What's Black and White and Blue and Yellow—And Less in the Red," *Business Week*, July 12, 1993, p. 30.

2. "Top 10 Newspapers," *USA Today*, November 25, 1992, p. 2B.

3. "USA Today, What Others Say," *USA Today* press release, Gannett Company Inc., Arlington, VA.

4. Albert Scardino, "USA Today Produces Readers But Not Profits," *The New York Times*, July 11, 1988, IV, p. 8.

5. Gannett Company Inc. 1982 Annual Report.

6. Peter Prichard, *The Making of McPaper* (Kansas City: Andrews, McMeel, Parker, 1987), p. 161.

7. Wright, John W., ed., *The Universal Almanac 1992* (Kansas City: Andrews and McMeel, 1991), p. 246.

8. *Standard & Poor's Industry Surveys*, 1984, Vol. 2, p. 78.

9. Patricia Aburdene and John Naisbitt, *Megatrends 2000* (New York: William Morrow and Company, Inc., 1990), p. 12.

10. Ibid., p. 138.

11. Arlie Schardt, "A New National Daily," *Newsweek*, December 29, 1980, p. 59.

12. Taylor Buckley, Senior Editor, *USA Today*, personal interview, November 24, 1992.

13. Alan Neuharth, *Confessions of an S.O.B.* (New York: Doubleday, 1989), p. 108.

14. Ibid., p. 108.

15. *Value Line Investment Survey* (New York: Value Line Publishing, Inc., March 1982).

16. Prichard, op. cit., p. 86.

17. Ibid., p. 95.

18. Buckley, op. cit.

19. Howard Kurtz, "We Want News, McPaper Discovers," *The Washington Post*, December 26, 1991, p. 1.

20. Prichard, op. cit., p. 100.

21. Ibid., pp. 124–125.

22. Eamonn Fingleton, "Citizen Kane in Rochester," *Forbes*, February 15, 1982, p. 23.

23. "Gannett's National Gamble," *Newsweek*, September 20, 1982, p. 121.

24. Prichard, op. cit., p. 361.

25. Buckley, op. cit.

26. Rance Crain, "Readers Find Newspapers 'Boring . . . Dull'," *Advertising Age*, September 1992, p. 64.

27. Buckley, op. cit.

28. The information in this success story is based primarily on the following sources: Greg Bowens, "Taurus Goes for the Title," *Business Week*, May 18, 1992, pp. 50+; Rebecca Fannin, "Ford Taurus/Mercury Sable: The Road Warriors," *Marketing & Media Decisions*, 22 (March 1987), pp. 60–66; Robert L. Shook, *Turnaround: The New Ford Motor Company* (New York: Simon & Shuster, 1990); David W. Scott, Ford Motor Company, personal communication, August 15, 1994; Eric Taub, *Taurus: The Making of the Car that Saved Ford* (New York: The Penguin Group, 1991); Alex Taylor, III, "Why Fords Sell Like Big Macs," *Fortune*, November 21, 1988, pp. 122+; Alex Taylor, III, "Caution: Bumps Ahead at Ford," *Fortune*, December 18, 1989, pp. 93+.

29. Taub, op. cit., p. 13.

30. Ibid., p. 49.

31. Cited in Taub, p. 52.

32. Shook, op. cit., p. 145.

33. Taylor, op. cit., p. 80.

34. Robert L. Simison and Neal Templin, "Ford Motor Co. Shakes Up Staff of Finance Unit," *The Wall Street Journal*, June 14, 1994, pp. A3+.

35. See Joseph B. White and Oscar Suris, "How a 'Skunk Works' Kept Mustang Alive—On a Tight Budget," *The Wall Street Journal*, September 21, 1993, pp. A1+; Neal Templin, "Ford Plans Capacity Boost for Mustang," *The Wall Street Journal*, December 10, 1993, pp. A3+; and Valerie Reitman, "Mustang Leads Ford's Charge on Japan," *The Wall Street Journal*, June 9, 1994, pp. B1+.

36. The information in this success story is based primarily on the following sources: *Canon Fact Book 1992/93* (Tokyo, Japan: Canon Inc., 1992); Axel Johne, "How to Pick a Winning Product," *Management Today*, February 1992, pp. 72–74; Louis Kraar, "Canon Focuses on America," *Fortune*, January 12, 1981, pp. 83+; Kazumi Nakano, Marketing Manager, Canon U.S.A., Inc., Washington, DC, office, personal interview; Ikujiro Nonaka and Teruo Yamanouchi, "Managing Innovation as a Self-Renewing Process," *Journal of Business Venturing*, 4 (September 1989), pp. 299–315; "The Squeeze on Copier Dealers," *Business Week*, July 6, 1981, pp. 78+; Teruo Yamanouchi, "Breakthrough: The Development of the Canon Personal Copier," *Long Range Planning*, 22 (October 1989), pp. 11–21.

37. Yamanouchi, ibid., p. 16.

Chapter 6: Creating New Product Ideas

1. The authors are indebted to Gordon Clayton and Bruce Kirby for their personal interviews and information about the Laser's success. In addition,

information used in the story was obtained from the following sources: Kurt Hoehne, "The Grown-Up Laser," *Sailing,* 1992; Dave Lavallee, "Sunfish Laser Sailboat Maker Riding High on Wave of Success," *The Newport Daily News,* September 2, 1992, pp. C1+; Mark Mitchell, "Peter L. Johnstone," interview, *Providence Business News,* June 29, 1992, pp. 2+.

2. The information in this success story was derived primarily from the following sources: Phil Baechler, personal interview, November 1992; Tom Carter, "Now Baby Can Train for Boston, Too," *The Washington Times,* March 21, 1985, p. 2B; "Firm's Success Rolls on Three Wheels," *USA Today,* January 9, 1989, p. 6B; Janice L. Kaplan, "Bringing Up Baby on Wheels," *The Washington Post,* Weekend Section, September 18, 1992, p. 59; Barbara Lloyd, "Joggers' Kids Can Roll Along," *The New York Times,* January 25, 1988, p. C11; Kelly Prior, "Go, Baby, Go," *New York,* July 11, 1988, p. 14; "Racing Strollers," *Washington CEO,* July 1990, p. 10; Racing Strollers, Inc., press releases; "Some Joggers Take the Baby Along," *Los Angeles Times,* November 5, 1987, Part IV, p. 2; Craig Troianello, "Racing Strollers Keeps Rolling on Fast Track to World Markets," *Yakima Herald-Republic,* February 29, 1992, pp. 4DD+.

3. Phil Baechler, op. cit.

4. "Racing Strollers," op. cit.

5. Autumn Alexander, "Racing Stroller Firm Off to a Running Start," *Costco Home,* Member/Vendor Profile, no date.

6. Troianello, op. cit., p. 4DD.

7. Baechler, op. cit. See also, Mary Baechler, "Learning to Live with Patent Copycats," *The Wall Street Journal,* July 18, 1994, p. A12.

8. See Mary Baechler, "Tom Peters Ruined My Life," *The Wall Street Journal,* October 25, 1993, p. A20.

9. "Carmen Sandiego Series Fact Sheet," Broderbund Software, Inc., July 1992.

10. *Where in the World Is Carmen Sandiego: User's Manual,* Broderbund Software, Inc., 1986, p. 12.

11. Andrew Kupfer, "Identify a Need, Turn a Profit," *Fortune,* November 30, 1992, pp. 78+.

12. Ibid., p. 78.

13. "Carmen Sandiego Series Fact Sheet," Broderbund Software, Inc., July 1992.

14. Lawrence M. Fisher, "Carmen Sandiego Leaps Out of PC," *The New York Times,* July 9, 1991.

15. Ibid.

16. Carla Lazzareschi, "In Pursuit of Carmen," *Los Angeles Times,* September 30, 1989.

17. Kupfer, op. cit.

18. Michael Rogers, "Crime Doesn't Pay: It Teaches," *Newsweek,* March 19, 1990.

19. "Carmen Sandiego Series Backgrounder," Broderbund Software, Inc.

20. Rogers, op. cit.

21. Lazzareschi, op. cit.

22. Rogers, op. cit.

23. Lazzareschi, op. cit.

24. Kathleen Burke, Public Relations Coordinator, Broderbund Software, Inc., personal interview, December 10, 1992.

25. Rogers, op. cit.

26. Roy Schwedelson, "Microcomputer Marketing: Act III," *Direct Marketing*, October 1990, pp. 24+.

27. Ibid., p. 30.

28. Carrie Dolan, "Childish Pursuits Pay at Broderbund, Home of Carmen Sandiego," *The Wall Street Journal*, March 10, 1993, pp. B1+.

29. Rogers, op. cit.

30. Ibid.

31. Michael Selz, "Small Software Companies Crack the Educational Market," *The Wall Street Journal*, March 10, 1993, pp. B1+.

32. Ralph T. King, Jr., "Broderbund Jilts Electronic Arts; Scraps Agreement To Be Acquired," *The Wall Street Journal*, May 4, 1994, p. B5.

33. "Carmen Sandiego Series Fact Sheet," op. cit.

Chapter 7: Designing New Products from Concepts

1. Mark Lewyn, "MCI Is Coming Through Loud and Clear," *Business Week*, January 25, 1993, pp. 84+.

2. Tara Clyne, Sandra Gauntt, and Nicholas Kouwenhoven, MCI Communications Corporation, personal interviews, November 18, 1992.

3. Peter Coy and Mark Lewyn, "Waging Long-Distance Wars from the Back Office," *Business Week*, April 8, 1991, p. 85.

4. MCI Communications Corporation, company information.

5. Kate Fitzgerald, "Roberts Brings Real Branding to Long-Distance Phones," *Advertising Age*, December 20, 1993, pp. 8+.

6. Regina Eisman, "Calling All Customers," *Incentive*, February 1992, p. 40.

7. Coy and Lewyn, op. cit.

8. 1990 MCI Annual Report.

9. Coy and Lewyn, op. cit.

10. Junu Kim et al., "Marketing 100: The People Behind Today's Marketing Success Stories," *Advertising Age*, July 6, 1992, p. S6.

11. Clyne, op. cit.

12. Ibid.

13. Fitzgerald, op. cit.

14. Clyne, op. cit.

15. Kate Fitzgerald, "MCI, Sprint Ads Hit AT&T Outage," *Advertising Age*, September 23, 1991, p. 3.

16. Clyne, op. cit.

17. Ibid.

18. Fitzgerald, 1993, p. 9.

19. John Keller, "Reaching Out, AT&T, MCI, Sprint Raise the Intensity of Their Endless War," *The Wall Street Journal,* October 20, 1992, pp. A1+; John Keller, "MCI Earnings Increased 14 Percent in Third Period," *The Wall Street Journal,* October 22, 1992, p. B10.

20. Fitzgerald, 1993, p. 8.

21. Marriott 1983 Annual Report, p. 25.

22. "Bill Marriott's Grand Design for Growth: Upscale and Down in the Lodging Market," *Business Week,* October 1, 1984, p. 61.

23. Ibid., p. 60.

24. Steve Swartz, "How Marriott Changes Hotel Design to Tap Mid-Priced Market," *The Wall Street Journal,* September 18, 1985, pp. A1+.

25. Craig Lambert, vice-president of marketing for Courtyard and Fairfield Inns, personal interview, December 2, 1992. Lambert joined Courtyard in 1983 as Marriott was preparing to begin its test market in Atlanta.

26. Christopher Hart, "Product Development: How Marriott Created Courtyard," *The Cornell H.R.A. Quarterly,* November 1986, pp. 68+.

27. This section is based on the following article from this award-winning research project: Jerry Wind, Paul Green, Doug Shifflet, and Marsha Scarbrough, "Courtyard by Marriott: Designing a Hotel Facility with Consumer-Based Marketing Models," *Interfaces,* 19 (January-February 1989), pp. 25–47.

28. For an overview of hybrid conjoint analysis, see Paul E. Green, "Hybrid Models for Conjoint Analysis: An Expository Review," *Journal of Marketing Research,* 21 (May 1984), pp. 155–169.

29. Wind et al., ibid., pp. 33–37.

30. Ken Koepper, "Creating Hotel Services for the Mid-Market Psychology," *Lodging,* October 1988, pp. 55–56.

31. Swartz, op. cit., p. A1.

32. Lambert, op. cit.

33. Hart, op. cit., p. 69.

34. Lambert, op. cit.

35. Ibid.

36. Ibid.

37. Wind et al., op. cit., p. 37.

38. Lambert, op. cit.

39. Ibid.

40. Swartz, op. cit., p. A1. An article in the October 1, 1984, issue of *Business Week* (p. 61) cites Marriott senior vice-president Francis Cash as saying the breakeven occupancy rate was 60 percent.

41. Marriott 1991 Annual Report, p. 24.

42. Lambert, op. cit.

43. Koepper, op. cit., p. 57 and "Courtyard Invests $1 Million per Year To Learn Guest Preferences," *Corporate Travel,* November 1989, p. 20.

44. Marriott Annual Report, 1987 and 1991.

45. Lambert, op. cit.

46. This success story is based on information from the following sources: Stuart Elliott, "An Enthusiastic Pitchman at the Helm of Lever Bros.," *The New York Times,* August 20, 1992, p. D18; Martin Everett, "Why Special Events Wash Well with Lever Brothers," *Sales & Marketing Management,* 141 (September 1989), pp. 86+; Thomas Exter, "It's a Man's Soap," *American Demographics,* 9 (December 1987), pp. 36+; Jefferson Grigsby, "Unilever: Gulliver Awakes," *Financial World,* October 3, 1989, pp. 36–39; Walecia Konrad, "The New, Improved Unilever Aims to Clean Up in the U.S.," *Business Week,* November 27, 1989, pp. 102+; George Lazarus, "Lever 2000 Soap May Go National," *Chicago Tribune,* July 13, 1989, Section 3, p. 4; George Lazarus, "Lever 2000 Awash in Soapy Success," *Chicago Tribune,* September 13, 1991, Section 3, p. 2; Gregory Morris, "Soap & Detergents," *Chemical Week,* January 18, 1989, pp. 24+; Christopher Power, "Everyone Is Bellying Up to This Bar," *Business Week,* January 27, 1992, p. 84; Valerie Reitman, "Buoyant Sales of Lever 2000 Soap Bring Sinking Sensation to Procter & Gamble," *The Wall Street Journal,* March 19, 1992, pp. B1+; Iris Rosendahl, "Soaps Are Steady Sellers in Drugstore," *Drug Topics,* September 23, 1991, pp. 83+; Lynda Singletary, "Bar Soaps: No-Soap Soaps Up," *Chemical Marketing Reporter,* January 27, 1992, pp. SR23+; Pat Sloan, "Olay Bath Bar Aims at Dove," *Advertising Age,* February 4, 1991, p. 9; Pat Sloan and Bradley Johnson, "P&G Slips on Soap," *Advertising Age,* September 30, 1991, pp. 3+; Pat Sloan and Jennifer Lawrence, "Olay Bath Bar Makes Splash," *Advertising Age,* August 2, 1993, p. 9.

Chapter 8: Refining the New Product

1. The information in this success story is based largely on company documents provided by Kimberly-Clark Corporation. Other sources used are: Stephanie Anderson Forest, "Kimberly-Clark's European Paper Chase," *Business Week,* March 16, 1992, p. 94; Laurie Freeman, "The People Behind Today's Marketing Success Stories," *Advertising Age,* July 6, 1992, p. S6; Thomas Jaffe, "Huggable Shares," *Forbes,* May 29, 1989, p. 346; Jennifer Lawrence, "Private Label Forces P&G's Hand; Slumping Luvs Becomes a Lower-Price Diaper Brand," *Advertising Age,* April 19, 1993, p. 43; Jennifer Lawrence, "P&G Makes Advances in Diaper Derby," *Advertising Age,* March 7, 1994, pp. 3+; Barbara E. Lencheck, "Cashing In on the Baby Boom," *Progressive Grocer,* May 1990, p. 65; Lynn O'Shaughnessy, "Lawsuits Fly in the Battle to Cover the Most Baby Bottoms, a Fracas Insiders Call . . . The Diaper Wars," *Los Angeles Times,* July 10, 1992, pp. E1+; "P&G Takes First Steps with Training Pants, but Focus Is Abroad," *The Wall Street Journal,* June 21, 1993, p. B3; Valerie Reitman, "Diaper Firms Fight to Say on the Bottom," *The Wall Street Journal,* March 23, 1993, p. B1; Alecia Swasy, "Kimberly-Clark

Bets, Wins on Innovation," *The Wall Street Journal,* November 22, 1991, p. A5; *Your Growing Child* (Morristown, NJ: Time Life Books, 1987), pp. 110–117.

2. George Creswell, Gerber Products Company, personal interview, November 17, 1992.

3. This success story is based on the following sources: Jerry E. Bishop, "Bacterium Causes Most Peptic Ulcers," *The Wall Street Journal,* February 10, 1994, p. B6; John R. Dorfman, "Glaxo's Dependence on Zantac Inspires Fears that the Drug Maker Could Develop an Ulcer," *The Wall Street Journal,* May 11, 1994, p. C2; FDC Reports, "SmithKline Has Two of Top Five Products," *The Pink Sheet,* February 2, 1981, p. 6; FDC Reports, "List of Top Twenty Products," *The Pink Sheet,* January 25, 1982, p. 6; FDC Reports, "Zantac New Rxs Well Over 40,000 Per Week," *The Pink Sheet,* November 21, 1983, p. 7; Julia Flynn et al., "Having an Ulcer Is Getting a Lot Cheaper," *Business Week,* May 9, 1994, pp. 30+; David Gerrie, "Can Marketing Keep Glaxo in Pole Position?" *Marketing,* October 18, 1990, pp. 24+; Matthew Lynn, *The Billion-Dollar Battle* (London: William Heinemann Ltd., 1991); Gautam Naik, "SmithKline Will Sell Generic Version of Tagamet, Its Popular Ulcer Drug," *The Wall Street Journal,* May 11, 1994, p. A4; Adrian Slywotzsky and Benson P. Shapiro, "Leveraging To Beat the Odds: The New Marketing Mind-Set," *Harvard Business Review,* 71 (September-October 1993), pp. 97–107; Robert Teitelman, "Oh, Henry," *Financial World,* March 7, 1989, pp. 30+.

4. This new product success story is based on the following sources: Richard J. Coletti, "Leading Edge," *Financial World,* January 8, 1991, no page number; Kathleen Deveny, "Sensor Gets Big Edge in Women's Razors," *The Wall Street Journal,* December 17, 1992, pp. B1+; *Gillette Sensor: A Case History,* The Gillette Company; Keith H. Hammonds, "How a $4 Razor Ends Up Costing $300 Million," *Business Week,* January 20, 1990, pp. 62+; Keith H. Hammonds, "It's One Sharp Ad Campaign, But Where's the Blade?" *Business Week,* March 5, 1990, p. 30; Lawrence Ingrassia, "Gillette Holds Its Edge by Endlessly Searching for a Better Shave," *The Wall Street Journal,* December 12, 1992, pp. A1+; Mark Maremont, "A New Equal Right: The Close Shave," *Business Week,* March 29, 1993, pp. 58+; Joseph Pereira, "Gillette to Launch New Sensor Razor in Europe This Fall," *The Wall Street Journal,* June 28, 1993, p. B6C.

Chapter 9: Tracking the New Product

1. This new product success is based primarily on the following sources: Riccardo A. Davis, "Single-Use Cameras Put Some Snap in Market," *Advertising Age,* March 8, 1993, p. 16; Fuji Photo Film Company, personal communication, September 2, 1994; Rod H. King, senior marketing manager, Fuji Photo Film USA, Inc., personal interview, December 3, 1992; Brett Lerner, Eastman Kodak Company, public relations, personal interviews, November-December 1992; Stephen Lukow, "Fuji Leads in Disposable Camera Market," *Tokyo Business Today,* October 1989, pp. 44–45; Mark Maremont, "The Hottest Thing Since the Flashbulb," *Business Week,* September 7, 1992, p. 72; Joan E. Rigdon, "For Cardboard Cameras, Sales Picture Enlarges and Seems Brighter than Ever," *The Wall*

Street Journal, February 11, 1992, pp. B1+; "Special Report," *Drug Store News,* February 1992 (Supplement); "Throw-Away High Tech," *The Economist,* February 29, 1992, p. 76.

2. This new product success story is based primarily on R. Serge Denisoff, *Inside MTV* (New Brunswick, NJ: Transaction Publishers, 1991). Other sources are: Mark Landler, "I Want My MTV—Stock," *Business Week,* May 18, 1992, pp. 55+; Mark Landler and Geoffrey Smith, "The MTV Tycoon," *Business Week,* September 18, 1992, pp. 57+; Laura Lipton, "The Shaping of a Shapeless Generation," *The Los Angeles Times,* November 10, 1991, pp. 86+; Patrick MacDonald, "As MTV Notes Birthday, Future Seems Limitless," *Seattle Times,* July 28, 1991, pp. L1+; Sharon D. Moshavi, "MTV Announces Move to Multiplexing," *Broadcasting Publications,* August 5, 1991, pp. 39+; Sean Piccoli, "Pop Revolution Triumphs," *The Washington Times,* August 1, 1991, pp. E1+; Matthew Schifrin, "I Can't Even Remember the Old Star's Name," *Forbes,* March 16, 1992, pp. 44+; Chris Willman, "Traveling Along the MTV Timeline," *The Los Angeles Times,* July 28, 1991, pp. 6+.

3. This success story is based on the following sources: Elena Bowes and Laurel Wentz, "Snapple Beverage War Spills onto Continent," *Advertising Age,* April 18, 1994, pp. 11+; Alison Fahey, "Snapple Faces Flood of New Drinks," *Advertising Age,* April 13, 1992, p. 12; Kevin Goldman, "Snapple Goes Big Time for New Age Drink," *The Wall Street Journal,* April 20, 1993, p. B7; Kevin Goldman, "Ads Seek to Make Iced Tea the Hot Drink," *The Wall Street Journal,* August 17, 1993, p. B6; Laurie M. Grossman, "Iced-Tea Products Get Off to a Slow Start," *The Wall Street Journal,* September 28, 1992, pp. B1+; Suein L. Hwang, "Outlook Is Murky for Clear, Fruity Drinks," *The Wall Street Journal,* August 17, 1993, p. B1; Elizabeth Lesly, "Does Snapple Have the Juice To Go National?", *Business Week,* January 18, 1993, pp. 52+; Marcy Magiera, "Lipton Tea Leaves Snapple Smarting," *Advertising Age,* November 1, 1993, p. 48; Marcy Magiera, "Snapple Spends Hard To Fight Big Guys," *Advertising Age,* March 21, 1994, p. 15; Marcy Magiera and Melanie Wells, "New Age Road Leads Coke to Fruitopia," *Advertising Age,* March 7, 1994, pp. 4+; Ronald A. Margulis, "Snapple Leads in 'New Age' Beverage Sector," *US Distribution Journal,* 11 (November 1989), p. 13; Michael J. McCarthy, "Competition Heats Up Iced-Tea Industry," *The Wall Street Journal,* June 15, 1993, pp. B1+; Cynthia Rigg, "Snapple Cracks Tough Pop Market," *Crain's New York Business,* August 14, 1989, p. 3; Cynthia Rigg, "Snapple, Misreading Tea Leaves, Prepares for Entrees from Giants," *Crain's New York Business,* May 2, 1992, p. 33; Cara S. Trager, "Niche Entrepreneurs," *Beverage World,* October 2, 1989, p. 34; Snapple Beverage Corporation prospectus, 1992; *Standard and Poor's Industry Surveys,* 1987–1992.

Index